BRITISH AND AMERICAN PLAYWRIGHTS,
1750–1920

General editors: Martin Banham and Peter Thomson

W.S. Gilbert

OTHER VOLUMES IN THIS SERIES

To be published in 1982:

TOM ROBERTSON edited by William Tydeman
HENRY ARTHUR JONES edited by Russell Jackson
DAVID GARRICK and GEORGE COLMAN THE ELDER
  edited by E.R. Wood

Further volumes will include:

THOMAS MORTON and GEORGE COLMAN THE YOUNGER
  edited by Barry Sutcliffe
J.R. PLANCHÉ edited by Don Roy
A.W. PINERO edited by Martin Banham
DION BOUCICAULT edited by Peter Thomson
CHARLES READE edited by M. Hammet
TOM TAYLOR edited by Martin Banham
ARTHUR MURPHY and SAMUEL FOOTE edited by George
  Taylor
H.J. BYRON edited by J.T.L. Davis
WILLIAM GILLETTE edited by Don Wilmeth and Rosemary Cullen
AUGUSTIN DALY edited by Don Wilmeth and Rosemary Cullen

Plays by
W. S. Gilbert

THE PALACE OF TRUTH
SWEETHEARTS
PRINCESS TOTO
ENGAGED
ROSENCRANTZ AND GUILDENSTERN

Edited with an introduction and notes by
George Rowell

CAMBRIDGE UNIVERSITY PRESS
Cambridge
London   New York   New Rochelle
Melbourne   Sydney

Published by the Press Syndicate of the University of Cambridge
The Pitt Building, Trumpington Street, Cambridge CB2 1RP
32 East 57th Street, New York, NY 10022, USA
296 Beaconsfield Parade, Middle Park, Melbourne 3206, Australia

First published 1982

Printed in Great Britain at the University Press, Cambridge

Library of Congress catalogue card number: 81–12248

British Library cataloguing in publication data
Gilbert, W.S.
Plays by W.S. Gilbert. – (British and American
playwrights, 1750–1920)
I. Title II. Rowell, George III. Series
822'.8   PR 4713
ISBN 0 521 23589 8 hard covers
ISBN 0 521 28056 7 paperback

GENERAL EDITORS' PREFACE

It is the primary aim of this series to make available to the British and American theatre plays which were effective in their own time, and which are good enough to be effective still.

Each volume assembles a number of plays, normally by a single author, scrupulously edited but sparingly annotated. Textual variations are recorded where individual editors have found them either essential or interesting. Introductions give an account of the theatrical context, and locate playwrights and plays within it. Biographical and chronological tables, brief bibliographies, and the complete listing of known plays provide information useful in itself, and which also offers guidance and incentive to further exploration.

Many of the plays published in this series have appeared in modern anthologies. Such representation is scarcely distinguishable from anonymity. We have relished the tendency of individual editors to make claims for the dramatists of whom they write. These are not plays best forgotten. They are plays best remembered. If the series is a contribution to theatre history, that is well and good. If it is a contribution to the continuing life of the theatre, that is well and better.

We have been lucky. The Cambridge University Press has supported the venture beyond our legitimate expectations. Acknowledgement is not, in this case, perfunctory. Sarah Stanton's contribution to the series has been substantial, and it has enhanced our work.

Martin Banham
Peter Thomson

CONTENTS

ILLUSTRATIONS

ACKNOWLEDGEMENTS

The 'Early Doors' which first ushered me (like many others before and since) into stageland bore the greatly loved names of Gilbert and Sullivan; they also led me to the study of the Victorian theatre, and to the discovery that the Gilbert in whose Savoy operas I delighted wrote plays as well, although these were not to be found on the playbills and only after much searching on the library shelf.

I am therefore especially grateful to the Cambridge University Press, and in particular to Diane Speakman and Sarah Stanton, for their invitation to undertake a volume of Gilbert's plays, and to the Editors of the British and American Playwrights series, Martin Banham and Peter Thomson, for their encouragement and guidance at every stage of the book's preparation.

I must also place on record the good offices of Colin Prestige in granting permission, on behalf of the Royal General Theatrical Fund Association, 11 Garrick Street, London WC2, owners of the copyrights in the estate of the late Sir William Gilbert, to draw on the original text of *Princess Toto* (from the copy deposited for licensing with the Lord Chamberlain's Office, and now in the British Library).

I have numerous reasons to be grateful to Peter Joslin, for his help with illustrations and with the text of *Princess Toto*. I am also indebted to John Cannon, Curator of the Gilbert and Sullivan Museum, for his kindness in making available to me the prompt-copy of the original production of *The Palace of Truth*.

My last and most substantial acknowledgement must be to my fellow-student of Gilbert's work, Brenda Jackson, whose support and dedication to the task of producing the various sections of the book can most aptly be termed Adamant-ine.

GEORGE ROWELL

INTRODUCTION

Of the many hundreds of writers who supplied the fiery furnaces of the British theatre between the decline of Sheridan and the rise of Shaw, William Schwenck Gilbert was alone in consistently displaying originality over more than seventy plays during more than forty years. Such an achievement — in a field which has always suspected originality and worshipped novelty — is all the more remarkable in an age when the theatre was struggling to recover its self-respect after almost a century of mass-production for mass-consumption. Writers were still so poorly rewarded that economics alone drove them to pillage fiction, French drama, the popular theatre itself, rather than invest their time and talent in original work likely to be rejected on the grounds of its originality. When in the 1890s Gilbert was himself eclipsed, his narrowness of range was censured but his highly individual style was ignored.

It could further be argued that outside Shakespeare no other writer has been more widely cited on and off the stage, and throughout the English-speaking world. His lines, his characters, even his attitudes have found their way into everyday expression; that the adjective 'Gilbertian' should be regularly applied to situations far removed from the theatre is a tribute as much to his comic consistency as to his popularity. A less individual writer could not have fathered so immediately identifiable a description. A term such as 'Byronic' can be applied to someone's appearance, 'Dickensian' to a scene or character, but 'Gilbertian' is universally used of a situation at once ordinary and extraordinary.

Of course Gilbert owes this unique attribute to the popularity of his collaboration with Arthur Sullivan, and the relationship between the Savoy operas and Gilbert's other theatre work presents problems of definition and distinction. Some are purely semantic: the term 'Savoy operas' is itself by way of a misnomer, since out of the fourteen joint works of Gilbert and Sullivan, only eight were first performed at the Savoy. Again Gilbert himself rejected the term 'playwright' (citing parallels with 'wheelwright', 'millwright', 'wainwright' and 'shipwright'[1] which doubtless touched him nearly in an age of universal theatrical carpentry, including dramaturgic carpentry), in favour of 'dramatist' to cover all his theatrical output, although paradoxically publishing his collected works, including the operas, as *Original Plays*. Nevertheless convenience — to put it no more strongly — suggests a division of his work into that of the 'librettist' (with a composer) and 'playwright' (without one), while 'dramatist' can acceptably serve for both functions.

The popularity of the Gilbert and Sullivan operas has also produced an imbalance in the knowledge of Gilbert's work as a whole. They are played, sung, loved, and studied with an enthusiasm unique in the Victorian repertoire and rarely equalled outside it, but that enthusiasm does not extend to the collaborators' individual work. It is a little as though the *Essays of Elia* have been buried under the

1

monument of Charles and Mary Lamb's *Tales from Shakespeare*. All invidious comparison apart, one result is a Savoy feast and a Gilbert famine. The operas have remained in print, singly and collectively, since their first productions; the last representative edition of Gilbert the dramatist was published in 1911. This discrepancy is of course greatly exaggerated by the availability, often in recent years in an embarrassingly rich variety, of the operas in performance, live and recorded, in many forms. For this edition, therefore, itself strictly limited by space, the sacrifice of the Savoy operas seemed justified, although an example of Gilbert the librettist was judged desirable.

Again alone amongst the vast majority of nineteenth-century dramatists, Gilbert's work found published form almost from the outset. Where older men had feared to print their plays lest they forfeit copyright (or had been driven to sell them outright to publishers of 'acting editions'), Gilbert early established as firm a control of his plays in print as in performance. The first volume of his *Original Plays* appeared in 1876, and by 1882 William Archer, the critic, noted in *English Dramatists of Today* that of all his subjects only Gilbert's work was widely available in an acceptable reading edition.[2] Even ten years later so successful a writer as Pinero had scarcely a play in print, though the copyright position had been transformed in the meantime by the passing of the International Berne Convention of 1886 and the American Copyright Act of 1891.

Gilbert's assertion of his rights simplifies an editor's task, since he can usually accept the text of the *Original Plays* reissued between 1909 and 1911 as the author's considered thoughts. Only one piece in the present selection — *Princess Toto* — presents particular textual problems. First performed in 1876, it does not appear to have been published until a few years later, and was never included in the collected edition. Since Gilbert deliberately included in the fourth series of his *Original Plays* several early works not printed as the volumes first appeared, this omission may be taken as intended. One possible explanation lies in his making over his interest in the work of his collaborator, Frederick Clay, under whose auspices revivals both in North America and London were given.[3] By collating the Lord Chamberlain's licensed text with the only published edition a comprehensive version of this elusive work has been prepared.

Most English playwrights, at least until the 1890s, were either actors or journalists who wrote for the theatre in a part-time capacity. Unlike fiction, poetry, or even philosophy, the drama was certainly not a profession to which an author chose to devote himself alone. If a writer for the theatre was not born into a theatrical family, he usually approached it by way of journalism, including theatrical journalism. The links between the law, Fleet Street, and the stage door were particularly close in the mid-Victorian period, and W.S. Gilbert made contact at all these points. By the time he turned to the theatre he was already an unsuccessful barrister and a successful journalist and writer of humorous verse. Again like most of his fellows, he obtained the ear of the managers and the eye of the spectators by modelling himself on established practitioners, some of them his personal acquaintances.

Certainly his most influential friend was T.W. Robertson, to whom he paid explicit tribute, both as 'stage manager' (meaning director of his own plays) and as the leading writer who introduced him to the St James's management as the man to write their Christmas 1866 entertainment, *Dulcamara: or The Little Duck and the Great Quack*. Gilbert's assertion that this was his first staged piece has been queried by the emergence of *Uncle Baby*, acted three years earlier at the Lyceum,[4] and we may conclude either that Gilbert was not particularly proud of *Uncle Baby* or that he was particularly proud of Robertson's introduction, or even that he wished to gloss over the debt Robertson owed in *Caste* (1867) to the younger man's first piece, which centred on an elderly relative's selfish dependence on two young and dutiful girls: an Eccles family in embryo.

If so, the debt was immediately repaid. *Highly Improbable* (1867) opens with a game of croquet played by a group of girls on a country lawn. Act I of *Ours*, which Robertson had brought out the previous year, introduces a game of bowls. The croquet is conducted with just that theatrical neatness and sweetness associated with Robertson's Prince of Wales's comedies:

> POLLY: Who's tired of croquet? . . . Nonsense — it's a flirtation in effigy — the best substitute for the real thing I know. You get your admirer sighing at your feet — thus (*placing the balls, with her foot on one of them, as though she were about to 'croquet' it*) — one indignant blow (*striking her ball with her mallet*) — and away you send him into the next county.

In the next few years Gilbert regularly paid lip-service to his tutor, from whose rehearsals, in a much quoted passage, he stoutly affirmed he had derived valuable instruction:

> He invented stage-management. It was an unknown art before his time. Formerly, in a conversation scene, for instance, you simply brought down two or three chairs from the flat and placed them in a row in the middle of the stage, and the people sat down and talked, and when the conversation was ended the chairs were replaced. Robertson showed how to give life and variety and nature to the scene by breaking it up with all sorts of little incidents and delicate by-play. I have been at many of his rehearsals and learnt a great deal from them.[5]

His most explicit debt was the title of *Charity* (1874), though the play itself took awkwardly to the stage. The lady in need of that greatest of gifts, Mrs Van Brugh, was something of a heavyweight by 'cup-and-saucer' standards: claiming married status and legitimacy for her child was not a Robertson heroine's line of business, and Robertson's sister, Madge Kendal, found herself fighting not only suspicion as a 'woman with a past' but the rapidly developing irony of her author, who depicted the 'villain', Smailey Senior, as a rascal with protoplasmal ancestors:

> the Smaileys are a very old and very famous family. Caius Smaileius came over with Julius Caesar: his descendants have born an untarnished scutcheon for eighteen hundred years.

A much neater piece of thanksgiving to Robertson was *Sweethearts*, played at the Prince of Wales's in the same year, by Robertson's leading lady, Mrs Bancroft, and later (in a revival at the Haymarket) with her husband, Squire Bancroft, opposite her. It is short — the only form in which Gilbert could imitate successfully — and Robertsonian not only in tone but in treatment: the transformation of the garden between the acts admirably sums up his mentor's trick of telling by showing, not saying, and in the first act the flirtatious heroine's use of the gardener to keep her admirer from declaring his suit recalls Robertson's control of motive by movement (as Polly controls Hawtree by domestic drill in *Caste*):

> SPREADBROW: . . . Wilcox is hard at work, I see.
> JENNY: Oh yes, Wilcox is hard at work. He is very industrious.
> SPREADBROW: Confoundedly industrious! He is working in the sun
> without his hat (*significantly*).
> JENNY: Poor fellow.
> SPREADBROW: Isn't it injudicious, at his age?
> JENNY: Oh, I don't think it will hurt him.
> SPREADBROW: I really think it will. (*He motions to her to send him
> away*.)
> JENNY: Do you? Wilcox, Mr Spreadbrow is terribly distressed because
> you are working in the sun.
> WILCOX: That's mortal good of him . . . Well, sir, the sun is hot, and I'll
> go and look after the cucumbers away yonder, right at the other end
> of the garden. (WILCOX *going* — SPREADBROW *is delighted*.)
> JELLY: No, no, no! — Don't go away! Stop here, only put on your hat.
> That's what Mr Spreadbrow meant. (WILCOX *puts on his hat*.)
> There, *now* are you happy?

The ending too has Robertson's affable acceptance, although Gilbert's own style would suggest the middle-aged man's rejection of the woman who rejected him in his youth. 'So far from the play being over, the serious interest is only just beginning' is a metaphor from the theatre rather than a lesson from life. But *Sweethearts* is virtually unique in that Gilbert tells a story in contemporary terms on its face values, without disguise (of period, place or habit) and without head-on collision between outward signs and inward searchings. 'Charm' was rarely a self-sufficient quality for him; here it sufficed and suffices.

In his apprentice days he turned to earlier models than Robertson. *Allow Me To Explain* (1867) is a brief farce which not only borrows its setting (a hotel corridor with several rooms all occupied by a different 'Mr Smith') from the early Victorian school of Maddison Morton, but even the occasional phrase from *Box and Cox*:

> CADDERBY: You're a clumsy fellow, sir!
> JOHN SMITH: You're a fool, sir!
> CADDERBY: Where are you going to, sir?
> JOHN SMITH: Well, if it comes to that, where are *you* shoving to, sir?

More immediately he found himself directed to the French drama, with its clockwork construction and lure of sophistication behind a discreet wink. Both *An Old Score* (1869) and the much later *Ne'er-Do-Weel* (1878) resolve their personal and financial issues by producing and polishing off a rich and titled relation, unmentioned until exterminated, to rescue the central character from ruin. In the former play we are told:

> Lord Ovington and his sons and his son's wife were crossing the Channel in his yacht this morning — a sudden squall upset the vessel, and he, with all hands —

which makes the less than noble Colonel Calthorpe the next Lord Ovington, while in the latter

> Lord Dunueggan, his cousin, died suddenly yesterday, and my father succeeds to the title and estates.

Often in these early plays Gilbert had to battle with second-rate models and second-rate standards of performance. *On Guard* (1871) presents seriously a 'school-chums-through-life' relationship between Guy Warrington and Dennis Grant threatened by their love for the same girl, and more seriously menaced by the use of an actress *en travestie* as Warrington, another nail in the coffin of transvestism as far as Gilbert was concerned.

A feature of English comedy in the 1870s was the coy introduction of 'Palais Royal' farce in homespun English habits. Gilbert found himself called on to play his part in this re-dressing, twice adapting Meilhac and Halévy's *Le Réveillon* (as *Committed for Trial* in 1874 and as *On Bail* in 1877), and twice working on Labiche and Marc-Michel's *Chapeau de Paille d'Italie* (as *The Wedding March* in 1873 and nearly twenty years later in musical form as *Haste to the Wedding*). It does not appear to have been a labour of love; in particular he wrote scornfully of the financial success of *The Wedding March*, 'the author thereof' having been paid 'considerably more than £2000 in return for two days' labour',[6] although it 'was little more than a bald translation' and 'the dialogue was, in itself, contemptible'. When a month earlier he was responsible for 'a free and easy version' of Meilhac and Halévy's *Le Roi Candaule*, he diverted the audience's attention from the 'sophisticated' nature of the original play-within-a-play by substituting his own *Happy Land*, which had offended the Lord Chamberlain on political, not sexual, grounds.[7] Nevertheless both the French piece and Gilbert's version were shortly to provide more than a hint for the *risqué Dominos Roses* and its popular English adaptation, *Pink Dominos* (1877).

During these years he also did a great deal of work in the flourishing but amorphous and largely indistinguishable fields of burlesque, extravaganza, and pantomime. It would be comforting to find these early musical pieces fostering the Savoy operas, but the Victorian burlesque was really too cramping a formula for so individual a writer as Gilbert to transcend. Not only were the subjects ready-made (though not necessarily topical: Gilbert's operatic targets during this period included *La Sonnambula*, *La Figlia del Regimento*, *L'Elisir d'Amore*, *Norma*, *Robert le Diable*, and *The Bohemian Girl*, all long-established favourites), but the lyrics were

governed by the music, always preselected. Gilbert's views on writing words to exist-
ing music, later loudly expressed, were doubtless formed at this time. Occasionally
he was driven to despair, as with

> Picky wicky, picky wicky, gay, gay, gay
> Very in a quiet sort of way, way, way,
> Showee, showee, showee time o' day, day, day,
> Ticky, wicky, picky, picky, pay, pay, pay.

(from *The Merry Zingara*, although the melody was drawn from Offenbach's *Robin-
son Crusoe*).

Much Victorian stage humour turned on the pun, and it is hard to convince a
theatrical public inured to the belief that all bad language is good stage fun that the
pun could be — and was — skilfully and wittily used by Victorian writers. Under
pressure Gilbert at this juncture sometimes settled for nonsense, as a little later in
The Merry Zingara:

> COUNT: A common gypsy, going through life's scene
>   With Miss Arline's an awful *misarleence.*

or, in *The Pretty Druidess*:

> NORMA: Go, close the gates, or otherwise, you know,
>   Some foe may come — which were not *cummy fo!*

where the primary rule of punning (that the *sound* of the words must be identical)
is flouted.

But immediately after this solecism the ear is beguiled with a lyric that has
Gilbert's own signature:

> NORMA: Young ladies, I'm going to superintend
>   Our Family Fancy Fair —
>   So gather around, if you would befriend
>   Our Family Fancy Fair.
>   For if we desire our funds to feed,
>   And make all our enemies freely bleed,
>   No weapons are ours, except indeed,
>   A Family Fancy Fair!
> ALL: A Family Fancy — Family Fancy —
>   Family Fancy Fair!
>   A Family Fancy — Family Fancy —
>   Family Fancy Fair!
> NORMA: In yonder domain we'll hold our tryst —
>   Our Family Fancy Fair —
>   A liberal gentleman can't resist
>   A Family Fancy Fair.
>   To flatter and wheedle and dazzle and coax,
>   These racketty, rollicking, Roman folks,
>   We're carefully planning that splendid hoax
>   A Family Fancy Fair!
> ALL: A Family Fancy — Family Fancy *etc.*

It is as though another voice has taken over. The setting was 'composed by T. German Reed, Esq., for *No Cards*, and introduced here by his kind permission'.

This attribution is significant, since *No Cards* (1869) was Gilbert's own work. Undoubtedly the restrictions placed on him in his early career riled. His article, 'Actors, Authors, and Audiences', published in 1890 but evidently written during the 1870s (and much later recast in dialogue as *Trying a Dramatist*), depicted another trial by jury, in this case of an author by his audience in the playhouse at the end of a performance. The unsuccessful piece, entitled *Lead* (it is not clear whether the mineral or the act of leading is intended, but either way the title is plainly fair comment), has resulted in its author being charged

> with one of the greatest offences that a man with any pretension to a literary position could commit — that of having written, and caused to be produced, an original stage-play which had not come up to the expectations of the audience.[8]

Much of the evidence throws light on the bad old ways of the bad old theatre days: the leading lady reveals that 'Two minor parts were fused with mine to make it worthy of my reputation'; the comedian wore 'a remarkably clever mechanical wig'; while the soubrette (who 'played a young governess in a country rectory who is secretly in love with the Home Secretary') wore short petticoats 'because the audience expected it of me', and introduced a song-and-dance, 'Father's pants will soon fit brother', in order to give briskness to the part; and the manager admits:

> I did not read the play before accepting it, because I do not profess to be a judge of a play in manuscript. I accepted it because a French play on which I had counted proved a failure.[9]

As has been seen, *Lead* was condemned because it was 'original' (unlike *The Wedding March*, which a witness praises for its 'inimitable' construction), and Gilbert's early plays were often an awkward amalgam of imitation and originality. *Randall's Thumb*, a substantial success at the Court in 1871, introduces a recognizably Gilbertian quartet: an old married couple who bill and coo to conceal their long partnership and two newly weds who bicker to cover up their status as novices, but they are the comic relief in a contrived story of crime, blackmail, and retribution. Gilbert's early essays for the commercial theatre, whether musical, like the pantomimes and burlesques, or 'legitimate', seem written 'down' to his audience, not 'up' to his own taste. The contrary is true of his work (including *No Cards*) for the Gallery of Illustration, a 'non-theatrical' enterprise by a former theatrical pair, Thomas German Reed and his wife, Priscilla Horton, once Macready's leading *comédienne*, catering to an audience that looked askance at the theatre. Between 1869 and 1875 Gilbert contributed five pieces to their repertoire, and in them a new and authentically Gilbertian voice can consistently be heard. The conditions of performance at the Gallery of Illustration were restrictive: no chorus, perhaps half a dozen principals, piano and harmonium instead of an orchestra, less than full length plays. But the actors had talent and taste, the audience intelligence, and Gilbert responded to their challenge.

The links between his work for the Reeds and the Savoy operas have been skilfully traced.[10] *Ages Ago* (1869) points clearly to *Ruddigore*; *Our Island Home* (1870) to *The Pirates of Penzance*. What is even more germane to Gilbert's career in the playhouse is the virtue he and the company made of necessity. Lacking numbers, they delighted in multiple impersonation: simple disguises (in *No Cards*); transmigration (in *Ages Ago*); playing 'themselves' as very-far-from-themselves (*Our Island Home*); switching minds and bodies (including trans-sexuality in *Happy Arcadia*); fictional characters taking over their own fates (*A Sensation Novel*). These brief pieces nevertheless achieved new levels of intellectual comedy for the Victorian theatre, and show Gilbert in a far more characteristic light. At the same time he was striving to refine his burlesques, but here the audience held him back. Both *The Princess* (1870) and *Thespis* (1871) mix Gilbertian originality with the commonplaces of the Victorian stage, including low comedians and actresses *en travestie*. Even more influential than the legacy handed down from the Gallery of Illustration to the Savoy operas was the shaping there of Gilbert's essential comic position: the assumption by one character of different roles (achieved at the Gallery for light-hearted laughter) led him to the consistent standpoint of his major comedies – the contention that human nature conceals its wholly selfish motivation behind the good manners of polite society.

In the brief musical plays Gilbert contributed to the commercial theatre at the start of the 1870s this message is wrapped in magic spells. *The Gentleman in Black* (1870) has the power to transfer one human soul to another's body, and exchanges Hans Gopp's with Baron Otto Von Schlachenstein's (who then turn out to have been exchanged at birth); the Bad Fairy in *Creatures of Impulse* (1871) transforms those who cross her into characters diametrically opposed to their established selves. In both cases the tone is noticeably sharper than that which Gilbert adopted for the Gallery of Illustration. In his full-length pieces, chiefly staged at the Haymarket during this decade, his cynical and sometimes even despairing point of view is given complete expression. These works (often termed the 'fairy plays', though the description could only strictly be applied to *The Wicked World*) mark an important step in Gilbert's dramatic development, and, it should be added, the development of contemporary theatrical taste. Any comparison of the demands they make on the audience's understanding with other 'schools' of the day – Robertson's 'cup-and-saucer' comedies, 'sophisticated' farce as purveyed by Wyndham at the Criterion, Lyceum melodrama with Irving triumphing over shallow if spectacular material – underlines the intelligence which the Haymarket public displayed in appreciating Gilbert's closely-argued and deeply pessimistic exposition.

Evidently the author at first felt nervous of both his theme and the audience, seeking to cloak the one and coax the other by 'make-believe': the Arabian Nights setting of *The Palace of Truth*; the classical framework of *Pygmalion and Galatea*; Fairyland itself in *The Wicked World*. Although increasingly confident in his 'originality', he still sought to vary its tone. *The Palace of Truth* (1870) includes a facetious variation on the underlying theme, in which the flirt, Azèma, spellbound by the magic palace of the title, betrays her motives while maintaining her manner:

PHILAMIR: I beg your pardon, but the furniture
               Has caught your dress.
AZEMA: (*rearranging her dress hastily*) Oh, I arranged it so,
               That you might see how truly beautiful
               My foot and ankle are (*as if much shocked at the exposé*).
PHILAMIR: I saw them well;
               They're very neat.
AZEMA: I now remove my glove
               That you may note the whiteness of my hand.
               I place it there in order that you may
               Be tempted to enclose it in your own.

Pygmalion and Galatea (1871) combines a semi-tragic theme of innocence, causing unhappiness and sacrificed to restoring propriety, with a passage of coy Victorian comedy between the wealthy patron, Chrysos, and the statue come to life:

GALATEA: How awkwardly you sit.
CHRYSOS: I'm not aware that there is anything
               Extraordinary in my sitting down.
               The nature of the seated attitude
               Does not leave scope for much variety.
GALATEA: I never saw Pygmalion sit like that.
CHRYSOS: Don't he sit down like other men?
GALATEA: Of course!
               He always puts his arm around my waist.
CHRYSOS: The deuce he does! Artistic reprobate!
GALATEA: But you do not. Perhaps you don't know how?
CHRYSOS: Oh yes; I *do* know how!
GALATEA: Well, do it then!
CHRYSOS: It's a strange whim, but I will humour her.
               You're sure it's innocence? (*Does so.*)
GALATEA: Of course it is.
               I tell you I was born but yesterday.

The Wicked World (1873) comes nearest to unity of tone, and even touches tragedy when Selene, the Fairy Queen, discovers that from her earthly gallant, Sir Ethnais, she has learnt not only love but jealousy:

Thou phantom of the truth — thou mimic god —
Thou traitor to thine own unhappy soul —
Thou base apostate to the lovely faith,
That thou hast preached with such false eloquence,
I am thine enemy! (*to her sisters*) Look on your work,
My gentle sisters. (*They look in horror.*) Are ye not content?
Behold! I am a devil, like yourselves!

The Palace of Truth may be regarded as the keystone of Gilbert's original drama, even though it derives from a French source (a story, not a play: Madame de Genlis's

Palais de la Vérité). Not only was it his first fully-developed essay in ironic contrast; it made extensive use of the 'lozenge' later to prove so dyspeptic to Sullivan – in this case a 'talisman' which nullifies the Palace's magic powers – and offers several character studies in greater detail than Gilbert had yet attempted: the reserved but deeply loving Princess Zeolide; the vain but worldly-wise Prince Philamir, the devious and semi-tragic Lady Mirza. *Pygmalion and Galatea* was to eclipse its predecessor's success, both initially and in a number of prestigious revivals, but it risked less to please more. William Archer's comment that 'Gilbert could never quite escape from that Palace of Truth which was the scene of his first serious play'[11] begs the question of whether Gilbert wanted to escape, but underlines the work's centrality.

All three plays were written in blank verse, a form Gilbert employed when aspiring to dramatic heights, but the aspiration outran the achievement. There is in this dramatic verse regularity and clarity, but none of the adroit surprise (both sweet and sour) which distinguished his *Bab Ballads* and was to lend enchantment to his best lyrics. In the operas the lyrics gained from the discipline of rhyme and brevity; in the fairy plays the verse rarely rises to emotional force, and often stretches humour unduly to conform to the metre. Not surprisingly after the success of *Pygmalion and Galatea* and *The Wicked World* Gilbert was tempted towards tragic themes, but seemed to confuse intensity with simplicity. *Broken Hearts* (1875) is the most economical of his full-length plays (a single scene, strict unity of time, a quartet of characters with two supernumeraries), but despite being set on a tropical island, the result is bleak and barren. Even his version of the Faust legend, *Gretchen* (1879), seems determined to sacrifice the theatrical elements in the story; there is no magic after the initial vision of Gretchen; Faust has no need of rejuvenation, since he is in the prime of life (though a renegade priest), and Mephistopheles thus mostly superfluous. But if there is no magic in the stage directions, there is no magic in the verse either.

The fairy plays served to distract both audience and author from the full force of his irony, and he skirted round contemporary scenes until his style was completely formed. But he was moving steadily towards a definition of that style, insisting increasingly on the seriousness of his furthest flights of fancy. His introductory note to *Engaged* (1877) is regularly cited:

> It is absolutely essential to the success of this piece that it should be
> played with the most perfect earnestness and gravity throughout. There
> should be no exaggeration in costume, make-up, or demeanour; and the
> characters, one and all, should appear to believe, throughout, in the per-
> fect sincerity of their words and actions. Directly the characters show that
> they are conscious of the absurdity of their utterances the piece begins to
> drag.

Less familiar but equally relevant is his preliminary directive to an earlier play, *The Wedding March*:

The dresses of the Wedding Party should be quaint, countrified and rather old-fashioned in character, but not too much exaggerated. Indeed the success of the piece depends principally on the absence of exaggeration in dress and 'make-up'. The characters should rely for the fun of their parts on the most improbable things being done in the most earnest manner *by persons of every-day life.* (Gilbert's italics)

The depiction of persons of every-day life was a task he tended to avoid. But in *Tom Cobb* (1875) and *Engaged*, its extended and uncompromising successor, he undertook this task while maintaining his characteristic comic position. Both plays are apparently realistic pictures of contemporary society, and forswear magic, whether from palaces or pills. They share a common theme and common ground: each features a barbed encounter between old schoolchums on which Wilde was to draw for Gwendolen's and Cecily's tea-party in *The Importance of Being Earnest*;[12] both present a heroine espoused to a man of whom she knows next to nothing; both pivot on the dead-or-alive status of the hero, and the financial expectations of the other characters which depend thereon.

In addition *Tom Cobb* develops the 'multiple identities' of Gilbert's Gallery of Illustration plays, replacing the magic of the earlier pieces with legal facts and fictions. To avoid his creditors one Tom Cobb assumes another (dead) Tom Cobb's identity; later he pretends to be a duke and then a major-general, an alias which involves him with a jilted fiancée and a suit for breach of promise. By the end of act II he is enmeshed in a web of Pirandello-esque proportions:

> (BULSTRODE *presents writ, which* CAROLINE, *kneeling at* TOM's *feet, reaches and hands to him, kissing his hand as she places the writ in it.*)

TOM: (*looking at writ*) Breach of promise! (*wildly*) Don't bring any actions, don't resort to any violent measures. You say I'm engaged to you. I dare say I am. If you said I was engaged to your mother I'd dare say it too. I've no idea who I am, or what I am, or where I am, or what I am saying or doing, but you are very pretty and you seem fond of me. I've no objection. I think I should rather like it: at least — *I'll try*!

Predictably, he discovers that he is in fact the grandson and heir of the man he first impersonated.

Similarly in *Engaged* the complications of a Scots 'marriage by declaration' leave the matrimonial status of Cheviot Hill and his three fiancées in total confusion. Inevitably others are caught in the imbroglio, in particular his friend Belvawney who, in a passage Gilbert was to draw on for *The Gondoliers*, expresses his divided loyalties in precisely calculated terms, such as a man-of-law could execute:

> Ladies — one word before I go. One of you will be claimed by Cheviot, that is very clear. To that one (whichever it may be) I do not address myself — but to the other (whichever it may be), I say, I love you

whichever you are) with a fervour which I cannot describe in words. If you (whichever you are) will consent to cast your lot with mine, I will devote my life to proving that I love you and you only (whichever it may be) with a single-hearted and devoted passion, which precludes the possibility of my ever entertaining the slightest regard for any other woman in the whole world. I thought I would just mention it. Good morning!

Finally the border-line between England and Scotland which has run through the play is shown to have run through the scene of the marriage ceremony, and the matter is decided on territorial grounds.

This legal usage supplies another clue to the character of the two comedies. In making the transition from the verse of the fairy plays Gilbert dropped the distinction between assumed altruism and basic selfishness which various devices (the Palace itself, the 'incarnation' of Galatea, the 'invisibility veil' in *Broken Hearts*) had emphasised. Instead contrast is achieved by dressing naked self-interest in elegant phrasing. Caroline Effingham does not have the music talents of the Plaintiff in *Trial by Jury*, but she stakes her claim just as lyrically:

> CAROLINE: . . . my poet-soldier – by our old vows – by the old poetic
> fire that burns in *your* heart and kindled mine, tell them – tell *me* –
> that you can explain everything. (*Falls on her knees to him.*)
> TOM: Upon my word, I shouldn't like to undertake to do that. Why, I
> never saw you before in all my life . . .
> CAROLINE: . . . I am told by those who understand these things that you
> have indeed compromised yourself to the extent required by our
> common law. But you will not – oh, you will *not* compel me to
> bring our sacred loves into Court. You are a poet – a great, great,
> poet – you will be faithful – you will be true.
> MRS EFFINGHAM: (*kneels*) Oh, sir, do not compel us to lay bare the
> workings of her young affections – do not force us to bring her very
> heartstrings into Court, that ribald minds may play upon them!
> BULSTRODE: (*gloomily*) To the tune of £5000.

In the same key Uncle Symperson in *Engaged*, having persuaded Cheviot he has nothing left to live for, finds himself denied his legacy when his nephew changes his mind, and expresses himself just as loftily:

> SYMPERSON: . . . My dear young friend, these clothes are symbolical;
> they represent my state of mind. After your terrible threat, which I
> cannot doubt you intend to put at once into execution –
> CHEVIOT: My dear uncle, this is very touching; this unmans me. But
> cheer up, dear old friend . . . I have consented to live.
> SYMPERSON: Consented to live? Why, sir, this is confounded trifling. I
> don't understand this line of conduct at all; you threaten to commit
> suicide; your friends are dreadfully shocked at first, but eventually
> their minds become reconciled to the prospect of losing you, they
> become resigned, even cheerful; and when they have brought

themselves to this Christian state of mind, you coolly inform them
that you have changed your mind and mean to live.

Engaged is undoubtedly Gilbert's most characteristic play. It exposes all its
dramatis personae as motivated by money. Cheviot is 'a young man of large
property, but extremely close-fisted'; to the impressionable Belinda Treherne
'business is business' and her pockets prove deeper than her passions; poor little
Minnie Symperson 'don't pretend to have a business head' but knows that 'the
Royal Indestructible Bank was not registered under the Joint-Stock Companies Act
of '62'. Angus Macalister rates his lost love at 'twa pound', and the lost love herself
is prepared to settle for 'thirty shillings'. There is a thoroughness about the calcu-
lations in the play which chilled the audience's admiration for its dexterity and
deftness. Even Gilbert himself seems to have reconsidered his position, for he
reverted to 'magic' in *The Sorcerer* a month later, and in his next comedy,
Foggerty's Fairy (1881), after which he abandoned 'straight' comedy altogether.
Yet *Engaged* earned several revivals,[13] and more significantly the flattery of
imitation by Shaw (in the prevailing tone of *Arms and the Man*) and Wilde (in both
tone and specific incidents in *The Importance of Being Earnest*).

His abjuration of comedy left a gap in his writing which he filled increasingly
with melodrama. This enormously popular Victorian genre inspired Gilbert to love
and laughter in roughly equal proportions. Some of his earliest journalism consisted
of parodies of the favourite melodramas of the day — an easy target but one he hit
fairly and squarely. The contrivances and coincidences of the plots especially
amused him, for example in *East Lynne*, as parodied in *Fun*, the husband's failure
to pursue his erring wife is justified in the following terms:

> I will not run after her, for I might catch her as she has only been gone a
> few minutes, and that would spoil the plot. I will simply tear my hair.
> (*Simply tears his hair.*)[14]

Coincidence was his target when parodying Wilkie Collins's *The Frozen Deep* (set in
Newfoundland), and at the same time laughing at his friend, Robertson, who in
Ours, produced earlier the same year (1866), despatched his two heroines to make
roly-poly pudding in the middle of the Crimean War:

> CLARA: . . . Suppose we should come across the explorers from the
> North Pole. Wouldn't that be a coincidence?
> LUCY: It would indeed. Ha! Here they are!
> (*Enter* LIEUTENANTS CRAYFORD, STEVENTON, *and
> other* EXPLORERS.)
> LIEUT. CRAYFORD: Lucy! You here? Who *would* have thought of seeing
> you? How dedo?[15]

A Sensation Novel too, although literary in subject and treatment, showed an affectionate understanding of stage melodrama. As with comedy, Gilbert tended to take
refuge in 'fancy dress' when first writing melodrama. *Dan'l Druce, Blacksmith*
(1876), a somewhat surprising stable-companion at the Haymarket for *Pygmalion
and Galatea* or *Engaged*, and suggested by *Silas Marner*, was dressed in seventeenth-

century stage English (it has happily been described as 'a play of the "second person singular" variety')[16] and the uniforms of Roundheads and Cavaliers. Even so something of the authentic Gilbert slipped into the Quaker Girl dialect of Dorothy, the foundling-heroine, on confronting the sailor-hero:

> I am rejoiced that I am decked in my new gown — it is more seemly than the russet, in which, methinks, I did look pale . . . Pity that I have not my new shoes, for they are comely; but they do compress my feet, and so pain me sorely. Nevertheless, I will put them on, for it behoveth a maiden to be neatly apparelled at all seasons.

Comedy and Tragedy (1884) was written to complete the bill for a revival of *Pygmalion and Galatea* by the American actress, Mary Anderson, and not only assumed period costume but deployed the role-playing of the Gallery of Illustration by making the central character an actress whose 'performance' takes place while hero and villain fight a duel for her reputation. It succeeds because it ends before the author has had time to sign it.

At the height of his fame as a librettist Gilbert chose to write two 'society' melodramas, such as filled the stage and auditorium of a number of London theatres like Drury Lane and the Adelphi in the 1880s and '90s. Success in contemporary melodrama proved even more elusive than in contemporary comedy. *Brantinghame Hall* (1888) takes a leaf from Charles Reade's book by opening in the Australian 'diggings' and moving on to ancestral England. It overtaxed both Gilbert's protégée, Julia Neilson (as a heroine who declares herself 'fallen' in order to save her lost husband's parents from ruin because of a will in her favour), and his manager, the Savoy stalwart, Rutland Barrington. *The Fortune Hunter* (1897) offers some comic relief, and seems aimed at the Adelphi public of William Terriss, but again the central situation is sadly miscalculated: the scheming suitor of the title, finding himself to be a father, forswears his fortune-hunting and provokes a rival to kill him in a duel, thus ensuring his wife's and child's future. Gilbert's adoption of melodrama as an alternative mode to comedy suggests that he found the simple conflict of honour and dishonour a welcome change from the complex ironies of his comedies.

At the very end of his career he achieved in *The Hooligan* (1911), written as a music-hall sketch, something quite outside his established range. It is an extended character-study in a cockney idiom he had scarcely ever attempted. Only by turning back to his adaptation of *Great Expectations* over thirty years before could a companion to this passage be found:

> SOLLY: Oh, it's 'ard — it's 'ard! I ain't like a ordinary bloke. I'm feeble-
> minded; the doctor said so, and 'e'd know. Then I've never 'ad no
> chanst — I've never been taught nuffin', and I've got a weak 'eart. I
> was in 'orsepital six weeks wiv a weak 'eart. Oh, my Gawd, it's 'ard;
> see 'ere — my fa'ver was a high toby cracksman;* my muvver was a

---

high toby cracksman: highway robber ('toby' derives from 'tobar', meaning 'road' in the secret language of the Irish tinkers).

> prig and did two stretches; my bruvvers and sisters were all prigs, and every chap as I ever knowd was a thief o' sorts — cracksmen, cly-fakers, and wot not! Am I to be judged like a bloke wot's been brought up fair and strite, and taught a tride, and can look on a ticker wiv 'is hooks safe in 'is trowsers' pockets? Oh, my Gawd, it's 'ard, it's 'ard! (*Sobs on bed.*)

At the end irony is combined more effectively with melodrama than in any of Gilbert's earlier essays in this vein.

> SOLLY: (*who has been gazing wildly at the* GOVERNOR *during this speech as one who is completely dazed*) Commuted! Penal servitude! Then — then I'm not to be 'ung? I'm to live?
>
> > (GOVERNOR *nods assent. The* CHAPLAIN *goes to* SOLLY *to raise him from the floor.* SOLLY *springs up, straightens himself, looks wildly around, gives an agonized cry as of a man in acute pain, and falls senseless on the stage. They bend over him — the* DOCTOR *turns him face upwards, feels his heart, and puts his ear to* SOLLY's *mouth.*)
>
> DOCTOR: Heart failure.
> GOVERNOR: Dead?
> DOCTOR: Dead. (*Movement.*)
> > CURTAIN

Gilbert also died of heart failure, but while assisting a girl who was in difficulties when swimming, and the parallel between the Hooligan's end and the author's, which has been pointed out, is really more arbitrary than apt. Gilbert had lived a long and enormously productive life. His Hooligan died young, but in dying was saved from the living death to which his reprieve sentenced him. What does strike the imagination is the endeavour of an author, who consistently found 'persons of everyday life' outside his range, to depict at the end of his life not indeed an every-day situation, but a situation seen without distortion. The irony lies in the plot, not the perspective.

The apprenticeship to comic opera which Gilbert served from the outset of his theatrical career took diverse forms: pantomime, burlesque, extravaganza, and the musical plays for the German Reeds which confirmed him in the belief that intelligence and originality could find a hearing in the musical theatre of his day. These exercises pointed to two works: *Thespis* (1871) and *Princess Toto* (1876), both full-length though neither fully-formed. *Thespis*, his first collaboration with Sullivan and also his first extended libretto to an original score (which was promptly lost and, contrary to its comic opera origins, has never reappeared), still retained a foot-hold in the world of burlesque. Written for the Gaiety, a house distinguished for its burlesque performers, including in this instance J.L. Toole, Nellie Farren, and the Brothers Payne, it brought together Greek gods and theatrical mortals, both elements of traditional burlesque, although not a 'travesty' of any particular piece.

For *Princess Toto* (apparently written before the partnership with Sullivan was cemented in *Trial by Jury*, though not staged until the following year), Gilbert returned to Frederick Clay, his collaborator on *Ages Ago* for the German Reeds and *The Gentleman in Black*, as well as the gentleman who introduced him to Sullivan. Like *Thespis* it voiced his challenge to the restrictive practices of the musical stage. In this piece he managed to throw off the conventions of Victorian burlesque; the well-known picture of Kate Santley in the title part,[17] although regarded as illustrating a concession to the travesty role, more properly illustrates a concession to the lady's legs as lady's legs. He was still struggling, however, to achieve both originality and the full-length form. In effect *Princess Toto* consists of three acts with different settings, choruses, and identities (the proprieties of King Portico's court; the laxities of the Brigand Barberini's lair; the indolence of the Indian Chief's island), welded uncertainly by the lamentable lapses of the Princess's memory.

On the other hand the lyrics include both the kindest and the most complete statement of that dichotomy of expressed intention and performance which underlies so much of Gilbert's work. Toto explains her vacillation by distinguishing between the world in which she lives and the world of which she dreams, and concludes:

> Oh, if we, who are wide awake,
> And very shrewd and deep,
> Could wipe out every sad mistake
> By falling fast asleep;
> If from our folly we were freed
> Whene'er a nap we take,
> How very, very few indeed
> Would ever keep awake!

Later she demonstrates her somnambulist state by singing to Prince Caramel the first verse of her *credo*:

> My simple heart knows no deceit.
> It loves but thee alone,
> And while I live that heart will beat
> For thee, my own — my own

and singing the second verse to Prince Doro 'not noticing that any change has taken place'.

Within this framework are placed both novel touches and features soon to be familiar from the Savoy operas; amongst the latter a Tremendous Swell who, before his eyesight deteriorated, was known as 'Pish-tush-pooh-bah or the Oxy-hydrogen Microscope'; an early example of the parable-in-song ('The pig with a Roman nose'); and a set-piece finale with brigands who repeatedly sing 'Let us follow' and a leader who protests:

> It's all very well to cry 'Follow'
> But why the dickens don't you do it?

The dramatis personae also illustrate Gilbert's curious association of appetites, for in the original version the distaff side includes Jelly, Sago, Tapioca, and Vermicelli. The text itself contains two unusually elaborate parodies, one of Longfellow:

> If you ask me if I'm equal
> To sustain the part of Red Man
> So as to defy detection,
> I would answer, I would tell you,
> If the being quite familiar
> With the metre and construction
> Of the poem 'Hiawatha'
> Is enough to qualify me,
> Apprehend no kind of danger!
> For I'd give to Paw-puk-ke-wis,
> Paw-puk-ke-wis the great boaster,
> Or the lovely Mi-ne-ha-ha,
> Six to four and beat 'em easy!

The other suggests 'Nigger Minstrels' (or as the Victorians liked to style them 'Ethiopian Serenaders'):

> With skip and hop,
>   With jerky jump,
> We come down plop,
>   And come down plump;
> We are installed
>   In Indian rig,
> Our name is called
>   Hop — pe — de — gig.
> Hoppedegig, Hoppedegig,
> Hoppedegig are we,
> Hoppedegig, Hoppedegig,
> From an isle beyond the sea,
> Hoppedegig, Hoppedegig,
> You think our colour's paint.
> Hoppedegig, Hoppedegig,
> I do not say it ain't.

The stage history of *Princess Toto* winds intriguingly through the early collaboration of Gilbert and Sullivan, the partnership which took over from Gilbert and Clay. Its first performance was soon eclipsed by the success of *The Sorcerer*; its first American production took place between D'Oyly Carte's staging there of *HMS Pinafore* and *The Pirates of Penzance*; and it was revived at the Opera Comique when *Patience* moved across to the newly built Savoy. Its omission from Gilbert's collected works has caused it to be more referred to than read; nevertheless the forgetful Princess should not be forgotten.

The popular and artistic success of Gilbert's partnership with Sullivan not only terminated his collaboration with Clay but substantially restricted his work as a playwright. As has been seen, *Engaged* and *Gretchen* mark the consummation of his comic and tragic endeavours, with significantly contrasted results. In comic opera he found an ideal expression for his central philosophy, through the mouths of characters who sing like sirens but speak polished and pointed prose. In Sullivan he found a partner who could enhance his gift of irony and match his lyrical litheness, while offsetting the pessimism and callousness some detected in his plays. The curiously distant tone of their collaboration has been emphasized — not only their 'quarrels', but the formality of their communication even when on friendly terms, always calling each other by surname, which was not the universal Victorian practice, though doubtless more common than today. Where Gilbert was concerned, working at arm's length like this may have been an artistic stimulus. Certainly he needed criticism to produce perfection, and the operas he wrote with (though not necessarily for) other, lesser men during breaks in the collaboration — *The Mountebanks* (1892) and *His Excellency* (1894) — betray the flaws of grotesquerie and overemphasis which Sullivan sought to refine and mostly succeeded.

The Savoy series itself took time to develop. The theatrical and topical elements in *The Sorcerer*, *HMS Pinafore*, *The Pirates of Penzance*, *Patience*, and *Iolanthe* commended them strongly to a public which, although outgrowing the crudities of burlesque performance, retained a taste for burlesque. The maturity of *The Mikado*, *The Yeomen of the Guard*, and *The Gondoliers*, with their self-sufficient stories and extended scores, reflects the collaborators at their most confident, and celebrates a musical theatre which is effectively independent of the past and fearless for the future. In this sense *Princess Ida* and *Ruddigore*, for all their charms, marked a reversion to secondary sources, just as the final operas, *Utopia Limited* and *The Grand Duke*, were not only products of failing inspiration but a return to the political and theatrical Aunt Sallies of Victorian burlesque. Nevertheless whatever comparisons or reservations individual operas may occasion, the Savoy series remains unique, both in the success its creators sustained over twenty years and in the delight they and their interpreters have provided since. It is sometimes objected that Gilbert and Sullivan cannot be translated and only appeal to English-speaking audiences; if they could be translated, they would not be unique, and they would appeal less to those who prize the originals.

For Victorian audiences the Savoy shared with the Lyceum under Henry Irving the credit of restoring theatregoing to the fashionable calendar during the 1880s. If the Lyceum was a National Theatre before the days of the Arts Council, the Savoy was an English National Opera without subsidy. The achievements of the two enterprises run in fascinating parallel. Irving built his undisputed leadership on Shakespeare and melodrama — often Shakespeare *as* melodrama — and brought this popular but sometimes despised form to the pitch of an English Romantic revival in the theatre. D'Oyly Carte by staging Gilbert and Sullivan at the Savoy raised the suspect genre of comic opera to an entertainment which was not only respectable and respected but enjoyable and enjoyed.

The reaction to their achievements was strongly contrasted, though no less instructive. Irving's concentration on costume drama and neglect of contemporary playwrights provoked a demand for intellectual drama which his competitors in the

1890s satisfied to their own and their audiences' profit. Alexander at the St James's sponsored Wilde's and Pinero's society plays; Wyndham at the Criterion staged the fashionable dramas of Henry Arthur Jones. The popularity of Gilbert and Sullivan on the other hand led to a rejection of satire in favour of sentiment, and George Edwardes (briefly D'Oyly Carte's assistant at the Savoy) met this at the Gaiety and elsewhere with the newly devised musical comedy, far less intellectual than Savoy opera, but offering broader comedy and simpler music. Thus the Lyceum's emphasis on 'sensation' provoked a taste for 'problem plays', but the Savoy's sophistication encouraged a turn to naïveté. It should be noted, however, that whereas society drama itself spurred on the Shavian 'play of ideas', musical comedy could not long exclude Gilbert and Sullivan, and in due course the Savoy operas regained and extended their public, while the serious drama of Pinero and Jones lost its hold.

The termination of his partnership with Sullivan after *The Grand Duke* led to seven years' silence for Gilbert. But three of his works staged late in his career illustrate diversely his preoccupation with established theatrical formulae. *The Fairy's Dilemma* (1904) waves a somewhat uncertainly magic wand, though the notion of reviving the combination of pantomime 'opening' and Harlequinade by blending a Drury Lane melodrama, including Bad Baronet and Lady of Lineage, with the traditional figures of Clown, Pantaloon, Harlequin, and Columbine, is intriguing. However, Gilbert's insistence that the actors 'double' both sets of characters defeats his purpose; the mock-melodramatics may tickle the intelligence and the traditional slapstick the senses, but since the performers cannot carry out both tasks simultaneously or equally well, it follows that one or other of the spectator's faculties will be left unsatisfied. *Fallen Fairies* (1909), a musical version of *The Wicked World*, demonstrates like *Princess Ida* that though Gilbert often found inspiration in his non-dramatic work, particularly *The Bab Ballads*, drawing on his own plays was something of a sterile process. The adaptation coarsens the passionate moments of the play, and cheapens the comic.

Rosencrantz and Guildenstern boasts a different pedigree, one in fact largely literary. Not only did it derive from Shakespeare's tragedy, but it first appeared in the pages of *Fun* (between 12 and 26 December 1874),[18] and was occasioned by the success and controversy attending Irving's *Hamlet* at the Lyceum. Its performance nearly twenty years later in 1891 marked a graceful swan-song for Victorian burlesque, by this date almost completely absorbed in comic opera, pantomime, and before long musical comedy.

No doubt because he was writing to be read, Gilbert forswore many of the usual comic aids of the 'travesty'. There are no songs, no low sentiments from lofty mouths, or lofty sentiments from lowly mouths, and a positive prohibition on broad comedy in this Hamlet's Advice to the Players:

> I pray you, let there be no huge red noses, nor extravagant monstrous wigs, nor coarse men garbed as women, in this comi-tragedy; for such things are as much as to say, 'I am a comick fellow — I pray you laugh at me, and hold what I say to be cleverly ridiculous'. Such labelling of

humour is an impertinence to your audience, for it seemeth to imply that they are unable to recognize a joke, unless it be pointed out to them. I pray you avoid it.

In fact the piece is almost wholly a reworking of the play scene, by-passing the rest of the plot, and once again Gilbert in imitative vein proves happiest when briefest. In performance the trifle shows its theatrical quality, and was regularly used for 'mixed' bills. Gilbert the 'stage manager' emerges in the sly comment that whatever the nationality of the principal actor,

Whether he's dark or flaxen − English − French −
Though we're in Denmark, AD, ten − six − two −
He always dresses as King James the First!

and in the skilful handling of Rosencrantz's and Guildenstern's interrupting 'To be or not to be', leading Hamlet to the unchallengeable conclusion:

It must be patent to the merest dunce
Three persons can't soliloquize at once!

What particularly commends the piece to the collector is the knowledge that Claudius (like the Associate in *Trial by Jury*) was a part Gilbert himself played 'on request', for Claudius is here the author of the 'Tragedy of Gonzago', on which its creator's verdict is final:

QUEEN: And how long did it run?
CLAUDIUS: About ten minutes.
          Ere the first act had traced one-half its course
          The curtain fell, never to rise again!

It is intriguing too to note that the central position of Rosencrantz and Guildenstern in the story of Hamlet was to be taken up in mid-twentieth century by another playwright whose approach could be described as partly Gilbertian: Tom Stoppard.

This survey of Gilbert the dramatist began by stressing his originality, a quality which often denied him the popular success accorded less talented contemporaries, and discouraged complete acceptance of his most individual work, as opposed to compromises, either (like *Pygmalion and Galatea*) of his own devising, or (like the Savoy operas) the product of collaboration. Perhaps it could most fittingly conclude by stressing another quality: his thoroughness. This is easily demonstrated by statistics, for in an age of enormous theatrical output and much ephemera, his was still an extraordinary record: at least seventy-one works for the stage over a period of forty-five years, an impressive tally both quantitatively and qualitatively. During 1871, for instance, London saw first productions of *Randall's Thumb*; *A Sensation Novel*; *Creatures of Impulse*; his adaptation of *Great Expectations*; *On Guard*; *Pygmalion and Galatea*; and *Thespis*. The texts of at least the major plays testify to the thoroughness with which Gilbert the writer matched the fully-documented methods of Gilbert the 'stage manager'. If he was Robertson's disciple in this, he was by reason of his much longer career and subtler range a disciple who outstripped his master, and himself inspired such director−dramatists as Pinero and Shaw.

When Gilbert was knighted in 1907, he took some pains to point out that 'no dramatic author as such ever had it [the accolade] for dramatic authorship alone',[19] evidently a reference to Burnand (knighted for services to literature in 1902) amongst others. Pinero was similarly honoured two years later, but it seems certain that with their names this particular roll of honour is complete. J.M. Barrie, created a baronet in 1922, was also recognized for services to literature, and the great diversity of dramatic writing since the introduction of film and television suggests that those knights who follow in the steps of Noel Coward and Terence Rattigan will not be singled out solely for their dramatic authorship.

Gilbert's dramatic reputation has followed the exceptional character of his official honours: for at least twenty years recognized as the leader of his profession, he suffered almost total eclipse during his last years and in the decade following his death. His plays, with their scrupulously crafted structure and elegant dialogue, served as models for a generation of writers who, like Pinero and Henry Arthur Jones, struck a serious, socially relevant note or, like Wilde and Shaw, applied his command of paradox and fancy to themes which appealed to the sophisticated audiences Gilbert had himself helped to create. Conversely the musical theatre increasingly rejected the satire and irony of his libretti, turning instead to the simple charms of musical comedy. For ten years the Savoy operas were banished from the West End stage, but starting with the 1919 season they recaptured the public they had once conquered, and have never lost again.

It has been suggested in this account of the plays that by their nature they now appeal more strongly to the reader than the playgoer, but that is in itself a powerful argument for making a selection available once more after seventy years. The Gilbert of Gilbert-and-Sullivan needs no advocate; the Gilbert whose *Original Plays* re-established the drama in England as worth publishing has been neglected. Both for what they inspired and what they are, the plays of W.S. Gilbert deserve attention.

NOTES

1   Letter quoted in Sidney Dark and Rowland Grey, *W.S. Gilbert: His Life and Letters* (1923), p. 196.
2   William Archer, *English Dramatists of Today* (1882), pp. 6–7.
3   See Robert Binder, 'Gilbert's Other Princess' in the *Gilbert and Sullivan Journal* vol. X no. 15 (Autumn 1978).
4   See Terence Rees (ed.), *Uncle Baby: A Comedietta by W.S. Gilbert* (privately printed, London, 1968).
5   Interview with William Archer in *Real Conversations* (1904), p. 114, and widely reprinted, e.g. in Dark and Grey, *W.S. Gilbert*, p. 59.
6   'Actors, Authors, and Audiences' in *Foggerty's Fairy and Other Tales* (1890), p. 228.
7   See Terence Rees (ed.), *The Realm of Joy* (privately printed, London, 1969).
8   'Actors, Authors, and Audiences', pp. 215–16.
9   *Ibid.* p. 217.

10 See Jane W. Stedman, *Gilbert Before Sullivan: Six Comic Plays by W.S. Gilbert* (1967).
11 *The Old Drama and the New* (1923), p. 276.
12 Noted by Lynton Hudson in *The English Stage 1850–1950* (1951), pp. 102–5, and others.
13 For example, at the Court in 1881, by Tree at the Haymarket in 1886, and more recently by the National Theatre at the Old Vic in 1975. *Engaged! or Cheviot's Choice*, a comic opera adapted from the play, with music arranged from Sullivan, was first produced in 1962 and published by Chappell (1963).
14 *Fun* 17 February 1866, p. 233.
15 *Fun* 17 November 1866, p. 101.
16 Hesketh Pearson, *W.S. Gilbert: His Life and Strife* (1957), p. 64.
17 Reproduced in R. Mander and J. Mitchenson (eds.), *A Picture History of Gilbert and Sullivan* (1962), p. 17.
18 For details of the play's published and stage history, see Stanley Wells (ed.), *Nineteenth Century Shakespeare Burlesques* vol. IV (1978), pp. xiv–xix.
19 Dark and Grey, *W.S. Gilbert*, p. 196.

BIOGRAPHICAL RECORD

18 November 1836	William Schwenck Gilbert born at 17 Southampton Street, Strand, London, eldest child and only son of William Gilbert, retired naval surgeon, and his wife Anne, née Morris.
c. 1839	Kidnapped by brigands at Naples. Ransomed for £25.
1842	Sent to school at Boulogne, France.
1846–9	Attended Western Grammar School, Brompton, London.
1849–52	Attended Great Ealing School. Head boy.
1853–7	Attended King's College, London. BA 1857.
1855	Entered Inner Temple, London, as law student.
1857–61	Assistant clerk in Education Dept of Privy Council offices, at a salary of £120 p.a.
1857–83	Served in 5th West Yorkshire Militia and later the Royal Aberdeenshire Militia.
1858	Translation of 'Laughing Song' from *Manon Lescaut* (Auber) sung by Mlle Parepa at Promenade Concert, Covent Garden.
1861–71	Contributed regularly to *Fun*, occasionally to *Punch*, *Illustrated Times* etc.
1862	Inherited £300 and resigned clerkship.
1863	Called to Bar.
31 October 1863	*Uncle Baby* (his first identified play) produced at the Lyceum.
1865	Illustrated his father's novel, *The Magic Mirror*.
1866	Joined Northern Circuit as barrister.
29 December 1866	*Dulcamara* (his first acknowledged piece for the theatre, written at the suggestion of T.W. Robertson) produced at the St James's.
6 August 1867	Married Lucy Blois Turner at St Mary Abbot's, Kensington, and set up house at Eldon Road, Kensington.
1868	Moved to 8 Essex Villas, Kensington. 'Trial by Jury' published in *Fun*.
1869	*The Bab Ballads* published. Illustrated his father's novels, *King George's Middy* and *The Seven League Boots*.
29 March 1869	*No Cards* produced at the Gallery of Illustration (his first work here).
1870	Served as correspondent for *The Observer* in Paris during the Franco-Prussian War.

19 November 1870	*The Palace of Truth* (his first 'fairy play') produced at the Haymarket.
9 December 1871	*Pygmalion and Galatea* produced at the Haymarket.
26 December 1871	*Thespis* (his first collaboration with Sullivan) produced at the Gaiety.
1873	Unsuccessfully sued the *Pall Mall Gazette* for calling parts of *The Wicked World* 'coarse and indecent'. *More Bab Ballads* published.
4 January 1873	*The Wicked World* produced at the Haymarket.
7 November 1874	*Sweethearts* produced at the Prince of Wales's.
12–26 December 1874	'Rosencrantz and Guildenstern' published in *Fun* (his last contribution).
25 March 1875	*Trial by Jury* (his first association with Richard D'Oyly Carte) produced at the Royalty.
1876	*Original Plays* published. Moved to 24 The Boltons, Kensington. Comedy Opera Company formed by Richard D'Oyly Carte.
2 October 1876	*Princess Toto* produced at the Strand.
1877	*Fifty Bab Ballads* published.
June 1877	Sued by Henrietta Hodson, actress and manageress, for 'conspiracy' etc.
3 October 1877	*Engaged* produced at the Haymarket.
17 November 1877	*The Sorcerer* produced at the Opera Comique.
25 May 1878	*HMS Pinafore* produced at the Opera Comique.
1879	Partnership formed between Gilbert, Sullivan, and D'Oyly Carte. Profits from the production of their operas to be divided equally.
31 July 1879	Attempt by directors of the Comedy Opera Company to seize scenery of *HMS Pinafore* at the Opera Comique.
October 1879	Gilbert, Sullivan and D'Oyly Carte travel to New York for première of 'authorized' *HMS Pinafore* and world première of *The Pirates of Penzance*.
3 April 1880	*The Pirates of Penzance* produced at the Opera Comique.
October 1880	*The Martyr of Antioch* (oratorio, adapted by Gilbert from H.H. Milman, music by Sullivan) performed at the Leeds Festival.
1881	*Original Plays*, second series, published.
23 April 1881	*Patience* produced at the Opera Comique.
10 October 1881	Savoy Theatre opened by D'Oyly Carte and let to the D'Oyly Carte Opera Company at £4000 p.a.
15 October 1881	Revival of *Princess Toto* at the Opera Comique.
1882	Moved to 39 Harrington Gardens, Kensington.

25 November 1882	*Iolanthe* produced at the Savoy.
3 February 1883	New, 5-year, agreement signed by Gilbert, Sullivan, and D'Oyly Carte.
22 May 1883	Knighthood conferred on Sullivan.
5 January 1884	*Princess Ida* produced at the Savoy.
11 October 1884	Revival of *The Sorcerer* at the Savoy (in lieu of new opera).
14 March 1885	*The Mikado* produced at the Savoy.
22 January 1887	*Ruddigore* produced at the Savoy.
12 November 1887	Revival of *HMS Pinafore* at the Savoy.
17 March 1888	Revival of *The Pirates of Penzance* at the Savoy.
7 June 1888	Revival of *The Mikado* at the Savoy.
3 October 1888	*The Yeomen of the Guard* produced at the Savoy.
24 April 1889	Opening of the Garrick Theatre (financed by Gilbert).
7 December 1889	*The Gondoliers* produced at the Savoy.
1890	*Foggerty's Fairy and Other Tales* published. Quarrelled with D'Oyly Carte and withdrew from partnership with him and Sullivan.
September 1890	Moved to Grim's Dyke, Harrow Weald, Middlesex.
1891	*Songs of a Savoyard* published. Appointed Deputy Lieutenant for County of Middlesex.
6 May 1891	Command Performance of *The Gondoliers* before Queen Victoria at Windsor.
3 June 1891	*Rosencrantz and Guildenstern* produced at the Vaudeville.
4 September 1891	Command performance of *The Mikado* before Queen Victoria at Balmoral.
1892	Appointed Justice of the Peace for the division of Gore, Middlesex.
27 April 1892	Revival of *Rosencrantz and Guildenstern* at the Court.
1893	Reconciled with D'Oyly Carte and resumed collaboration with Sullivan.
7 October 1893	*Utopia Limited* produced at the Savoy.
1895	*Original Plays*, third series, published.
7 March 1896	*The Grand Duke* produced at the Savoy.
1898	*The Bab Ballads, with which are included Songs of a Savoyard* published.
22 November 1900	Death of Sullivan, aged 58.
3 April 1901	Death of D'Oyly Carte, aged 56.
1905	Entered into new agreement with Mrs D'Oyly Carte, granting her exclusive performing rights in Gilbert and Sullivan operas.
1906	Elected to Garrick Club.

12 June 1906	Played Associate in *Trial by Jury* at Ellen Terry Jubilee Matinee, Drury Lane.
March 1907	Revival of *The Mikado* by D'Oyly Carte Company forbidden, in deference to State Visit to London by Prince Fushimi of Japan.
30 June 1907	Knighted by King Edward VII at Buckingham Palace.
2 February 1908	Congratulatory dinner on his knighthood given at the Savoy Hotel.
August 1909	Gave evidence to Parliamentary Committee on Stage Censorship.
11 December 1909	*Fallen Fairies* (his last libretto) produced at the Savoy.
1911	*Original Plays*, fourth series, published.
27 February 1911	*The Hooligan* produced at the Coliseum.
27 May 1911	Died while swimming at Grim's Dyke.
2 June 1911	Buried at Great Stanmore, Middlesex.
1914	Unveiling of memorial by George Frampton in Embankment Gardens; inscribed 'His Foe was Folly and his Weapon Wit'.

THE PALACE OF TRUTH*

A fairy comedy

First produced at the Theatre Royal, Haymarket, London, on 19 November 1870, with the following cast:

KING PHANOR	Mr Buckstone
PRINCE PHILAMIR betrothed to Zeolide	Mr Kendal
CHRYSAL a complimentary courtier	Mr Everill
ZORAM a musical courtier	Mr Clark
ARISTAEUS an outspoken courtier	Mr Rogers
GELANOR chamberlain of the Palace of Truth	Mr Braid
QUEEN ALTEMIRE	Mrs Chippendale
PRINCESS ZEOLIDE	Miss Madge Robertson
MIRZA Zeolide's companion	Miss Caroline Hill
PALMIS the Queen's companion	Miss Fanny Wright
AZEMA a coquette	Miss Fanny Gwynne

ACT I: Gardens of KING PHANOR's country house. Morning. Mr Morris†
ACT II: Interior of the Palace of Truth. Noon. Mr O'Connor†
ACT III: The Avenue of Palms within the precincts of the Palace of Truth. Night.
    Mr O'Connor

---

*Text used: *Original Plays*, first series (1876, reissued 1909), collated with Lacy's acting edition no. 1332 (?1870).
  Here and subsequently minor variants in stage directions are not listed.
† John O'Connor was the resident scene painter at the Theatre Royal, Haymarket, and also painted the scenery for *Engaged*. 'Mr Morris' seems to have been his assistant.

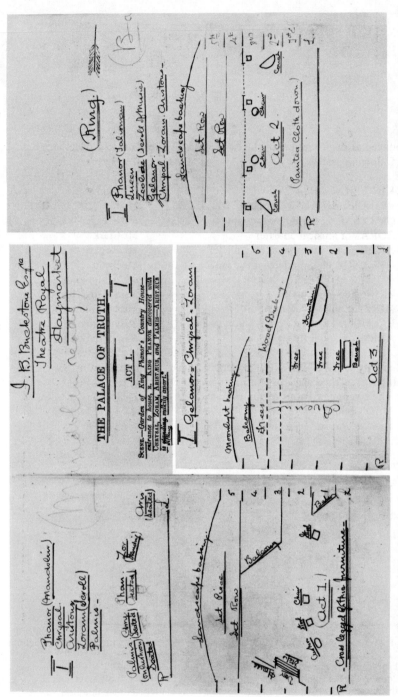

I *The Palace of Truth.* Detail from the prompt-copy, once in the possession of J.B. Buckstone (lessee of the Theatre Royal, Haymarket), who created the part of King Phanor. No sketches of the original production appear to have survived, but these diagrams give some indication of the settings. Act I, left; act III, below, centre; act II, right

28

ACT I

Garden of KING PHANOR'*s country house.* KING PHANOR *discovered with*
CHRYSAL, ZORAM, ARISTAEUS, *and* PALMIS. ARISTAEUS *is standing sulkily
apart. As the curtain rises,* KING PHANOR *is finishing a recitation which he is
accompanying on a mandolin, in a very affected manner.*

PHAN: 'Oh, I would not — no, I would *not* be there!'
         (ZORAM *and* CHRYSAL *applaud vigorously.*)

CHRYS: My lord, I pray you read it once again,
         My ears are greedy for the golden sound.

PHAN: Chrysal, you make me blush!

CHRYS: My lord, a blush
         Is modesty's sole herald — and true worth
         Is ever modest. Pray you, sir, again!

PHAN: It's a poor thing — a string of platitudes —
         Stale metaphors — time-honoured similes.
         I'm a poor poet, gentlemen!

CHRYS: I swear
         There never lived a poet till now!

ZORAM: And then
         The music you have wedded to the words
         (I speak of this with some authority)
         Shames, in its flow of rhythmic melody,
         The counterpoint of Adam de la Halle!

PHAN: (*bashfully*) The merit is not altogether mine.
         I wrote the music — but I did not make
         This dainty instrument. Why, who could fail
         To charm, with such a mandolin as this?

ZORAM: Believe me, the result would be the same,
         Whether your lordship chose to play upon
         The simple tetrachord of Mercury
         That knew no diatonic intervals,
         Or the elaborate dis-diapason
         (Four tetrachords, and one redundant note),
         Embracing in its perfect consonance
         All simple, double and inverted chords!

PHAN: (*to* CHRYSAL) A wonderful musician — and a man
         Of infinite good taste!

ZORAM: Why, from my birth
         I have made melope and counterpoint
         My favourite study.

PHAN: And you really care
          To hear my work again, O melodist?

ZORAM: Again, my lord, and even then again!

PHAN: (*recites*) 'When pitch-encrusted night aloft prevails;
         When no still goddess through the mid-air sails;
         When scorpions vomit forth their poisonous scum;

When to the demon tryst gaunt witches come;
When noisome pestilence stalks through the glen,
Bellowing forth its enmity to men;
When ghastly toads scream loudly through the air;
Oh, I would not — no, I would *not* be there!'

CHRYS: (*in raptures*) Why, where's the cunning of the sorcerer
    Placed by the magic of such words as these?
    'When pitch-encrusted night aloft prevails';
    Why, there's an epithet might make day night,
    And shame the swallows to their couching place!
    'When no still goddess through the mid-air sails'!
    Why, here's a blackness, Zoram, so intense
    It scares the very deities away!

PHAN: (*explaining*) 'Still goddess' means the moon.

CHRYS: The moon — my lord?
    Of course — the moon! See how, in ignorance,
    We seek upon the surface of the wave
    For pearls that lie uncounted fathoms deep.
    The darkness frightens e'en the moon away!
    The metaphor is perfect!

PHAN: (*annoyed*)   No, no, no!
    The moon has not yet risen, sir! The moon
    Frightens the darkness — darkness don't frighten *her*!
    Why sits the genial Aristaeus there
    All solitary? How d'you like my work?
    (*aside to* CHRYSAL) We'll have some fun with him.
                 (*aloud*) Your verdict, come!

ARIST: I'm blunt and honest. I can't teach my tongue
    To lie, as Zoram here, and Chrysal do.
    I tell the truth, sir. If you want to know
    My estimate of what you've given us,
    I think your poetry contemptible —
    Your melody, my lord, beneath contempt.

PHAN: That's rather strong.

ARIST: It's strong, my lord, but true.
    I'm blunt — outspoken. If I've angered you,
    So much the worse; I always speak the truth.

CHRYS: Heed not the yelpings of this surly cur;
    Nought satisfies him, Phanor!

ARIST: There you're wrong,
    For I was satisfied to hear it once;
    'Twas you that wanted it a second time.

CHRYS: Back to your kennel, sham Diogenes!

ARIST: I'm no Diogenes. *He* spent his life
    Seeking an honest man. *I* live in courts.

ZORAM: My lord, I pray you send this fellow hence,
    For he and we are always out of tune.

An inharmonious bracketing of notes,
Whose musical extremes don't coalesce:
He's sharp and we are flat.

ARIST: Extremely flat!

CHRYS: He's vinegar, my lord, and we are oil.

ARIST: Oil is a sickening insipid food
Unless it's qualified with vinegar.
I'm rough and honest. If I've angered you,
I'll go.

PHAN: No, no, you have not angered us.
(*aside to* ZORAM) I like the fellow's humour — he may rave!
I'm tired of hearing truths, so let him lie!
But where's Queen Altemire?

CHRYS: My lord, she comes —
A perfect type of perfect womanhood.
The dew of forty summers on her head
Has but matured her beauty, by my life!
For five-and-thirty years, a bud — and now
A rose full blown!

ARIST: Say over-blown.

PHAN: What's that?

ARIST: My lord, the Queen's too fat.

PHAN: Well, that may be.
But don't you tell her so. Your insolence
Amuses me — it won't amuse the Queen:
She has no sense of humour. So take care.

ARIST: My lord, I'm rough, but honest. I've a tongue
That cannot frame a lie.

PHAN: But bear in mind
Besides that very rough and honest tongue,
You have a palate, and a set of teeth,
And several delicate contrivances
That aid digestion. Tell her she's too fat,
And she may take offence; and, if she does,
She'll throw that apparatus out of work:
That's all.
        (*Enter the* QUEEN *and* MIRZA.)
                Good morning, Altemire, my Queen.
Why, you seem sad.

ALTEM: My lord, I'm very sad.

PALMIS: The Queen is sad! Zoram, attune your lyre
And soothe her melancholy.

ALTEM: No, no, no —
I'm not in cue for music — leave us, pray —
I would take counsel with my lord — look, sirs,
I am not well.
        (*The three* COURTIERS *exeunt into house.*)

PHAN: (*aside to* PALMIS) Palmis, what's here amiss?
            What causes this? Have *I* done anything?
PALMIS: I know not, but I think it bears upon
            Your daughter's troth to brave Prince Philamir.
            Whenever we have spoken on the point
            She has commanded silence.
PHAN: Well, we'll see.
            Chrysal awaits you — you may go to him;
            Talk to him of your pledge to marry *him*,
            And he'll not silence you. There, you may go.
               (*Exit* PALMIS *into house.*)
            Now what's the matter?*
ALTEM: Oh, I'm sick at heart
            With apprehension! Our dear Zeolide
            Tomorrow is betrothed to Philamir,
            The bravest and the most accomplished Prince
            In Christendom. Phanor, she loves him not!
PHAN: What makes you think so?
ALTEM: Phanor, you are blind!
            Why, see how coldly Zeolide receives
            His songs of love — his bursts of metaphor;
            'I love you, Philamir', and there's an end.
            She will vouchsafe her spouse-elect no more —
            No tenderness — no reciprocity;
            A cold, half-sullen and half-wayward smile,
            And that is all. The maiden lavishes
            More love upon her horse!
PHAN: Perhaps she thinks
            Her horse will bear such tokens of regard
            With more discretion than her lover would!
ALTEM: Phanor, I tell you she loves him not.
            I am a woman, with a woman's tact.
PHAN: She *says* she loves him.
ALTEM: So indeed she says,
            And says no more. Phanor, had I been woo'd
            With ardent songs of overwhelming love,
            Framed by so fair a poet as Philamir,
            It would have turned my giddy woman's brain,
            And thrilled my reason to its very core!
PHAN: I never thought my wooing poetry,
            Now I begin to think it may have been.
MIRZA: Oh, sir, *I* love the Princess. Pause before
            You sacrifice her earthly happiness
            For sordid ends of selfish policy.

---

*Lacy adds: '*They sit . . .* MIRZA *standing, at some distance.'*

The Prince is rich. What then? The girl is poor.
But what is wealth of gold to wealth of love?
What famine's so deplorable as his
Who hungers for a love he cannot find?
What luxury so wearisome as hers
Who's surfeited with love she values not?
King Phanor, let the Princess be released!

ALTEM: My lady Mirza, you forget yourself!

MIRZA: I do forget myself, remem'bring her;
I have her happiness at heart. The maid
Is more than life to me. Forgive me, Queen.
I could not help but speak.

PHAN: Well, say no more.
I'll question her, and if it then appears
She loves not Philamir, she shall be free.
I also love the girl — but, here she comes.
I'll find some test which shall decide the point. (*Exit into house.*)
          (*Enter* ZEOLIDE.)*

ALTEM: My daughter, where's the Prince?

ZEO: I cannot say;
I saw his Highness yesterday, but since
Have not set eyes on him.

ALTEM: Has he returned
From hunting?

ZEO: Yes, I heard the Prince's voice
Not half an hour ago.

ALTEM: And, in return,
You made no sign to him?

ZEO: No sign, indeed.
I heard his song — 'twas very sweetly sung;
It told of love — it called for no reply.

ALTEM: A song of love that called for no reply?

ZEO: It asked no question, mother.

ALTEM: Surely, girl,
There may be questions that are not expressed.

ZEO: And answers, mother — mine was one of them!

ALTEM: Come, Zeolide, I've much to say to you.
Renounce Prince Philamir ere 'tis too late!
He will release you; he is proud and brave,
And would not force a hated life on you.
Come, Zeolide, throw off this weary bond,
And marry whom you love, or marry none!

ZEO: As I am bound, dear mother, I'll remain,
So let me stay with Mirza.

---

*Lacy adds: 'MIRZA *hastens to embrace her.*'

ALTEM: (*annoyed*)   You can stay!
        (*Exit* QUEEN ALTEMIRE *into house, glancing angrily at* MIRZA;
        ZEOLIDE *notices this with some surprise.*)

ZEO: Why, Mirza, how my mother frowns at you!
        How have you angered her?

MIRZA: I love you well;
        And when I told her of my sister-love,
        In words more passionate than politic,
        The Queen rebuked me sternly.

ZEO: Oh, for shame!

MIRZA: She is your mother, and she claims your love,
        And cannot brook that I should share that love.
        I can forgive the noble jealousy
        That comes of woman's love for woman.

ZEO: Yes;
        For you are Mirza — queen of womankind —
        The best, the noblest woman in the world!

MIRZA: Why, here is warmth! And people call you cold,
        Because you are so cold to Philamir.

ZEO: Why, Mirza, he's a man!
        (*Enter* PHILAMIR *from house — he overhears* MIRZA.)

MIRZA: A man indeed!
        The bravest warrior that wields a sword;
        The rarest poet that ever penned a lay;
        An admirable knight — gay, handsome, young,
        Brave, wealthy, and accomplished — with a tongue
        Might shame a siren's!

ZEO: Hush! A siren's tongue
        Is not renowned for much sincerity.

MIRZA: *He* is sincere.

ZEO: Indeed, I hope he is!

PHIL: (*coming forward*) I thank you, Lady Mirza, for those words.

MIRZA: (*coldly*) I little thought that they were overheard.
        This is ungenerous, Prince Philamir. (*Bows coldly and exit.*)
        (PHILAMIR *rushes to* ZEOLIDE, *who receives him very quietly.*)

PHIL: Dear Zeolide, at last we are alone!
        Oh, I have longed for this!

ZEO: Indeed! And why?

PHIL: And why? We can converse without reserve.

ZEO: What should I say when we are quite alone
        That I should leave unsaid were others here?
        I can but say, 'I love you', Philamir.

PHIL: And is that all?

ZEO: And is that not enough?

PHIL: All the world knows you love me!

ZEO: That is why
        I do not blush to own it in the world.

PHIL: But give me more — *I* love *you*, Zeolide,
            As the earth loves the sun!

ZEO: The earth is glad
            To see the sun, and asks no more than that.
            You would do well to imitate the earth.

PHIL: I am content to imitate the earth —
            I am content to sit and gaze at you,
            Tranced in a lazy glow of happiness;
            But if you speak and wake me from that trance,
            Wake me, dear Zeolide, with warmer words.
            'I love you!' Why, I know you love me well!
            Say nothing, Zeolide, and I'm content,
            If you say anything, say more than that!

ZEO: What words could I employ which, tested in
            The crucible of unimpassioned truth,
            Would not resolve themselves into those three?
            Now I must go — your sun's about to set —
            So farewell earth!

PHIL: And when the sun is down
            The earth is inconsolable!

ZEO: Until
            The moon appears! Perhaps there is a moon
            That fills my place until I rise again?

PHIL: No more, dear Zeolide; or, if there be,
            She floats in one perpetual eclipse!

ZEO: The moon is not the less a moon because
            The earth thinks fit to hide her from the sun!

PHIL: Nay; you pursue the metaphor too far.
            If I, the earth, conceal a nightly moon,
            Why, you, the sun, have many worlds to warm,
            And some are nearer to you than this earth!

ZEO: Hush, Philamir! I'm ready to believe
            That you're an earth that knows no moon at all,
            If you'll allow that I, although a sun,
            Consent to warm no other world than this! (*kissing his forehead, and
            going*)

PHIL: Oh, do not leave me thus, dear Zeolide.
            I am a beggar, begging charity;
            Throw me more coin that bears the stamp of love!

ZEO: I have one coin that bears that holy stamp —
            I give you that — I have no more to give.

PHIL: Tell me its value, then, in words of love!

ZEO: What! Would you have me advertise my alms,
            And trumpet forth my largess to the world?

PHIL: Not to the world, dear Zeolide — to me!

ZEO: Ah, you would have me say, '*You* are my world!'
            You see, I have the trick of ardent speech,

And I could use it, were I so disposed.
But surely, Philamir, the mendicant
Who is not satisfied to take my alms
Until he know how much that alms be worth,
Can scarcely stand in need of alms at all!
I love you, Philamir — be satisfied.
Whose vows are made so earnestly as hers
Who would deceive you by her earnestness?
Why, if I sought to trick you, Philamir,
I should select such phrases for my end —
So passionate — and yet so delicate,
So fierce — from overflow of gentle love,
So furious — from excess of tenderness,
That even your expressions of regard,
Unbounded in their hot extravagance,
Would pale before the fury of *my* words,
And you, for very shame, would call them back,
And beg my pardon for their lack of warmth!
I love you, Philamir — I'll say no more! (*Exit.*)

PHIL: Gone! But I'll follow her — (*going*)
    (*Enter* PHANOR *from house.*)

PHAN: Stop, Philamir,
If, as she says, she loves you, well and good;
She'll give you proof of it in her good time;
But if she don't, why, take an old boy's word
(Who speaks of love with some authority),
She'll love you none the better for the warmth
That prompts you to perpetual persecution.
The girl has taken this road — take you that.
    (PHILAMIR *stands irresolute, then goes off slowly in the direction*
    indicated.)
That's good advice!
    (*Enter* QUEEN ALTEMIRE *from house.*)

ALTEM: My lord, old Gélanor,
The steward of your palace, has arrived
And waits without.

PHAN: We'll see him presently.

ALTEM: (*with some hesitation*) Now, do you know, I often wonder why,
Possessing such a palace, furnished with
The rarest luxuries that wealth can buy,
You hold your court in this secluded place?
I have been married to you eighteen years,
Yet I have never seen this palace, which
Stands barely twenty miles away, and which
You visit regularly once a month.

PHAN: (*rather confused*) There are good reasons, Altemire.

ALTEM: (*angrily*)   No doubt!

                    Exceedingly good reasons! When a man
                    Maintains a bachelor establishment,
                    He has the best of reasons to decline
                    To take his wife there!
PHAN: You're a jealous fool.
ALTEM: Jealous I am, and possibly a fool,
                    But not a fool for being jealous.
PHAN: Peace,
                    And I will tell you why I take you not.
                    That palace is enchanted. Everyone
                    Who enters there is bound to speak the truth —
                    The simple, unadulterated truth.
                    To every question that is put to him
                    He must return the unaffected truth.
                    And, strange to say, while publishing the truth
                    He's no idea that he is doing so;
                    And while he lets innumerable cats
                    Out of unnumbered bags, he quite believes
                    That all the while he's tightening the strings
                    That keep them from a too censorious world.
                    What do you say to that?
ALTEM: (*amazed*)   Say? Would the world
                    Were one such palace, Phanor!
PHAN: If it were,
                    At least we all should meet on equal terms;
                    But to be taken from a world in which
                    That influence don't exist, and to be placed
                    Inside a fairy palace where it does
                    (Accompanied, moreover, by one's wife),
                    Might take one at a disadvantage!
ALTEM: Well,
                    I am prepared to undergo the test
                    If you'll accompany me.
PHAN: No, no, no!
                    You are a worthy woman, Altemire,
                    But, Altemire, you have your faults!
ALTEM: My lord,
                    I am a woman!
PHAN: Yes, exactly so!
                    If you were *not* a woman, Altemire,
                    Or, being one, were someone else's wife,
                    I'd take you there tomorrow!
ALTEM: But, my lord,
                    Why won't you take me, being what I am?
PHAN: Because, my wife, I don't know what you are.
ALTEM: You know, at least, that I'm a faithful wife.
PHAN: I think you're more than faithful. I believe

You are a perfect woman, Altemire,
A pattern as a mother and a wife —
And, so believing, why, I do not care
To run the risk of being undeceived!

ALTEM: (*annoyed*) My lord, you are unjust! Can you believe
I should expose myself to such a test
Had I been guilty of unfaithfulness?
I am no perfect woman, Phanor. I have faults
That advertise themselves. No need to say
That I'm quick-tempered, jealous, over-prone
To underrate the worth of womankind —
Impetuous — unreasonable — vain —
I am a woman, with a woman's faults.
But, being woman, Phanor, I'm a wife;
And, in that I am one, I need not blush.
You have some better reason. Possibly
You dread the palace on your own account?

PHAN: *I* dread the palace, Altemire? No, no.
I am a child of impulse. All my faults
Lie on the surface. I have nought to hide.
Such little faults as sully me you know.

ALTEM: Or guess.

PHAN: Ha! Am I then to understand
My Queen suspects her husband?

ALTEM: Yes, you are!

PHAN: Then this decides me. You *shall* go with me.

ALTEM: But —

PHAN: Not a word — King Phanor cannot brook
The breath of jealousy. With all his faults,
His married life has been as pure as snow.
We two will go this morning.

ALTEM: Stay! A thought!
Let us take Zeolide and Philamir,
They shall not know the fairy influence
To which they are subjected. If the maid
Does not love Philamir, she'll show it then,
And the betrothal can be cancelled. If
She loves him, why, she'll show it all the more:
Then the betrothal shall be ratified.

PHAN: We *will* take Zeolide and Philamir,
Chrysal and Zoram — Aristaeus too,
And Palmis — yes, and blameless Lady Mirza —
Mirza, the good, the beautiful, the pure!

ALTEM: Mirza! Eternal Mirza! Everywhere
I hear her irritating virtues praised!
I'm weary of the woman!

PHAN: Stop a bit,

Till we are in the palace. Then we'll learn
Not only your opinion of her worth,
But also why you hold it.

ALTEM: Well, well, well!
The maid is young and beautiful, and I
Am envious of that youth and beauty. See,
I can anticipate the influence
To which I'm going to subject myself.
There I was wrong. Mirza *shall* go with us,
And by her conduct under such a test,
Prove the injustice of my estimate.
I'll go and warn the court. (*Exit into house.*)

PHAN: The course I take
Is rather rash, but the experiment
Will not be destitute of interest.
          (*Enter* GELANOR *from house.*)
Well, Gélanor, what tidings do you bring?
About our palace?

GELAN: Sir, the old, old tale.
Men come and go — and women come and go.
Although the palace gates are opened wide
To rich and poor alike — and rich and poor
Alike receive full hospitality
For any length of time they care to stay,
Few care to stay above a day or two.
Free entertainment in a princely home
Is little valued when it's coupled with
The disadvantage of a dwelling-place
Where everyone is bound to speak the truth.
When does my lord propose to start?

PHAN: Today.
But this time not alone, good Gélanor.

GELAN: And who is to accompany you, sir?

PHAN: My wife.

GELAN: Your wife?

PHAN: My wife.

GELAN: Great heavens, my lord,
Have you reflected?

PHAN: Yes.

GELAN: To any place
Where one is bound to speak the baldest truth
Concerning all the actions of one's life,
It's hardly politic to take one's wife!

PHAN: Oh, I've the fullest confidence in her.
She's a good woman, Gélanor.

GELAN: Ah, sir,
I have seen married couples, by the score,

Who, when they passed within our crystal walls,
Have boldly advertised themselves prepared
To stake their souls upon each other's faith —
But who, before they've spent an hour at most
Under the castle's mystic influence,
Have separated ne'er to meet again!
Oh, have a care!

PHAN: Queen Altemire knows all,
And, knowing all, she fears not for herself,
So I've no fear for her!

GELAN: But *you*, my liege —
How will *you* bear yourself 'neath such a test?
You have been married nearly eighteen years:
That's a long time!
              (*Enter* MIRZA, *unobserved.*)*

PHAN: Well, yes — I've thought of that.
I'm a good husband — as good husbands go.
I love my wife — but still — you understand —
Boys will be boys! There *is* a point or two —
Say two, as being nearer to the mark —
On which I do not altogether care
To stand examination by my wife.
Perhaps I may have given out that I've
Been dining *here* — when I've been dining *there* —
I may have said 'with A' — when 'twas with B —
I may have said 'with *him*' — when 'twas with *her* —
Distinctions such as these, good Gélanor,
Though strangely unimportant in themselves,
Still have a value, which the female mind's
Particularly quick to apprehend.
Now here's a talisman — a crystal box — (*producing it*)
Whoever carries this within those walls
May overcome the castle's influence,
And utter truth or falsehood as he wills.
I should do well, I think, to take this box?

GELAN: From all accounts, my lord, I think you would! (*Sees* MIRZA.)
Ahem! We are observed!

MIRZA: My lord, I trust
My presence here is not inopportune?
I will withdraw.

PHAN: No, Lady Mirza, no!
I was exhibiting to Gélanor
A curious specimen of crystal work —
He understands such things.

---

*Lacy adds: 'She occupies herself with flowers.'

MIRZA: (*taking box*)   And so do I.
         How marvellously pure! No single flaw
         Affects its exquisite transparency!
         A perfect emblem of a spotless life!
GELAN: But, Lady Mirza, perfect spotlessness
         Is apt to smack of insipidity.
MIRZA: No — hold it to the light, and see the change!
         See how its exquisite prismatic hues,
         Under the influence of searching light,
         Are instantly made clear and manifest.
         As shines this crystal in the sun, so shines
         A perfect woman in the light of truth.
         The modest beauties of a spotless life
         Remain unknown and unsuspected, till
         A ray of truth-light starts them into life,
         And shows them — all unwilling — to the world!
GELAN: But there are hidden qualities of soul
         That even truth cannot detect. Suppose
         This crystal, peerless in its spotlessness,
         Turned out to be a potent talisman,
         With power to work all kinds of devilry?
         There are such things!
PHAN: (*aside*)   Why, there are women, too
         (I have known many such), to whom the box
         Might still be very properly compared!
MIRZA: Impossible, my lord. I'll not believe
         That aught so beautiful could be so base.
         (*returning it*) I thank you, sir. I've read a lesson here
         That I shall take good heed to profit by.
            (*Enter the* QUEEN ALTEMIRE, *with* ZEOLIDE, PHILAMIR,
           ARISTAEUS, ZORAM, *and* PALMIS, *from house.*)
ALTEM: Here comes your court, my lord.
PHAN: That's well. My friends,
         I have a palace, twenty miles away —
         A lovely place, engirt with crystal walls;
         Its grounds will show fair flowers and shady groves,
         Huge forest trees, rare fountains, hill and dale,
         There's hunting, fishing — eighteen years preserved!
         There the sun shines unclouded all day long.
         What say you — will you go?
CHRYS: Go? What care I
         Whether it rain or shine so that I may
         Bask in the sunshine of my King and Queen!
PHAN: In half an hour we start. Once there, our life
         Shall be a song, and Aristaeus here,
         The jolly, genial, laughing Aristaeus,
         Shall strike the key-note!

ARIST: Well, I'll do my best.
ZORAM: But pray consider. If the intervals
                 Throughout the diatonic series, sir,
                 Were mathematically equal, why,
                 It would not greatly matter, as you know,
                 Upon what note your melody commenced.
                 But as it is not so, we must respect
                 The intervals the melody demands.
                 No key-note struck by Aristaeus could
                 Be correspondent with those intervals!
PHIL: *I'll* give the key-note. We will pass the day
                 By quivering willows at the waterside,
                 Lapped in a lazy luxury of love!
                 There we'll forget the world of work-a-day,
                 And crown our happiness with songs of love!
                 What say you, dearest Zeolide?
ZEO: I've said
                 As much as it is maidenly to say —
                 I love you, Philamir — be satisfied!

         ACT II

Interior of the Palace of Truth.
Enter GELANOR, *meeting* KING PHANOR *and* QUEEN ALTEMIRE *and*
ZEOLIDE.
GELAN: Welcome, my lord! Madam, I humbly trust
                 The palace realizes all the hopes
                 That you had entertained concerning it.
ALTEM: Indeed, it far exceeds them, Gélanor.
                 There is no lovelier abode on earth!
                 And so says Zeolide.
ZEO: Indeed she does!
                 Why, father, I have lived near eighteen years,
                 And never knew until three hours ago
                 That you possessed so lovely a domain!
                 Why have I wasted eighteen years on earth,
                 When such a heaven as this awaited me?
GELAN: *(aside to* PHANOR) You have not told the Princess or your court
                 The palace's peculiarity?
PHAN: Not I. The secret is our own, as yet —
                 The Queen's, and yours, and mine.
GELAN: With you and me
                 The secret's safe. But then — Queen Altemire —
                 If you have told *her* all —
PHAN: No, no — not all!
                 Here is a secret which is yours and mine; *(producing crystal box)*
                 And yours and mine the secret shall remain.

> Protected by this talisman, I stand,
> A sturdy rock amid the shifting sands —
> A salamander in a world of fire —
> Achilles in a crowd of myrmidons —
> Achilles, with an iron-plated heel!
> Go, send my courtiers — I anticipate
> No ordinary sport from watching them.
>> (*Exeunt* GELANOR *and* PHANOR.)

ALTEM: What are you reading, Zeolide?

ZEO: (*with scroll*)   A song
> Written by Chrysal set to Zoram's notes;
> They gave it me before we left our home,
> But in the hurry of the journey here,
> I managed to mislay it — here it is.
>> (*Enter* ZORAM, CHRYSAL *and* ARISTAEUS.)

ALTEM: And here are author and composer, too —
> And critic, teeming with humanity.
> Come let us hear it.*
>> (ZEOLIDE *sings a song.*† *At its conclusion* CHRYSAL *and* ZORAM *applaud.*)

CHRYS: (*coming forward with all the action of a man who is expressing extreme approval*) Oh, I protest, my ears have never heard
> A goodly song more miserably sung.
> (*clapping hands*) Oh, very poor indeed — oh, very weak;
> No voice — no execution — out of tune —
> Pretentious too — oh, very, very poor! (*applauding as if in ecstasies*)

ALTEM: (*amused*) Indeed! I think I've often heard you say
> No voice could rival Princess Zeolide's?

CHRYS: (*enthusiastically*) I've often said so — I have praised her voice,
> Because I am a courtier — paid to praise.

---

*Lacy adds:
  (*aside*)   If you conveniently could mislay them,
           I'd bear the loss with equanimity.
†Buckstone's prompt-copy has written-in:
      SONG. — ZEOLIDE
      Return to me — thine anger soften.
      Whence comes this change? Where hast thou fled?
      Oh, let the voice that calms thee often
      For pardon sue, nor vainly plead.
      Thine image in this heart was dwelling
      So lately yet, but peacefully.
      Dost see how fast my tears are falling?
      Return to me. Return to me.
(MS. addition in prompt-copy, once in the possession of J.B. Buckstone, now in the Gilbert and Sullivan Museum.)

I never meant one word of what I said;
I have the worst opinion of her voice,
And so has Zoram.

ZORAM: I? Oh, dear me, no!
I can form no opinion on the point,
I am no judge of music.

CHRYS: Eh?

ZORAM: Not I!
I hardly know the treble from the bass,
And as to harmony — I know the word,
But hang me if I guess at what it means!

ZEO: Oh, Zoram, you are jesting — why, you wrote
The air I sung!

ZORAM: *I* wrote the air? Not I,
I paid a poor musician for his work,
And palmed it off upon you as my own.
A common trick with melodists who stand
Far higher in the world's esteem than I!

ALTEM: Well, Aristaeus there has still to speak,
What says that rollicking philosopher?
Come, growl it out!

ARIST: (*gruffly, as if finding fault*) It's sweetly pretty, ma'am,
And very nicely sung. I like it much.

ZEO: What! Aristaeus pleased?

ARIST: (*very savagely*)   Of course I am;
I'm always pleased with everything.

ALTEM: Indeed!
Men look on Aristaeus as a man
Whom nothing satisfies.

ARIST: (*with outrageous bluntness*) Then men are wrong.
No child's more easily amused than I.
But, here at court, where everyone is pleased
With everything, my amiability
Would go for nought; so I have coined myself
A disposition foreign to my own,
In hopes my clumsy boorish insolence
Might please you by its very novelty;
And prove, perchance, a not unwelcome foil
To Zoram's mockery of cultured taste,
And Chrysal's chronic insincerity!
I'm rough and honest, frank — outspoken — blunt.

CHRYS: Boor! When you dare to say I'm insincere
You tell the truth — there, make the most of that!

ZORAM: Chrysal, your hand; I'm glad to find at last
Your eyes are opened to your many faults.

CHRYS: How, sir, is this intentional affront?

ZORAM: No, not intentional. I tried to frame

                    A pleasant speech, but, by some awkward slip,
                    The truth escaped me quite against my will.
                    (*with great admiration*) You systematic liar!
CHRYS: Insolent!
ZORAM: Sir!
CHRYS: This shall cost or you or me his life.
                    In half an hour you shall hear from me!
                            (*Exit* CHRYSAL.)
ZORAM: (*in terror*) What *have* I said?
ALTEM: (*aside*)   These boobies must not fight,
                    But how to stop them? Here comes Philamir!
                    Now he and Zeolide can meet. But first
                    I must get rid of Zoram. (*to* ZORAM) Get you hence,
                    I will contrive to pacify your foe.
ZORAM: But —
ALTEM: Go!
ZORAM: (*piteously*) I'm sure I don't know what I've done!
                            (*Exeunt* ZORAM *and* QUEEN ALTEMIRE.)
                            (*Enter* PHILAMIR — ZEOLIDE *runs to him and embraces him — he
                            turns away.*)
ZEO: My love, is Philamir unhappy?
PHIL: Yes.
                    I have heard people talking of our troth,
                    And prophesying that it will soon cease.
ZEO: Indeed! They think you do not love me, then?
PHIL: They doubt not that — they doubt your love for me.
                    Some say it sleeps; some say that it is dead;
                    Some that it never lived. Oh, Zeolide,
                    If love for Philamir is yet unborn,
                    Why, bring it now to light! Where will you find
                    A fitter nursery for love than this?
                    If that love lives, but sleeps, why, wake it now
                    And let it revel in these golden groves.
                    If it is dead, why, here's a paradise
                    That well might summon it to second life!
ZEO: It sleeps not, Philamir, nor is it dead;
                    It lives and cannot die.
PHIL: But people say
                    That love should advertise itself in words
                    More fervid than the weary formula,
                    'I love you, Philamir'. You love your friends.
                    Why, Zeolide, I think I've heard you say
                    You love your horse!
ZEO: Unjust! You ask me, then,
                    To limit my illimitable love,
                    And circle, with a boundary of words,
                    A wealth of love that knows no bounds at all!

> There is a love that words may typify —
> A mere material love — that one may weigh
> As jewellers weigh gold. Such love is worth
> The gold one pays for it — it's worth no more.
> Why, Philamir, I might as well attempt
> To set a price upon the universe —
> Or measure space — or time eternity,
> As tell my love in words!

PHIL: (*astonished*)   Why, Zeolide,
> At last you speak! Why, this, indeed, is love!

ZEO: (*aside*) What have I said? (*aloud and coldly*) Indeed, I'm glad to think
> My words have pleased you!

PHIL: (*with enthusiasm*) Pleased me? They've done more —
> They've gratified my vanity, and made
> Me feel that I am irresistible!

ZEO: Indeed!

PHIL: Indeed, dear Zeolide, they have.
> Why, how you frown!

ZEO: (*coldly*)   If such a love as mine
> Serves but to feed your sense of vanity,
> I think it is misplaced.

PHIL: My vanity
> Must needs be fed, and with such love as yours.
> I have worked hard to gain it, Zeolide!
> You are not nearly as attractive as
> Five hundred other ladies I could name,
> Who, when I said I loved them, stopped my lips —

ZEO: (*astonished*) I'm glad they did!

PHIL: With kisses, ere I could
> Repeat the sentence; and it hurt me much
> That you, who are comparatively plain,
> Should give me so much trouble, Zeolide.

ZEO: (*aside*) What can he mean? (*aloud*) Oh, you are mocking me —

PHIL: Mocking you, Zeolide? You do me wrong!
> (*with enthusiasm*) Oh, place the fullest value on my words,
> And you'll not overvalue them! I swear,
> As I'm a Christian knight, I speak the truth!

ZEO: Why, Philamir, you've often told me that
> You never loved a woman till we met!

PHIL: (*with all the appearance of rapture*)
> I always say that. I have said the same
> To all the women that I ever woo'd!

ZEO: And they believ'd you?

PHIL: Certainly they did.
> They always do! Whatever else they doubt,
> They don't doubt that! (*He tries to embrace her.*)

ZEO: Away, and touch me not! (*horror-struck*)

PHIL: What! Has my earnestness offended you,
              Or do you fear that my impassioned speech
              Is over-coloured? Trust me, Zeolide,
              If it be over-charged with clumsy love,
              Or teem with ill-selected metaphor,
              It is because my soul is not content
              To waste its time in seeking precious stones,
              When paste will answer every end as well!
ZEO: Why, Philamir, dare you say this to me?
PHIL: All this, and more than this, I dare to say.
              I dare to tell you that I like you much,
              For you are amiable, refined, and good —
              Saving a little girlish diffidence
              I have no serious fault to find with you!
ZEO: You're very good!
PHIL: Indeed, I think I am,
              But let that pass. In truth I like you much.
              At first I loved you in an off-hand way!
ZEO: At first?
PHIL: Until the novelty wore off,
              And then, receiving but a cold response
              To all the seeming fury of my love,
              My pride was nettled, and I persevered
              Until I made you tell me of your love,
              In words that bore comparison with mine.
              I've done that, and I'm amply satisfied.
ZEO: (*in blank astonishment*) And this is Philamir, who used to breathe
              Such words of passion and such songs of love!
              Those words that fiercely burnt with such false fire,
              Those songs that sung so lovingly of lies,
              Bore unsuspected fruit — I gathered it
              And garnered it away. Oh, Philamir,
              As misers store up gold, I stored my love
              In all the inmost corners of my heart,
              Dreading to speak or look at Philamir,
              Lest some unguarded word or tell-tale glance
              Should give a clue to all the wealth within!
              I laughed within myself, as misers laugh,
              To find my hoard increasing day by day,
              And now — the coin I hoarded up is base —
              The flowers that decked my life are worthless weeds —
              The fruit I plucked is withered at the core —
              And all my wealth has faded into air!
PHIL: Faded? Why, Zeolide, what do you mean?
              I do not love you as a lover should,
              Yet you reproach me! Oh, you are unjust.
ZEO: Indeed, I'll not reproach you! Let me go.

My grief shall be as silent as my love.
Farewell! (*Exit.*)
PHIL: The woman's mad! Unquestionably mad!
My show of love has sent her brain adrift.
Poor girl! I really like her very much.
I tell her that I love her — and in words
Which never yet were known to miss their mark
When uttered by Prince Philamir — in words
So charged with passion that they well might charm
The very proudest maid in Christendom;
And off she bounces as indignantly
As if I'd told the very plainest truth!
(*Enter* CHRYSAL.)
CHRYS: Your Royal Highness seems disturbed.
PHIL: I am!
I'm much annoyed with Princess Zeolide.
You know how coldly she has hitherto
Received the protestations of my love?
CHRYS: (*politely*) I do indeed. You've been the laughing-stock
Of all the court for months on that account.
PHIL: (*amazed*) Oh, have I so?
CHRYS: Upon my soul, you have.
PHIL: You're candid, sir.
CHRYS: (*still as if paying a compliment*) I can afford to be
Extremely candid with Prince Philamir.*
But let that pass. You were reminding me
How coldly Princess Zeolide received
Your vows. What then?
PHIL: Why, not ten minutes since
Her manner changed, and all her pent-up love
Burst from her lips in frenzied eloquence.
I was astounded! — I, of course, began
To echo all her sentiments tenfold.
I picked the very fairest flowers that grow
Upon the dreamy plains of metaphor,
And showered them upon her. White with rage
She started from me — telling me, with tears,
Her dream of love had melted into air!
I see you don't believe me, Chrysal —

---

*Lacy adds:
No need to rack my brain for pleasant things
To say to him. The very plainest truths,
When told of such a prince as Philamir,
Bring more amusing fancies in their wake
Than any airy high-flown compliment
That courtly ingenuity could frame.

CHRYS: Well,
    I half believe you. I can scarcely think
    The Princess spoke with rapture of your love;
    But I can quite believe that when you spoke
    In what you're pleased to think is metaphor,
    The well-bred Princess shrank instinctively
    From such a florid prince as Philamir (*with a respectful bow*).

PHIL: (*haughtily*) This form of compliment is new to me!

CHRYS: My lord, my speciality consists
    In framing novel forms of compliment,
    But who comes here? — A modest little maid —
        (*Enter* AZEMA — *she starts on seeing* PHILAMIR *and* CHRYSAL.)
    And rather pretty, too.

PHIL: (*angrily*)   She hears you, sir!
    (*politely to* AZEMA) I fear we've frightened you?

AZEMA: Oh no, indeed,
    I am not frightened, though I seem to be.
        (AZEMA'*s manner is characterized by the extremest modesty and
        timidity throughout this scene.*)

CHRYS: But why affect a fear you do not feel?

AZEMA: (*with extreme timidity*) Because, although I entered here to seek
    Prince Philamir, I'm anxious he should think
    This meeting is a simple accident.
    Do not suppose that this is modesty;
    'Tis but an artifice to make you think
    That I am timid as a startled fawn!

CHRYS: (*aside to* PHILAMIR) This is a character. I'll open fire,
    And storm her weakest point — her vanity.
    Now, my artillery of compliments,
    A salvo, if you please.
    (*aloud, as if paying an elaborate compliment*)
                    I have remarked
    That you've a certain girlish prettiness,
    Although your nose is sadly underbred.
    (*aside*) That's rather neat!

AZEMA: Are you Prince Philamir?

CHRYS: Not I indeed, fair lady. This is he —
    The most conceited coxcomb in the world (*with an elaborate bow to*
    PHILAMIR, *who starts angrily*).
    No thanks — indeed 'tis true.

AZEMA: Then go your way —
    I don't want you! I only want the Prince.
    'Twas Philamir I came to captivate.

CHRYS: Here's candour if you like!

AZEMA: Oh, leave us, sir!
    Find some excuse to go, that he and I
    May be alone together.

PHIL: Leave me, sir.
         I'll give your tongue a lesson ere the night!
CHRYS: How has my tongue offended? — Oh, I see —
         Exactly — don't explain! (*aside*) Poor Zeolide! (*Exit.*)
PHIL: Insolent scoundrel! (*following him*)
AZEMA: Oh, don't follow him.
         I want you here alone. You can begin —
         I am not shy, though I appear to be.
         Indeed, I entered here ten minutes since,
         Because I heard from those outside the gates,
         That you, Prince Philamir, had just arrived.
PHIL: Then you're a stranger here?
AZEMA: I am, indeed!
         The people told me anyone was free
         To enter.
PHIL: Yes, quite right. Did they say more?
AZEMA: Oh yes, much more. They told me then that you
         Received but sorry treatment at the hands
         Of Princess Zeolide. They told me, too,
         That your betrothal might ere long collapse;
         (*with extreme modesty*) So, thought I, as I am beyond dispute
         The fairest maid for many a mile around —
         And as, moreover, I possess the gift
         Of feigning an enchanting innocence
         I possibly may captivate the Prince,
         And fill the place once filled by Zeolide. (*Sits; her ankle is exposed.*)
PHIL: The Princess has a candid enemy!
         I beg your pardon, but the furniture
         Has caught your dress.
AZEMA: (*rearranging her dress hastily*) Oh, I arranged it so,
         That you might see how truly beautiful
         My foot and ankle are (*as if much shocked at the exposé*).
PHIL: I saw them well;
         They're very neat.
AZEMA: I now remove my glove
         That you may note the whiteness of my hand.
         I place it there in order that you may
         Be tempted to enclose it in your own.
PHIL: To that temptation I at once succumb (*taking her hand — she affects to
         withdraw it angrily*).
AZEMA: (*with affected indignation*) Go on! If you had any enterprise,
         You'd gently place your arm around my waist
         And kiss me (*struggling to release herself*).
PHIL: It might anger you!
AZEMA: Oh no!
         It's true that I should start with every show
         Of indignation, just in order to

        Maintain my character for innocence —
        But that is all.

PHIL: (*puts his arm round her and kisses her*) There, then — 'tis done!

AZEMA: (*starting, with a great show of rage*) How, sir?
        I think it's time that I should take my leave.
        (*very indignantly*) I shall be in the Avenue of Palms.
        At ten o'clock tonight. I mention this
        That you may take the hint and be there, too! (*going*)

PHIL: One moment, pray. Let me assure you now,
        That such an unmistakeable coquette,
        And one who shows her cards so candidly,
        Will not supplant the Princess Zeolide!

AZEMA: (*surprised*) Supplant the Princess Zeolide? Why, sir,
        By what authority do you imply
        That I have cherished any such design?

PHIL: Your own admission.

AZEMA: Oh, impossible!
        (*indignantly*) But as it seems that I've no chance with you,
        I'll try the gentleman who left us here.
        He comes!
           (*Enter* CHRYSAL.)
             Oh, sir, I crave a word with you!
        Are you a wealthy man? (*with extreme delicacy of manner*)

CHRYS: I am, indeed.

AZEMA: And you've a title?

CHRYS: Yes, of highest rank.

AZEMA: A bachelor.

CHRYS: A bachelor as yet,
        Betrothed to Palmis.

AZEMA: Oh! (*hopefully*) But possibly
        You do not love her much?

CHRYS: (*with enthusiasm*)   Oh, not at all!

AZEMA: You'll do — give me your arm. (*He does so — she shrinks.*) Oh, sir, indeed.
        (*impatiently to* CHRYSAL, *who hesitates*)
        Do take my hand and put it through your arm. (*He does so.*)
        That's it! Oh, sir, indeed I know you not!
          (*Exeunt* CHRYSAL *and* AZEMA — AZEMA *affecting to try and*
         release herself. PHILAMIR *stands astounded for a moment.*)

PHIL: I've found a clue that solves these mysteries!
        This palace is enchanted ground! It's plain
        That there's some subtle influence at work,
        Affecting everybody here — but me!
        Chrysal, the honey-tongued, turns out to be
        A blunt and scurrilous outspoken boor;
        Zoram, the musical enthusiast,
        Can hardly tell the treble from the bass;
        Then Aristaeus, surly, blunt, and gruff,

Turns out to be the gentlest soul alive;
And, most inexplicable change of all,
The amiable but prudish Zeolide
Becomes a foolish vixen, blind with love,
Maddened with jealous and unreasoning rage!
Then comes a girl — a commonplace coquette —
Who, while she lays her plans with practised skill,
Explains their aim, and holds them to the light
That all may see their arrant hollowness!
It's evident there's some enchantment here
That shows up human nature as it is,
And I alone resist its influence!
Ah, here is Mirza — lovely paragon —
I'll notice how it operates on her.
          (*Enter* MIRZA.)

MIRZA: (*Starts.*) I beg your pardon. I was looking for
          My diary; I've dropped it hereabouts.
PHIL: Allow me to assist you in your search?
MIRZA: (*hastily*) No, no; that must not be. My diary
          Must ne'er be seen by other eyes than mine!
PHIL: Indeed! And why?
MIRZA: My very inmost thoughts —
          The secret utterances of my heart —
          Are there inscribed. I would not for my life
          That any eyes but mine should rest on it.
PHIL: Can Lady Mirza harbour any thought
          That all the world may not participate?
          I'll not believe it.
MIRZA: (*eagerly*)   Hush — I charge you, sir!
          Ask me no questions here — for I have learnt
          That this is fairy ground, where everyone
          Is bound, against his will, to speak the truth.
          If you interrogate me, I am bound
          To answer truly. I need say no more
          To such a courteous knight as Philamir.
PHIL: (*aside*) It is then as I thought! (*aloud*) I guessed the truth —
          This palace doubtless *is* enchanted ground,
          And I alone resist its influence!
MIRZA: Indeed!
PHIL: I had occasion some time since
          To feign unbounded love for Zeolide
          (For whom I don't particularly care):
          Well, notwithstanding my indifference,
          I spoke with all my usual gush of love,
          From which I venture to conclude that I
          Am unaffected by this magic power.
MIRZA: You do not love the Princess Zeolide?

          You who professed unutterable love?

PHIL: I liked her well enough at first, but now
          I'm weary of my liking. She displays
          So much unreasonable petulance,
          Such causeless anger — such unbridled wrath,
          That I'm resolved to break the weary link
          That binds us. I'll be free to love again (*taking* MIRZA's *hand*).

MIRZA: (*releasing herself*) Oh, Philamir! Oh, shame upon you, sir.
          She loves you! You are loved by Zeolide!
          Why, there's a heaven opened to your eyes,
          And you'll not enter, Philamir! Oh, shame
          To blight so true a heart as hers! Oh, fool,
          To throw aside in wrath so fair a prize!

PHIL: But listen — I've a fairer prize in view.
          Mirza — I love *you*!

MIRZA: (*shuddering with terror*) Spare me, sir, I pray!

PHIL: Now, by this castle's mystic influence,
          I challenge you to answer truthfully —
          Do you love me?

MIRZA: (*shrinking from him*) Have pity, Philamir!
          Withdraw your question, I beseech you, sir!
          If you insist, I must perforce reply —
          I charge you, on your knighthood, press me not!
            (PHILAMIR *pauses, struggling with his feelings.*)

PHIL: (*releasing her*) My Lady Mirza, you are free to go.
            (*Exit* MIRZA *hastily.*)
          How subtly works the mystic influence,
          That all seem subject to, — excepting me!
          And from the fearful ordeal only one
          Of all the women here comes out unscathed.
          The peerless Mirza — good, and wise, and pure,
          Most excellent and unapproachable!
          To know that Mirza loves me, is to know
          That she is mortal — that I knew before.
          To know that Mirza's worthy of my love,
          And that, despite the searching influence
          That I alone resist — oh, this indeed
          Is happiness! — I'm sure she loves me well!
            (*Enter* ZEOLIDE.)

ZEO: Indeed she does! If half an hour ago
          She spoke abruptly to her Philamir,
          She bitterly repents it. Oh, my love,
          Forgive me, for in truth I love you well!

PHIL: (*embracing her fondly*) But my remark did not apply to you;
          I spoke of Lady Mirza.

ZEO: (*recoiling*)   Mirza?

PHIL: Yes,

I'm quite convinced she loves me!

ZEO: Philamir,
You should not jest with such a sacred word.
You've played your joke upon me, and you've seen
How readily I fell into the trap;
Let that content you. There — I'm not annoyed —
I'll not be caught again!

PHIL: (*earnestly*)   Dear Zeolide,
Indeed I do not jest — nor did I when
You left me in unwarrantable rage.
I love the Lady Mirza — she loves me.

ZEO: (*horrified*) She told you so?

PHIL: Well, no. I'm bound to say
She did not tell me so in open words:
Her love for you restrained her. She's too good —
Too pure — too honourable — to allow
A passion for her dearest friend's betrothed
To master her. You should have heard her plead
Your hopeless cause. She struggles with her love,
And tries to keep it down — but still she loves.

ZEO: (*astounded*) And you return this love?

PHIL: Most heartily.
(*with affectionate gesture*) I'm getting weary of you, and I wish
That I could find sufficient argument
To justify me in releasing you. (*She shrinks from him.*)
Why, now you frown again! Oh, Zeolide,
This wilfulness is insupportable!

ZEO: (*enraged*) Support it then no longer, Philamir!
There — you are free — our bond is at an end;
Choose your path, I'll choose mine. Our roads diverge.
We part and may not meet again. Farewell!
(*changing her manner*) Oh, Philamir, heed not my words; I spoke
In reckless haste — I spoke my death-warrant!
Philamir, do not leave me, let me live;
See how I love you! I am at your feet —
I, Zeolide, whom once you thought so cold —
I, Zeolide, who am not wont to kneel!
Oh, give me till tonight, and pass the hours
That intervene in marshalling the past,
And let that plead my cause! You loved me once,
You asked me for my love — I gave my life,
For I must die if you abandon me!
Have mercy on me! Give me till tonight!
There's some enchantment in this fearful place.
This is not Philamir — it is his shape,
But does not hold his soul. Before the night
I'll seek my father, and I'll gain from him

The key that solves this fearful mystery.
Go now — nay, do not speak — no — not a word —
I'll not believe that this is Philamir.
Go, leave me now — and we will meet tonight!
     (*He hesitates; then exit.*)
Oh, Philamir, my love, my love, my love! (*She falls sobbing on couch.*)
     (*Enter* PALMIS.)
PALMIS: What? Zeolide in tears? Has Philamir
     Been too emphatic in his vows of love?
     Have pity on him!
ZEO: Palmis, pity *me* —
     He loves me not!
PALMIS: Indeed!
ZEO: He told me so.
PALMIS: (*relieved*) Oho! He told you so?
ZEO: Most openly.
PALMIS: Then there is hope for you. Come, dry your eyes;
     When men are over head and ears in love,
     They cannot tell the truth — they must deceive,*
     Though the deception tell against themselves!
     Here Chrysal comes — (*astonished*) a lady on his arm!
     (*Enter* CHRYSAL *and* AZEMA — *he leaves* AZEMA *abruptly on
     seeing* PALMIS.)
PALMIS: Why, Chrysal, who is this? Where have you been?
CHRYS: (*affectionately*) I have been wandering through shady groves
     With that exceedingly attractive girl.
PALMIS: You have been flirting, sir?
CHRYS: (*putting his arm round her waist*) Exceedingly!
     I always do when I'm away from you.
PALMIS: (*to* AZEMA) Oh, you're a brazen woman!
AZEMA: That I am!
     An ordinary everyday coquette

---

*Lacy adds:
     And if they really love, they'll say they don't.
  ZEO: But surely when a man declares his love
       In words of sheer indifference, he takes
       A most unusual course!
  PALMIS: Because it is
       Unusual for men to love at all.
       Oh doubt not that he loves you, Zeolide.
       When Chrysal tells me that he loves me well,
       I don't believe a syllable he says!
       But if he told me that he hated me,
       Why, then I should feel certain of his love!
       Believe me, Zeolide, I know them all —
       Man dealing with a woman *must* deceive,
       Though the deception tells against himself.
       Here Chrysal comes . . .

> Who lives on admiration, and resolves
> To gain it by whatever means she can.
>
> ZEO: (*aside to* PALMIS) Palmis, there's some enchantment in this place —
> I know not what — it influences all.
> Do not dismiss him yet, until we learn
> Its nature!
>
> CHRYS: (*with affection*) Yes, my Palmis, wait awhile,
> Do not dismiss me yet; although it's true
> I never loved you, yet I want your love
> Because you have much influence at court,
> And have it in your power to help me on
> To further favour.
>
> PALMIS: (*astounded*) Chrysal, are you mad?
> You never loved me?
>
> CHRYS: (*enthusiastically*)   Never, on my soul!
> In point of fact, I always hated you,
> And mean to tell you so when I have won
> The highest rank your mistress can confer.
> In the meantime, however, I am fain
> To make you think that I adore you still.
> Observe the heaving of my swelling heart;
> My fervid manner — my ecstatic gaze —
> It's all assumed!
>
> PALMIS: Oh, miserable man!
> Go — get you hence, sir.
>
> CHRYS: (*astonished*)   Palmis, what on earth
> Possesses you?
>
> PALMIS: Don't speak to me again;
> I can't endure you!
>   (*Re-enter* ZORAM.)
>
> ZORAM: I am glad of this.
> Dear Palmis, I for many a weary day
> Have sought to win your love from Chrysal here,
> By every mean, contemptible device
> That my unequalled cunning could suggest.
>
> CHRYS: (*amazed*) And you admit this to my very face?
>
> ZORAM: (*cordially*) With pleasure, Chrysal. I have sought in vain,
> By daily blackening your character,
> To sicken pretty Palmis of her love.
> I've told her you're an unexampled rake,
> A gambler and a spendthrift, mean, poor, base,
> Selfish and sordid; cruel, tyrannical;
> But all in vain, she loves you all the more.
> (*taking his hand*) Forget the angry words you spoke today;
> In the glad glow of hope that I shall gain
> Your Palmis' love, I freely pardon you.
>
> CHRYS: (*in furious rage*) This evening, in the Avenue of Palms,

> I shall await you, sir.

ZORAM: (*in blank astonishment*) Oh dear, oh dear,
>> What *have* I said?
>>> (*Enter* GELANOR.)

GELAN: Hush, gentlemen — the Queen.
>> (*Re-enter* QUEEN ALTEMIRE *hastily.*)

ALTEM: (*in a rage*) Where is the King? Go, send him here to me.
>> Oh, Zeolide, go, get you hence away,
>> For I have words for Phanor that 'twere best
>> His daughter did not hear.

ZEO: My father comes.
>> (*Re-enter* PHANOR *and* MIRZA.)

ALTEM: Now, sir, I've every reason to believe,
>> From what I've heard, that you're deceiving me!
>> I'll question you — oh, infamous old man!

PHAN: (*aside*) The Queen is jealous. Where's my talisman? (*Finds it.*)
>> All right — it's well I have it with me now.
>> (*aloud*) Interrogate me. Conscious innocence
>> Has little fear of palaces of Truth!

ALTEM: You have been walking in the shrubbery;
>> What were you doing there?

PHAN: (*with great show of love for* ALTEMIRE) Why, making love
>> To Mirza. I invariably do
>> Whenever I've a chance; but all in vain.
>> She's a good woman, and despises me.
>> (*to* MIRZA) Haven't I offered love to you?

MIRZA: You have.

PHAN: And you despise me, don't you?

MIRZA: Heartily.

PHAN: (*to* ALTEMIRE) I told you so, and she endorses it.
>> Believe me, I am bound to speak the truth!

ALTEM: (*bitterly*) I do believe you.

PHAN: (*taking her by the hand*)   Thank you, Altemire.

ALTEM: Stand off, don't touch me, horrible old man!
>> You tell me you've made love to Mirza?

PHAN: (*astonished*)   No!
>> Did I say that?

ALTEM: Most unmistakeably.

PHAN: Oh, come, I say!

ZORAM: You did indeed, my lord!

PHAN: I said that I made love to Mirza?

CHRYS: Yes,
>> Those were the very words!

PHAN: Oh, Mirza, come,
>> You can deny this!

MIRZA: Would, my lord, I could.
>> To spare the Queen I would be silent, but

Some unknown power masters me, and makes
Me own, against my will, that it was so!
ALTEM: There, sir — you hear her words!
PHAN: (*aside to* GELANOR)   Why, Gélanor,
How's this? The talisman is out of gear! (*showing box to* GELANOR)
GELAN: Let me examine it. (*Takes it and returns it.*) A forgery!
A clever imitation; virtueless!
It lacks the small inscription on the hinge!
(PHANOR *falls breathless into a chair.*)
PHAN: Tomorrow morning we go home again!

ACT III

The Avenue of Palms — night. CHRYSAL *discovered with a drawn sword in his hand.*
Enter GELANOR.
GELAN: Chrysal, alone! And with a naked sword!
CHRYS: I'm waiting Zoram. I have challenged him.
He meets me here — the Avenue of Palms.
GELAN: Has he offended you?
CHRYS: Most grievously.
You heard the words he used to me today?
GELAN: I did.
CHRYS: Then blood must flow. I am a knight,
My knightly honour claims this sacrifice.
I've been insulted — one of us must die!
GELAN: You are a valiant man, if one may judge
By your demeanour.
CHRYS: (*very valiantly*)   My demeanour? Bounce!
Mere idle empty froth and nothing more.
Why, notwithstanding that I look so brave,
I'd give the riches of a universe
To find some decent means of backing out;
But, no, my honour must be satisfied!
If I endured with patience Zoram's taunts,
I should deserve to have my knightly spurs
Struck from my heels! 'Sdeath, sir, I'm bound to fight!
GELAN: Is Zoram a good swordsman?
CHRYS: Not at all.
I'm far more skilled — but still I can't repress
A certain sense of terror. Accident
May give him victory.
GELAN: Apologize!
CHRYS: (*indignantly*) To Zoram? Never! Would you have me stain
My hitherto untarnished 'scutcheon? Shame!
Stand back — he comes!
(*Enter* ZORAM, *with drawn sword.*)

Well, sir, you've kept your word.

ZORAM: Of course I have!

CHRYS: (*very sternly*)   I'm very much surprised –
I may say disappointed – to remark
That you're prepared to fight and do not show
The signs of terror that I hoped to see.

ZORAM: (*very bravely*) Oh, sir, I pray you don't deceive yourself!
My valiant manner hides an inward fear
That almost robs me of the power of thought!
Chrysal, you've grievously insulted me;
My sense of honour forces me to fight!
But I would rather have my hand cut off
(Could that be done without inflicting pain)
Than measure swords with you!

CHRYS: You craven hound!

ZORAM: Craven yourself!

CHRYS: (*furiously*)   I am, but you don't know it,
You musical impostor!

ZORAM: Ha, what's that?
I can stand much abuse and never flinch,
But when you twit me with my ignorance
Of musical expressions, blood alone
(Unless we're interrupted) can extract
The venom of the insult! Come! On guard!
    (*They fight.*)

GELAN: (*aside*) These donkeys must not fight! (*aloud*) Come – let me try
To reconcile you.

CHRYS: Reconcile us? No!
But you can interfere to stop the fight!
    (*They desist.*)

ZORAM: (*looking reproachfully at* GELANOR) I little thought when I called
Chrysal on,
That such a venerable gentleman
Would suffer two impetuous headstrong youths
To cut each other's throats.

GELAN: Come, come – desist.

CHRYS: This hound abused me!
                                    He insulted me;

BOTH: Our honour *must* be satisfied! (*They cross swords.*)

GELAN: No, no –
Attend to me. Within these crystal walls
A strange mysterious influence prevails:
All men are bound to speak the plainest truth!
And this they do, without suspecting it.
(*to* ZORAM) When Chrysal spoke the words that angered you
He did not mean to speak them. He believed
That he was paying you a compliment.

(*to* CHRYSAL) When Zoram said that he considered you
A systematic liar, mean, poor, base,
Selfish, and sordid, cruel, tyrannical,
'Twas what he *thought* — not what he would have *said*!

CHRYS: I see — if that was only what he *thought*,
It makes a difference.

GELAN: What *could* he say?
He was compelled, you know, to speak the truth.

CHRYS: Of course, I understand. Zoram, your hand!

ZORAM: With pleasure (*shaking hands with* CHRYSAL). Chrysal, I should like to say
That I esteem you — but indeed I can't.
My detestation of you knows no bounds.

CHRYS: How, sir? A fresh affront?

ZORAM: What can I do?
I try my best to say agreeable things,
But you're so utterly contemptible!
I'd put it more politely, but I can't!
I'm bound against my will to speak the truth!
I'd not insult you openly, for worlds —
Indeed, it's only what I *think* of you!

CHRYS: If it is only what you *think* of me,
Why, say no more; give me your hand again —
My knightly honour's amply satisfied!
(*They sheathe their swords, then exeunt arm in arm.*)

GELAN: So dies that breeze away! Oh, honour, honour!
Let no one take you at the estimate
Your self-elected champions price you at!
More harm is worked in that one virtue's name,
Than springs from half the vices of the earth!
(*Enter* QUEEN ALTEMIRE, *in violent rage.*)

ALTEM: Why, Gélanor, this is no spot for you,
You'd better go — the King will wish you gone.

GELAN: Indeed! And why?

ALTEM: I'll tell you, Gélanor,
His Majesty has an appointment here.
Oh, Gélanor, I've been alone with him
This afternoon, and I have learnt such things!
Why, even here — despite the castle's charm,
Despite the sacred influence of the place,
He prosecutes his infidelities!
At first he persecuted Mirza, but
Failing to find much favour in her eyes,
He looked for other game. Why, Gélanor,
He meets some woman called Azèma here,
At ten o'clock tonight!

GELAN: The deuce he does!

ALTEM: Then I resolved to know the very worst.
   I locked him in my room and questioned him
   For full three hours about his married life.
   Oh, I elicited such fearful things!
   Why, Gélanor, there's not a woman's name
   In all the long baptismal catalogue
   That's not identified with his intrigue!
   Tall, short, stout, slender, fair, dark, old and young,
   High, low, rich, poor, good, bad, maid, widow, wife,
   Of every country and of every clime!
   All's fish that his nets catch!
GELAN: And a king's net
   Is very comprehensive. Here she comes!
    (*Enter* AZEMA.)
ALTEM: Is this the woman? Tell me, who are you?
AZEMA: I am Azèma.
ALTEM: And *I* am the Queen!
AZEMA: (*bowing*) Then, madam, you're extremely in the way.
ALTEM: How so?
AZEMA: I've an appointment with the King,
   Of which you are entirely unaware;
   But though I'm much annoyed to find you here,
   I'm glad to find you here with Gélanor.
ALTEM: And why?
AZEMA: If our intrigue should come to light,
   We can retaliate by giving out
   That you and Gélanor are just as bad.
ALTEM: Upon my word!
GELAN: Oh, this is past belief!
ALTEM: Infamous hussy, you shall pay for this!
AZEMA: Why, madam, how have *I* offended you?
ALTEM: How? – you are here to meet the King, alone;
   At night – by pre-arrangement – in the dark!
AZEMA: Oh, madam, this indeed is terrible!
   That poor Azèma should be charged with this!
   It's true I've an appointment with the King,
   But as you're not aware of it, your words
   Are utterly unjustifiable.
   These flashing eyeballs and this angry blush
   (At least I hope I'm blushing) represent
   The noble rage of outraged innocence.
   I'll to the King, and let him know at once
   How, as I wandered through the grove, alone,
   I found you here with wicked Gélanor,
   At night – by pre-arrangement – in the dark.
   Oh, shame upon you – shame upon you, Queen!
    (*Exit* AZEMA – ALTEMIRE *and* GELANOR *stand confounded.*)

GELAN: Your majesty, I think I'd better go.
ALTEM: Absurd! The notion is preposterous!
You're old enough to be my father.
GELAN: Quite!
And wise enough to know that proper folk
Will only say 'that makes the matter worse!'
ALTEM: But surely here, in this enchanted home,
Where all are bound to speak the truth, our word
Will guarantee our perfect innocence!
GELAN: Yes, if the King is pleased to take our word;
But, as you've brought a charge against the King,
Analogous to that which will be brought
Against ourselves, he may ignore the fact
That truth is truth. No, no, upon the whole,
I think, your Majesty, I'd better go! (*Exit.*)
          (*Enter* PALMIS *and* ZEOLIDE, ZEOLIDE *weeping.*)
PALMIS: Nay, do not weep, dear mistress.
ZEO: Ah, my friend,
What comfort can *you* offer me?
PALMIS: I've heard
That when one is oppressed with weight of woe,
Some solace may be found in dwelling on
The grief of one more sorely laden still.
ZEO: More sorely laden? Where will Zeolide
Find one whose misery outweighs her own?
PALMIS: Your misery, though great, is but a grain
When balanced in the scales with mine!
ZEO: With yours?
PALMIS: Yes; Philamir respects you. He esteems
Your moral excellence, although no doubt
He does not love you as a lover should;
But Chrysal always hated me, and sought
To gain that love I gave so willingly
To hasten his promotion at the court.
Your case and mine are different. Besides,
You angered Philamir. I never gave
My Chrysal any reason for his hate.
ZEO: How did I anger him?
PALMIS: Your petulance
Annoyed him.
ZEO: Petulance! He told me that
He only liked me!
ALTEM: (*coming forward*) True, but you forget
He was compelled to speak the plainest truth,
And knew not that he spoke it. He believed
(While he was telling you he loved you not)
That he was breathing ardent words of love;

Believing this, your reasonable rage
Seemed in his eyes irrational caprice,
And changed his waning love to sheer dislike.
ZEO: Is this the truth, then?
ALTEM: Yes, I think it is.
The test has been exceedingly severe.
ZEO: I'll wed no man who cannot stand this test.
PALMIS: Then, Zeolide, you'll surely die a maid!
ALTEM: Come, come, be reasonable, Philamir
Is but a man — a vain and idle one,
But under this veneer of coxcombry
There's sterling stuff. The man is honest gold,
And vanity has silver-plated him.
PALMIS: At all events, you know he *likes* you well.
How many maidens when they wed a man
Have reason to be sure of half as much!
ZEO: But then his love for Mirza?
ALTEM: Idle pique!
No doubt he hoped — as other lovers hope —
In the fierce whirlpool of a new-born love
To drown remembrance of the love just dead.
Here comes the Lady Mirza! We will go,
And leave you with her. Tell her everything;
She is a noble lady — wise and pure!
She will not rob you of your Philamir.
There — tell her all!
ZEO: Forgive me, mother dear,
My heart is softened. I have been unjust.
                    (*Exeunt* ALTEMIRE *and* PALMIS.)
                    (*Enter* MIRZA.)
MIRZA: Oh, Zeolide, I know what you would say.
Say on, dear Zeolide, and have no fear.
ZEO: Mirza, for three long years we two have been
As sisters are, and I would speak to you
As younger sister speaks to elder-born.
Give me your counsel, Mirza; it will be
As pure, as true, as honest as those eyes.
MIRZA: If counsel such as mine can serve you aught,
'Tis thine, dear Zeolide. My sister, speak.
ZEO: With all my soul I love Prince Philamir.
A lady — good and beautiful and wise —
Unwittingly hath robbed me of my love;
She is too pure, too gentle, too divine,
To seek a love that rightly is not hers.
No, no, this lady hath not sought his love —
Of that I'm certain, yet she hath his love!
Oh, Mirza, when my Philamir declared

His love for me, I cast away the world
To enter paradise. Now, Philamir
Has led this lady (all unwillingly)
Within its gates, and I am left without —
A lonely wanderer 'twixt earth and heaven.
Mirza, dear sister, say — what shall I do?
Give me thy counsel — I'll abide by it.

MIRZA: No need to speak to me in parable.
I am that lady whom you over-praise —
That most unhappy woman, Zeolide!
Despite myself, I must admit the truth,
I do love Philamir — shrink not from me.
Mine is no idle love. Four years ago,
Ere you had ever seen Prince Philamir,
I was a lady of his father's court.
He loved me even then, and I loved him —
No need to tell you, dearest Zeolide,
The nature of that love; you know too well
How women love who love Prince Philamir!
We were betrothed, but secretly. Alas!
I was a humble waiting lady, he
A mighty prince — so we concealed our love.
Then it was rumoured that he sought your hand,
That policy, the curse of kings, required
That he should marry you. Then I fell ill —
(*struggling with her emotion*) Pass over that. Let it suffice that I
Released him — for I loved him passing well!

ZEO: (*amazed*) I never knew of this!

MIRZA: No, Zeolide,
I've learnt to bear my sorrow silently.
But for the sacred genius of this spot,
Whose influence no mortal can resist,
My secret would have passed away with me.
But I was true to you; for though I saw
How coldly you received his vows of love —

ZEO: (*rising, astonished*) Coldly! Why, every word he spoke to me
Rang through my brain, and would have waked up love
Had love been dead!

MIRZA: I thought you loved him not.
But though I grieved for him, yet when he spake
(As he at times would speak) of our old love,
I checked him with a simulated scorn,
For then, dear Zeolide, I loved you both!

ZEO: You love me still?

MIRZA: Most heartily!

ZEO: Why, then,
Have mercy on me, give me Philamir —

He is the soul and essence of my life!
Dear sister Mirza, give him back to me.
Oh, rather take my life than take my love,
And leave me here to linger on, alone!

MIRZA: Fear not, dear Zeolide, I love him well,
But I will never see his face again!

ZEO: Promise me this — swear to renounce his love!

MIRZA: As there's a shining sun in heaven I swear!
See, I am brave, and I will fight my love
As I have fought ere this. Take courage, dear;
I'll leave this place tonight, and Philamir
Shall ne'er set eyes upon my face again.
There, go — I'll tell him this. He's coming now —
Go, dry your eyes — he should not see them so.
Come back again when they are at their best.

      (*Exit* ZEOLIDE.)
      (*Enter* PHILAMIR.)

PHIL: Mirza — I have some words to say to you —
The diary you lost today?

MIRZA: (*eagerly*)   Well, sir,
And have you found it?

PHIL: Mirza, I have found
A portion of it — one loose leaf — behold! (*producing page*)

MIRZA: And you have read it, Philamir?

PHIL: (*guilty*)   I have!

MIRZA: Oh, shame upon you — shame upon you, sir!
You gave your knightly word — you are forsworn!

PHIL: But, Mirza, hear me out, ere you condemn.
I saw a paper tossed before the wind
And little dreaming 'twas your diary,
I picked it up. I knew not what it was
Till I began to read it. Then I knew,
And knowing so much, burnt to know still more!

MIRZA: But when you knew it held my secret thoughts,
You read no further?

PHIL: (*abashed*)   Mirza, I read on!

MIRZA: Lost! Lost! Give me that leaf, Prince Philamir;
You have deceived me, sir — I trusted you.

PHIL: But, Mirza, where's the knight who would have stopped
When of himself he read such words as these? —
(*Reads.*) 'I still love Philamir, but I must strive
To battle with my love. Oh, give me grace
To fight this fight.'

MIRZA: I charge you read no more!

PHIL: 'By day his ev'ry look — his every word —
Renews some mem'ry that should be long dead;
By night the phantom of my loved one's face

Burns in my eyes and robs me of my rest!'
MIRZA: My secret has gone forth. I strove to keep
That love as silent as my silent heart;
But it was not to be. You now know all!
Yet no — not all!
PHIL: Then, Mirza, tell me all.
Speak openly — hide nothing from me now.
MIRZA: I will speak openly. I love you, sir
And, loving you, I leave the court tonight,
That I may never see your face again.
PHIL: Recall those words! — We will not — must not part! (*He detains her.*)
(*Enter* ZEOLIDE, *unobserved.*)
MIRZA: Release me, Philamir, and let me go!
I love you! Let me hide myself away.
I love you! Leave me with myself alone.
I love you! Show me gratitude for this,
And leave me free to sanctify my vow,
For I have sworn to see your face no more!
PHIL: To whom have you sworn this?
MIRZA: To Zeolide,
Whom you once loved so well — who still loves you.
PHIL: I never loved her, Mirza — who is she,
That she should come between me and my love?
She loves me not, and I have done with her.
MIRZA: Oh, this will kill her, sir!
ZEO: No — Mirza — no!
It will not kill me. I can bear this blow (*coming forward*).
Prince Philamir, we two have been betrothed —
Your word is plighted — well, I set you free.
(*She takes* MIRZA's *hand and places it in* PHILAMIR's.)
Oh, Philamir — this is indeed the end!
Be true to her — such sacred love as hers
Should purify its object — oh, be true!
I'm but a chapter in your book of life,
I who had thought to be the book itself!
The chapter's ended, and to Zeolide
The book is closed for ever! Philamir,
When you are tempted to do Mirza wrong,
Turn to that chapter — read it through and through —
And let the tale of all that I have borne
Warn you from fresh inconstancy; my grief
May thus be Mirza's safeguard to the end.
Mirza — my sister — he will love you well —
Here, in the home of truth, he tells you so.
May you be happy in his new-born love,
May he be worthy of such love as yours —
(*to* PHILAMIR) Speak not, but let me go. (*Kisses* MIRZA's *forehead.*)

                                        Farewell — farewell!
          (*Exit* ZEOLIDE, *weeping* — PHILAMIR *and* MIRZA *stand for a*
          moment gazing at each other — *then they fall into each other's arms.*)
PHIL: Mirza, my own! At last — at last my own!
MIRZA: Oh, Philamir! I am so cruelly racked
          By sentiments I cannot reconcile;
          I know not whether this is joy or grief!
          True, when I think of Philamir, the air
          Seems charged with music, and the earth I tread
          All flowers. When I remember Zeolide
          I could go mad with sorrow!
PHIL: Then, my love,
          Think not of Zeolide!
MIRZA: Ah, Philamir,
          You speak as men speak of a worn-out love.
          You only know one kind of love, you men!
          My love for Zeolide is otherwise,
          Unselfish, generous, a sister's love.
          Yet have I stolen from her gentle heart
          That which in all the world she loved the best!
PHIL: You are too sensitive. Say, rather, she
          Hath freely given that she prizes least.
MIRZA: Oh, Philamir, indeed you do her wrong,
          And may perhaps wrong me, as you wronged her.
PHIL: (*rising*) Impossible! For if the words I breathe
          Were dashed with any mockery of love,
          I should, against my will, confess it now.
          Mirza, I love you! These are idle words
          When spoken in the unenchanted world,
          But, spoken here, they bear significance
          That rivals in its worth a life-long test!
          Let us exchange some trinket which shall serve
          As evidence of this our solemn troth.
          Here is my pledge (*giving a ring*).
MIRZA: My love, what can I give?
          I have no trinkets — I am very poor!
PHIL: A handkerchief — a glove — no matter what!
          (*She feels in pocket and takes out handkerchief* — *the crystal box*
          falls out with it — *he picks it up and retains it.*)
          This crystal box — nay, give it me, 'twill serve
          To chronicle —
MIRZA: (*hastily*) No, no, Prince Philamir!
          Not that — not that! It is a talisman!
PHIL: Then I will steal it as I stole your heart,
          And I will keep it while I keep that heart.
MIRZA: Give me that box, or I must own the truth —
          That I am miserably false in all! (*throwing herself at his feet*)

That my morality is all assumed!
That I am mean, and base, and treacherous!
A shameless schemer! Heartless — impudent!
Give me that box, or I must own that I
Abstracted it from Phanor's cabinet,
And substituted one that I possessed
Exactly like it. I must own to you
That I'm unutterable infamous —
A hypocrite — a traitress to my friend —
All this, and more, I must admit, if you
Retain that talisman! Oh, give it me,
And let this locket testify our love!*
The King! The King! The King! I am undone! (*Exit hastily.*)

PHIL: Gone, gone! — and Philamir, who thought he knew
The ways of women well, had still to learn
That in one woman's body there is place
For such a goodly show of purity,
And such unequalled treachery of heart!
Oh, Zeolide, for how much infamy
Have I rejected thine unequalled love?

(*Enter* PHANOR *with* CHRYSAL *and* ZORAM.)

PHAN: Congratulate me, I'm half mad with joy;
Azèma comes to tell me that she found
The Queen and Gélanor together here —
Alone — at night!

PHIL: Well, sir, and what of that?

PHAN: Nothing at all, my boy! Why, that's the joke.
Old Gélanor has dandled Altemire
Upon his aged knee five hundred times!

PHIL: What — lately?

PHAN: No! I won't commit myself
By telling you how many years ago,
But long before her majesty was weaned.

PHIL: (*shrugging his shoulders*) I see no reason to condole with you,
Because her majesty and Gélanor
Were here together — neither do I see
Why you should be congratulated, sir!

PHAN: You're very dull! The Queen has just found out
That I had an appointment in this grove
To meet Azèma — don't you understand?
I can retort and take indignant ground.
What was she doing here with Gélanor?
You'll see! (*Sees box.*) Hallo! what's that?

PHIL: A talisman.

---

*Lacy adds: '(*embracing* PHILAMIR)'.

	It fell from Mirza's pocket as you came.
PHAN:	The deuce it did! Allow me; this is mine! (*taking it*)
PHIL:	I know; she stole it from your cabinet;
	She owned as much!
PHAN:	Confound her impudence!
PHIL:	Oh, I have been deceived!
PHAN:	And so have I!

PHAN: Most seriously deceived! Hush, here's the Queen,

And with that gay deceiver, Gélanor!

The talisman has turned up just in time.

(*Enter* ALTEMIRE *and* GELANOR, *with* AZEMA *and* MIRZA.)

So, madam, I've detected you!

ALTEM: (*indignantly*)   How, sir?

PHAN: Never mind how — and you too, Gélanor.

Oh, I'm ashamed of you! (*crossing to* GELANOR)

GELAN: Your Majesty,

I don't know what you mean.

PHAN: You bad old man!

(*affecting to weep*) You whom I trusted so! (*aside*) Don't be alarmed,

I'm not in earnest. (*aloud*) Oh, it's infamous!

Why, let me see — how old are you?

GELAN: My lord,

If you imply —

PHAN: Imply! (*aside*) Don't be a fool,

I'm not in earnest; I have found the box!

(*aloud*) Explain this conduct!

ALTEM: Sir, is this a joke?

PHAN: Well, not exactly, madam; you've been found

Philandering at night with Gélanor.

Being within the influence of these walls,

You're bound to speak the truth. If you can say

Your meeting's innocent, I'm satisfied.

ALTEM: As innocent as truth itself, I swear.

PHAN: I'm satisfied! Your hand —

ALTEM: Nay, hear me first.

I charge you with appointing here to meet

Azèma; you are bound to tell the truth,

Being within the influence of these walls.

If you can unreservedly deny

This charge, I also shall be satisfied.

PHAN: Emphatically I deny the charge!

ALTEM: (*astounded*)   You do?

PHAN: I do! (*piously*) This is the Home of Truth.

And all are subject to its influence.

ALTEM: (*puzzled*) But you admitted it when you confessed

Your gallantries to me this afternoon!

PHAN: Oh, you've been dreaming!

ALTEM: Do I understand
        That you deny th..t you confessed all this?
PHAN: Distinctly! (*piously*) This is the Abode of Truth.
ALTEM: I *have* been dreaming! Phanor, there's my hand,
        I've deeply wronged you.
PHAN: Altemire, you have!
        But say no more — we are good friends again.
ALTEM: Then you forgive me?
PHAN: Heartily I do!
ALTEM: I'll never be a jealous fool again.
PHAN: I'm very glad indeed to hear you say so.
                (Enter ZEOLIDE — ALTEMIRE retires with GELANOR and con-
                verses with ZEOLIDE — PHILAMIR, seeing ZEOLIDE, comes down
                stage abashed.)
PHAN: (*to* PHILAMIR) Well, and what's wrong with you?
PHIL: I've been a fool,
        A madman, and a true-born idiot!
PHAN: By the mysterious influence of this place,
        I can believe it!
PHIL: I have given up
        The noblest woman that I ever knew,
        For that abominable cockatrice
        Who quitted me as you arrived.
PHAN: Well! Well!
        You may regain her yet.
PHIL: Impossible!
PHAN: Oh, not at all! There — take this talisman.
                (ZEOLIDE *overhears this speech.*)
        With this you're proof against this influence
        That rules this place; you can declare to her
        That you adore the very ground she walks,
        And wallow in the foolish flummery
        That used to make you so ridiculous.
        She will believe it all — there, take it, boy,
        And make good use of it to win her back.
PHIL: I'll use it, Phanor, and I'll use it well!
ZEO: (*aside*) He takes the box. And thus he thinks to win
        The hand of his forsaken Zeolide!
        Oh, Philamir, this is contemptible,
        I think I could have loved you, but for this!
PHIL: Dear Zeolide, I hold a talisman,
        Enabling me to counteract the charm
        That reigns within these walls. With this in hand
        I can tell truth or falsehood as I please,
        And you must needs believe me. Zeolide,
        I've learnt to set a value on your love
        Transcending all the riches of the earth;

Yet I would rather live without that love —
A life of self-reproach without that love —
Repentant and alone without that love —
Than stoop to gain it by such treachery.
Here is the talisman. (ZEOLIDE *takes it.*) No longer armed
Against the sacred influence of Truth,
I tell you of my sorrow and my love
With all the warmth of a repentant heart!
    (He presses ZEOLIDE *to his heart and kisses her.)*

ALTEM: (*indignantly*) Give me that talisman! (*Takes it.*) I have a clue
To much that was a mystery: Behold!
    (She breaks it — a loud crash — all come forward.)
    (Enter ARISTAEUS.)

GELAN: You know not what you've done! The castle's charm
Is bound up with that mystic talisman!
Now that the box is broken, these fair walls
Are disenchanted!

PHAN: P'raps it's quite as well.
Now that the place has lost its influence
We shall get on much better. We have learnt
A lesson that should last us till we die —
We've learnt how matrimonial constancy
By causeless jealousy is sometimes tried — (*looking reproachfully at*
ALTEMIRE)

ALTEM: How jealousy is sometimes justified — (*looking reproachfully at* PHANOR)
CHRYS: How Zoram — music's vaunted pioneer —
Don't even know his notes — and has no ear!
Even his cant expressions are the wrong ones!

ZORAM: I *have* an ear!
PHAN: (*shaking his head*) You have — two very long ones!
PALMIS: You've learnt to doubt the love that those profess,
Who by such love gain temporal success — (*looking angrily at* CHRYSAL)

ZORAM: That surly misanthropes, with venom tainted —
ARIST: Are often not as black as they are painted!
AZEMA: To doubt all maids who of their virtue boast:
That they're the worst who moralize the most! (*looking at* MIRZA)

MIRZA: That blushes, though they're most becoming, yet
Proclaim, too oft, the commonplace coquette! (*looking at* AZEMA)
I can declare, with pardonable pride,
I never blush!

AZEMA: You couldn't if you tried!
PHIL: Under the influence that lately reigned
Within these walls I breathed my love unfeigned;
Now that that power no longer reigns above,
I ratify the accents of my love.
Forgive me, Zeolide, my life, my bride!

ZEO: (*very demurely*) I love you, Philamir — be satisfied!

II *Sweethearts*. Scene from act I: 'Spring'. Sketch by D.H. Friston, published in the *Illustrated London News*, 21 November 1874

III *Sweethearts*. Scene from act II: 'Autumn'. Sketch by D.H. Friston. Like no, II, it depicts Marie Wilton (Mrs Bancroft) and Charles Coghlan as Jenny Northcott and Harry Spreadbrow in the original production

SWEETHEARTS*

An original dramatic contrast

First produced at the Prince of Wales's Theatre, London, on 7 November 1874, with the following cast:

MR HARRY SPREADBROW (age 21 in act I)	Mr Coghlan
(age 51 in act II)	
WILCOX, a gardener	Mr Glover
MISS JENNY NORTHCOTT (age 18 in act I)	Miss M. Wilton
(age 48 in act II)	(Mrs Bancroft)
RUTH, a maidservant	Miss Plowden

ACT I: The garden of a pretty country villa. 1844.
ACT II: The same. 1874.

*Text used: *Original Plays* second series (1881, reissued 1909), collated with French's acting edition no. 1655.

ACT I

DATE – 1844

The garden of a pretty country villa. The house is new, and the garden shows signs of having been recently laid out; the shrubs are small, and the few trees about are moderate in size; small creepers are trained against the house; an open country in the distance; a little bridge over a stream forms the entrance to the garden. *

WILCOX *is discovered seated on edge of garden wheelbarrow, preparing his 'bass' for tying up plants; he rises and comes down with sycamore sapling in his hand; it is carefully done up in matting, and has a direction label attached to it.*

WILCOX: (*reading the label*) 'For Miss Northcott, with Mr Spreadbrow's kindest regards.' '*Acer Pseudo Platanus.*' Ay, Ay! Sycamore, I suppose, though it ain't genteel to say so. Humph! Sycamores are common enough in these parts; there ain't no call, as I can see, to send a hundred and twenty mile for one. Ah, Mr Spreadbrow, no go – no go; it ain't to be done with '*Acer Pseudo Platanuses*'. Miss Jenny's sent better men nor you about their business afore this, and as you're agoin' about your'n of your own free will tonight, and a good long way too, why I says, no go, no go! If I know Miss Jenny, she's a good long job, and you've set down looking at your work too long; and now that it's come to going, you'll need to hurry it; and Miss Jenny ain't a job to be hurried over, bless her. Take another three months, and I don't say there mightn't be a chance for you; but it'll take all that – ah, thank goodness, it'll take all that!

> (*Enter* JENNY *from behind the house, prepared for gardening.*)

JENNY: Well, Wilcox, what have you got there? (*He touches his forehead and gives her the sycamore.*) Not my sycamore?

WILCOX: Yes, miss; Mr Spreadbrow left it last night as the mail passed.

JENNY: Then he's returned already? Why, he was not expected for a week, at least.

WILCOX: He returned quite sudden last night, and left this here plant, with a message that he would call at twelve o'clock today, miss.

JENNY: I shall be very glad to see him. So this is really a shoot of the dear old tree!

WILCOX: Come all the way from Lunnon, too. There's lots of 'em hereabouts, miss; I could ha' got you a armful for the asking.

JENNY: Yes, I dare say; but this comes from the dear old house at Hampstead.

WILCOX: Do it, now?

JENNY: You remember the old sycamore on the lawn where Mr Spreadbrow and I used to sit and learn our lessons years ago? – Well, this is a piece of it. And as Mr Spreadbrow was going to London, I asked him to be so kind as to call, and tell the new people, with his compliments, that he wanted to cut a shoot from it for a young lady who had a very pleasant recollection of many very happy hours spent under it. It was an awkward thing for a nervous young gentleman to do, and it's very kind of him to have done it. (*Gives back the plant, which he places against upper porch of house.*) So he's coming this morning?

---

*French adds: '*Music in orchestra at rise of curtain* "Love's Young Dream".'
mail: mail-coach.

WILCOX: Yes, miss, to say goodbye.

JENNY: (*Busies herself at stand of flowers.*) Goodbye! 'How d'ye do?' you mean.

WILCOX: No, miss, goodbye. I hear Mr Spreadbrow's off to Ingy.

JENNY: Yes; I believe he is going soon.

WILCOX: Soon? Ah, soon enough! He joins his ship at Southampton tonight — so he left word yesterday.

JENNY: Tonight? No; not for some weeks yet? (*alarmed*)

WILCOX: Tonight, miss. I had it from his own lips, and he's coming today to say goodbye.

JENNY: (*aside*) Tonight!

WILCOX: And a good job too, say I, though he's a nice young gentleman too.

JENNY: I don't see that it's a good job.

WILCOX: I don't want no young gentleman hanging about here, miss. I know what they comes arter; — they comes arter the flowers.

JENNY: The flowers? What nonsense!

WILCOX: No, it ain't nonsense. The world's a haphazard garden where common vegetables like me, and hardy annuals like my boys, and sour crabs like my old 'oman, and pretty delicate flowers like you and your sisters grow side by side. It's the flowers they come arter.

JENNY: Really, Wilcox, if papa don't object I don't see what you have to do with it.

WILCOX: No, your pa don't object; but I can't make your pa out, miss. Walk off with one of his tupenny toolips and he's your enemy for life. Walk off with one of his darters and he settles three hundred a year on you. Tell 'ee what, miss; if I'd a family of grown gals like you, I'd stick a conservatory label on each of them — 'Please not to touch the specimens!' — and I'd take jolly good care they didn't.

JENNY: At all events, if Mr Spreadbrow is going away tonight, you need not be alarmed on my account. I am a flower that is not picked in a minute.

WILCOX: Well said, miss! And as he *is* going, and as you won't see him no more, I don't mind saying that a better-spoken young gentleman I don't know. A good, honest, straight-for'ard young chap he is — looks you full in the face with eyes that seem to say, 'I'm an open book — turn me over — look me through and through — read every page of me, and if you find a line to be ashamed on, tell me of it, and I'll score it through.'

JENNY: (*demurely*) I dare say Mr Spreadbrow is much as other young men are.

WILCOX: As other young men? No, no — Lord forbid, miss! Come — say a good word for him, poor young gentleman. He's said many a good word of you, I'll go bail.

JENNY: Of me?

WILCOX: (*Takes ladder which is leaning against the house and places it against upper porch of house, and, going a little way up it, speaks this speech from it. JENNY remains seated.*) Ay. Why, only Toosday, when I was at work again' the high road, he rides up on his little bay 'oss, and he stands talking to me over the hedge and straining his neck to catch a sight of you at a window; that was Toosday. 'Well, Wilcox,' says he, 'it's a fine day!' — it rained hard Toosday, but it's always a fine day with him. 'How's Miss Northcott?' says he.

'Pretty well, sir,' says I. 'Pretty she always is; and well she ought to be if the best of hearts and the sweetest of natures will do it!' Well, I knew *that*, so off I goes to another subject, and tries to interest him in drainage, and subsoils, and junction pipes; but no, nothin' would do for him, but he must bring the talk back to *you*. So at last I gets sick of it, and I up and says: 'Look ye here, Mr Spreadbrow,' says I, 'I'm only the gardener. This is Toosday, and Miss Northcott's pa's in the study, and I dessay *he'll* be happy to hear what you've got to say about *her*.' Lord, it'd ha' done your heart good to see how he flushed up as he stuck his spurs into the bay and rode off fifteen miles to the hour. (*laughing*) That was Toosday.

JENNY: (*very angrily*) He had no right to talk about me to a servant.

WILCOX: (*coming down from ladder*) But, bless you, don't be hard on him, he couldn't help it, miss. But don't you be alarmed, he's going away tonight, for many and many a long year, and you won't never be troubled with *him* again. He's going with a heavy heart, take my word for it, and I see his eyes all wet, when he spoke about saying goodbye to you; he'd the sorrow in his throat, but he's a brave lad, and he gulped it down, though it was as big as an apple. (*Ring.*) There he is. Soothe him kindly, miss — don't you be afraid, you're safe enough — he's a good lad, and he can't do no harm now.

(*Exit* WILCOX.)

JENNY: What does he want to go today for? He wasn't going for three months. He could remain if he liked; India has gone on very well without him for five thousand years: it could have waited three months longer; but men are always in such a hurry. He might have told me before — he *would* have done so if he really, really liked me! I wouldn't have left *him* — yes I would — but then that's different. Well, if some people can go, some people can remain behind, and some other people will be only too glad to find *some people* out of their way!

(*Enter* SPREADBROW, *followed by* WILCOX.)

JENNY: (*Suddenly changes her manner, rises and crosses.*) Oh, Mr Spreadbrow, how d'ye do? Quite well? I'm so glad! Sisters quite well? That's right — how kind of you to think of my tree! So you are really and truly going to India tonight? That *is* sudden!

SPREADBROW: Yes, very sudden — terribly sudden. I only heard of my appointment two days ago, in London, and I'm to join my ship tonight. It's very sudden indeed — and — and I've come to say goodbye.

JENNY: Goodbye (*offering her hand*).

SPREADBROW: Oh, but not like that, Jenny! Are you in a hurry?

JENNY: Oh dear no, I thought you were; won't you sit down? (*They sit.*) And so your sisters are quite well?

SPREADBROW: Not very; they are rather depressed at my going so soon. It may seem strange to you, but they will miss me.

JENNY: I'm sure they will. I should be terribly distressed at your going — if I were your sister. And you're going for so long!

SPREADBROW: I'm not likely to return for a great many years.

JENNY: (*with a little suppressed emotion*) I'm so sorry we shall not see you again. Papa will be very sorry.

SPREADBROW: More sorry than you will be?

JENNY: Well, no, I shall be very sorry, too — very, *very* sorry — there!

SPREADBROW: How very kind of you to say so.

JENNY: We have known each other for so long — so many years, and we've always been good friends, and it's always sad to say goodbye for the last time (*He is delighted.*) to anybody! (*He relapses.*) It's so very sad when one knows for certain that it *must* be the last time.

SPREADBROW: I can't tell you how happy I am to hear you say it's so sad. But (*hopefully*) my prospects are not altogether hopeless, there's one chance for me yet. I'm happy to say I'm extremely delicate, and there's no knowing, the climate may not agree with me (*very cheerfully*) and I may be invalided home!

JENNY: Oh! But that would be very dreadful.

SPREADBROW: Oh, yes, of course it would be dreadful in one sense; but it — it would have its advantages. (*Looking uneasily at* WILCOX, *who is hard at work.*) Wilcox is hard at work, I see.

JENNY: Oh, yes, Wilcox is hard at work. He is very industrious.

SPREADBROW: Confoundedly industrious! He is working in the sun without his hat (*significantly*).

JENNY: Poor fellow.

SPREADBROW: Isn't it injudicious, at his age?

JENNY: Oh, I don't think it will hurt him.

SPREADBROW: I really think it will. (*He motions to her to send him away.*)

JENNY: Do you? Wilcox, Mr Spreadbrow is terribly distressed because you are working in the sun.

WILCOX: That's mortal good of him. (*aside, winking*) They want me to go. All right; he can't do much harm now. (*aloud*) Well, sir, the sun is hot, and I'll go and look after the cucumbers away yonder, right at the other end of the garden.

          (WILCOX *going* — SPREADBROW *is delighted.*)

JENNY: No, no, no! — Don't go away! Stop here, only put on your hat. That's what Mr Spreadbrow meant. (WILCOX *puts on his hat.*) There, *now* are you happy?

SPREADBROW: I suppose it will soon be his dinner-time?

JENNY: Oh, he *has* dined. You *have* dined, haven't you, Wilcox?

WILCOX: Oh, yes, miss, *I've* dined, thank ye kindly.

JENNY: Yes; he has dined! Oh! I quite forgot!

SPREADBROW: What?

JENNY: I must interrupt you for a moment, Wilcox; I quite forgot that I promised to send some flowers to Captain Dampier this afternoon. Will you cut them for me?

WILCOX: Yes, miss. (*knowingly*) Out of the conservatory, I suppose, miss?

          (WILCOX *going*, SPREADBROW *again delighted.*)

JENNY: No, these will do (*pointing to open-air flower beds* — SPREADBROW *again disappointed*). Stop, on second thoughts perhaps you *had* better take them out of the conservatory, and cut them carefully — there's no hurry.

WILCOX: (*aside*) *I* understand! Well, poor young chap, let him be, let him be; he's going to be turned off tonight, and his last meal may as well be a hearty one.

(*Exit* WILCOX.)

SPREADBROW: (*Rises in great delight.*) How good of you — how very kind of you!

JENNY: To send Captain Dampier some flowers?

SPREADBROW: (*much disappointed*) Do you really want to send that fellow some flowers?

JENNY: To be sure I do. Why should I have asked Wilcox to cut them?

SPREADBROW: I thought — I was a great fool to think so — but I thought it might have been because we could talk more pleasantly alone.

JENNY: I really wanted some flowers; but, as you say, we certainly can talk more pleasantly alone. (*She busies herself with preparing the sycamore.*)

SPREADBROW: I've often thought that nothing is such a check on — pleasant conversation — as the presence of — of — a gardener — who is not interested in the subject of conversation.

JENNY: (*Gets the tree, and cuts off the matting with which it is bound with garden scissors which she has brought with her from the table.*) Oh, but Wilcox is very interested in everything that concerns you. Do let me call him back.

SPREADBROW: No, no; not on my account!

JENNY: He and I were having quite a discussion about you when you arrived (*digging a hole for the tree*).

SPREADBROW: About me?

JENNY: Yes; indeed we almost quarrelled about you.

SPREADBROW: What, was he abusing me then?

JENNY: Oh, no; he was speaking of you in the highest terms.

SPREADBROW: (*much taken aback*) Then — *you* were abusing me!

JENNY: N — no, not exactly *that*: I — I didn't agree with all he said — (*He is much depressed, she notices this.*) — at least, not openly.

SPREADBROW: (*hopefully*) Then you did secretly.

JENNY: I shan't tell you.

SPREADBROW: Why?

JENNY: Because it will make you dreadfully vain. There!

SPREADBROW: (*delighted*) Very — very dreadfully vain? (*He takes her hand.*)

JENNY: Very dreadfully vain indeed. Don't! (*Withdraws her hand. During this she is digging the hole, kneeling on the edge of the flower bed; he advances to her and kneels on edge of bed near her.*)

SPREADBROW: Do you know it's most delightful to hear you say that? It's without exception the most astonishingly pleasant thing I've ever heard in the whole course of my life! (*Sees the sycamore.*) Is that the tree I brought you? (*Rises from his knees.*)

JENNY: Yes. I'm going to plant it just in front of the drawing-room window, so that I can see it whenever I look out. Will you help me? (*He prepares to do so; she puts it in the hole.*) Is that quite straight? Hold it up, please, while I fill in the earth. (*He holds it while she fills in the earth; gradually his hand slips down till it touches hers.*) It's no use, Mr Spreadbrow, our both holding it in the same place! (*He runs his hand up the stem quickly.*)

SPREADBROW: I beg your pardon — very foolish of me.

JENNY: Very.

SPREADBROW: I'm very glad there will be something here to make you think of me when I'm many many thousand miles away, Jenny. For I shall be always thinking of *you*.

JENNY: Really, now that's very nice! It will be so delightful, and so odd to know that there's somebody thinking about me right on the other side of the world!

SPREADBROW: (*sighing*) Yes. It *will* be on the other side of the world.

JENNY: But that's the delightful part of it — right on the other side of the world! It will be such fun!

SPREADBROW: Fun!

JENNY: Of course, the farther you are away the funnier it will seem. (*He is approaching her again.*) Now keep on the other side of the world. It's just the distance that gives the point to it. There are dozens and dozens of people thinking of me close at hand. (*She rises.*)

SPREADBROW: (*taking her hand*) But not as I think of you, Jenny — dear, dear Jenny — not as I've thought of you for years and years, though I never dared tell you so till now. I can't bear to think that anybody else is thinking of you kindly, earnestly, seriously, as I think of you.

JENNY: (*earnestly*) You may be quite sure, Harry, quite, quite sure that you will be the only one who is thinking of me kindly, seriously, and earnestly (*He is delighted.*) in India. (*He relapses — she withdraws her hand.*)

SPREADBROW: And when this tree, that we have planted together, is a big tree, you must promise me that you will sit under it every day, and give a thought now and then to the old playfellow who gave it to you.

JENNY: A big tree! Oh, but this little plant will never live to be a big tree, surely?

SPREADBROW: Yes, if you leave it alone, it grows very rapidly.

JENNY: Oh, but I'm not going to have a big tree right in front of the drawing-room window! It will spoil the view, it will be an eyesore. We had better plant it somewhere else.

SPREADBROW: (*bitterly*) No, let it be, you can cut it down when it becomes an eyesore. It grows very rapidly, but it will, no doubt, have lost all interest in your eyes long before it becomes an eyesore.

JENNY: But Captain Dampier says that a big tree in front of a window checks the current of fresh air.

SPREADBROW: Oh, if Captain Dampier says so, remove it.

JENNY: Now don't be ridiculous about Captain Dampier; I've a very great respect for his opinion on such matters.

SPREADBROW: I'm sure you have. You see a great deal of Captain Dampier, don't you?

JENNY: Yes, and we shall see a great deal more of him; he's going to take the Grange next door.

SPREADBROW: (*bitterly*) That will be very convenient.

JENNY: (*demurely*) Very.

SPREADBROW: (*jealously*) You seem to admire Captain Dampier very much.

JENNY: I think he is very good-looking. Don't you?

SPREADBROW: He's well enough — for a small man.

JENNY: Perhaps he'll grow.

SPREADBROW: Is Captain Dampier going to live here always?

JENNY: Yes, until he marries.

SPREADBROW: (*eagerly*) Is — is he likely to marry?

JENNY: I don't know. (*demurely*) Perhaps he may.

SPREADBROW: But whom — whom?

JENNY: (*bashfully*) Haven't you heard? I thought you knew!

SPREADBROW: (*excitedly*) No, no, I don't know; I've heard nothing. Jenny — dear Jenny — tell me the truth, don't keep anything from me, don't leave me to find it out; it will be terrible to hear of it out there; and, if you have ever liked me — and I'm sure you have — tell me the whole truth at once!

JENNY: (*bashfully*) Perhaps, as an old friend, I ought to have told you before; but indeed, indeed I thought you knew. Captain Dampier is engaged to be married to — to — my cousin Emmie.

SPREADBROW: (*immensely relieved*) To your cousin Emmie. Oh, thank you, thank you, thank you! Oh, my dear, dear Jenny, do — do let me take your hand. (*Takes her hand and shakes it enthusiastically.*)

JENNY: Are you going?

SPREADBROW: No (*releasing it — much cast down*). I was going to ask you to do me a great favour, and I thought I could ask it better if I had hold of your hand. I was going to ask you if you would give me a flower — any flower, I don't care what it is.

JENNY: (*affecting surprise*) A flower? Why, of course I will. But why?

SPREADBROW: (*earnestly*) That I may have a token of you and of our parting wherever I go; that I may possess an emblem of you that I shall never — never part with, that I can carry about with me night and day wherever I go, throughout my whole life.

JENNY: (*Apparently much affected, crosses slowly, stoops and takes up large geranium in pot.*) Will this be too big?

SPREADBROW: (*disconcerted*) But I mean a flower — only a flower.

JENNY: Oh, but do have a bunch! Wilcox shall pick you a beauty.

SPREADBROW: No, no; I want you to pick it for me. I don't care what it is — a daisy will do — if *you* pick it for me!

JENNY: What an odd notion! (*Crossing to flower-stand, and picking a piece of mignonette — he puts down flower-pot by bed.*) There! (*picking a flower and giving it to him*) Will that do?

SPREADBROW: I can't tell you how inestimably I shall prize this flower. I will keep it while I live, and whatever good fortune may be in store for me, nothing can ever be so precious in my eyes.

JENNY: I had no idea you were so fond of flowers. Oh, do have some more!

SPREADBROW: No, no — but — you must let me give you this in return; I brought it for you, Jenny dear — dear Jenny! Will you take it from me? (*Takes a rose from his buttonhole and offers it.*)

JENNY: (*amused and surprised*) Oh yes! (*Takes it and puts it down on the table carelessly — he notices this with much emotion.*)

SPREADBROW: Well, I've got to say goodbye; there's no reason why it shouldn't be said at once. (*holding out his hand*) Goodbye, Jenny!

JENNY: (*cheerfully*) Goodbye! (*He stands for a moment with her hand in his — she crosses to porch.*)

SPREADBROW: Haven't — haven't you anything to say to me?

JENNY: (*after thinking it over*) No, I don't think there's anything else. No —
  nothing. (*She leans against the porch — he stands over her.*)

SPREADBROW: Jenny, I'm going away today, for years and years, or I wouldn't
  say what I'm going to say — at least not yet. I'm little more than a boy, Jenny;
  but if I were eighty, I couldn't be more in earnest — indeed I couldn't! Parting
  for so many years is like death to me; and if I don't say what I'm going to say
  before I go, I shall never have the pluck to say it after. We were boy and girl
  together, and — and I loved you then — and every year I've loved you more
  and more; and now that I'm a man, and you are nearly a woman, I — I —
  Jenny dear — I've nothing more to say!

JENNY: How you astonish me!

SPREADBROW: Astonish you? Why, you know that I loved you.

JENNY: Yes, yes; as a boy loves a girl — but now that I am a woman it's impossible
  that you can care for me.

SPREADBROW: Impossible — because you are a woman!

JENNY: You see it's so unexpected.

SPREADBROW: Unexpected?

JENNY: Yes. As children it didn't matter, but it seems so shocking for grown
  people to talk about such things. And then, not gradually, but all at once — in
  a few minutes. It's awful!

SPREADBROW: Oh, Jenny, think. I've no time to delay — my having to go has
  made me desperate. One kind word from you will make me go away happy:
  without that word, I shall go in unspeakable sorrow. Jenny, Jenny, say one
  kind word!

JENNY: (*earnestly*) Tell me what to say?

SPREADBROW: It must come from you, my darling; say whatever is on your lips
  — whether for good or ill — I can bear it now.

JENNY: Well, then: I wish you a very very pleasant voyage — and I hope you will
  be happy and prosperous — and you must take great care of yourself — and
  you can't think how glad I shall be to know that you think of me, now and
  then, in India. There!

SPREADBROW: Is that all?

JENNY: Yes, I think that's all. (*reflectively*) Yes — that's all.

SPREADBROW: Then — (*with great emotion which he struggles to suppress*) there's
  nothing left but to say goodbye — (*Music in orchestra till end of act, 'Goodbye, Sweetheart'.*) — and I hope you will always be happy, and that, when
  you marry, you will marry a good fellow who will — who will — who will —
  — Goodbye! (*Exit, rapidly.*)

> (JENNY *watches him out — sits down, leaving the gate open — hums
> an air gaily — looks round to see if he is coming back — goes on
> humming — takes up the flower he has given her — plays with it —
> gradually falters, and at last bursts into tears, laying her head on the
> table over the flower he has given her, and sobbing violently.*)

'*Goodbye, Sweetheart*': Sullivan's song, specially composed for this play and published by
Chappell (1875), is entitled 'Sweethearts'.

ACT II

The same as in act I, with such additions and changes as may be supposed to have taken place in thirty years. The house, which was bare in act I, is now entirely covered with Virginia and other creepers; the garden is much more fully planted than in act I, and trees that were small in act I are tall and bushy now; the general arrangement of the garden is the same, except that the sycamore planted in act I has developed into a large tree, the boughs of which roof in the stage; the landscape has also undergone a metamorphosis, inasmuch as that which was open country in act I is now covered with picturesque semi-detached villas, and there are indications of a large town in the distance. The month is September, and the leaves of the Virginia creepers wear their autumn tint.*

JENNY *discovered seated on a bench, at the foot of the tree, and* RUTH *is standing by her side, holding a skein of cotton, which* JENNY *is winding.* JENNY *is now a pleasant-looking middle-aged lady.*

JENNY: Have you any fault to find with poor Tom?

RUTH: No, miss, I've no fault to find with Tom. But a girl can't marry every young man she don't find fault with, can she now, miss?

JENNY: Certainly not, Ruth. But Tom seems to think you have given him some cause to believe that you are fond of him.

RUTH: (*bridling up*) It's like his impudence, miss, to say so! Fond of *him* indeed!

JENNY: He hasn't said so, Ruth, but I'm quite sure he thinks so. I have noticed of late that you have taken a foolish pleasure in playing fast and loose with poor Tom, and this has made him very unhappy — very unhappy indeed; so much so that I think it is very likely that he will make up his mind to leave my service altogether.

RUTH: (*piqued*) Oh, miss, if Tom can make up his mind to go, I'm sure *I* wouldn't stand in his way for worlds.

JENNY: But I think you would be sorry if he did.

RUTH: Oh yes, miss, I should be sorry to part with Tom!

JENNY: Then I think it's only right to tell you that the foolish fellow talks about enlisting for a soldier, and if he does it at all, he will do it tonight.

RUTH: (*with some emotion*) Oh, miss, for that, I do like Tom very much indeed; but if he wants to 'list, of course he's his own master, and if he's really fond of me, what does he want to go and 'list for? (*going to cry*) One would think he would like to be where he could talk to me, and look at me — odd times! I'm sure I don't want Tom to go and 'list!

JENNY: Then take the advice of an old lady, who knows something of these matters, and tell him so before it's too late — you foolish, foolish girl! Ah, Ruth, I've no right to be hard on you! I've been a young and foolish girl like yourself in my time, and I've done many thoughtless things that I've learnt to be very sorry for. I'm not reproaching you — but I'm speaking to you out of the fulness of my experience, and take my word for it, if you treat poor Tom lightly, you may live to be very sorry for it too! (*taking her hand*) There, I'm

---

*French adds: '*Music in orchestra for rise of curtain.*'

not angry with you, my dear, but if I'd taken the advice I'm giving you, I shouldn't be a lonely old lady at a time of life when a good husband has his greatest value. (*Ring.*) Go and see who's at the gate!

> (*Exit* JENNY. RUTH *goes to the gate, wiping her eyes on her apron – she opens it.*)
> (*Enter* SPREADBROW – *now* SIR HENRY.)

SPREADBROW: My dear, is this Mr Braybrook's?

RUTH: Yes, sir.

SPREADBROW: Is he at home?

RUTH: No, sir, he is not; but mistress is.

SPREADBROW: Will you give your mistress my card? (*feeling for his card-case*) Dear me, I've left my cards at home! Never mind – will you tell your mistress that a gentleman will be greatly indebted to her, if she will kindly spare him a few minutes of her time? Do you think you can charge yourself with that message?

RUTH: Mistress is in the garden, sir; I'll run and tell her, if you'll take a seat. (*Exit* RUTH.)

SPREADBROW: That's a good girl! (*He sits on seat.*) I couldn't make up my mind to pass the old house without framing an excuse to take a peep at it. (*Looks round.*) Very nice – very pretty – but, dear me, on a very much smaller scale than I fancied. Remarkable changes in thirty years! (*Rises and walks round trees, looking about.*) Why, the place is a town, and a railway runs right through it. And this is really the old garden in which I spent so many pleasant hours? Poor little Jenny! – I wonder what's become of her? Pretty little girl, but with a tendency to stoutness; if she's alive, I'll be bound she's fat. So this is Mr Braybrook's, is it? I wonder who Braybrook is – I don't remember any family of that name hereabouts. (*looking off*) This, I suppose, is Mrs Braybrook. Now, how in the world am I to account for my visit?

> (*Enter* JENNY – *she curtsies formally, he bows.*)

I beg your pardon, I hardly know how to explain this intrusion. Perhaps I had better state my facts, they will plead my apology – I am an old Indian civilian, who, having returned to England after many years' absence, is whiling away a day in his native place, and amusing himself with polishing old memories – bright enough once, but sadly tarnished – sadly tarnished!

JENNY: Indeed? May I hope that you have succeeded?

SPREADBROW: Indifferently well – indifferently well. The fact is, I hardly know where I am, for all my old landmarks are swept away; I assure you I am within the mark, when I say that this house is positively the only place I can identify.

JENNY: The town has increased very rapidly of late.

SPREADBROW: Rapidly! When I left, there were not twenty houses in the place, but (*politely*) that was long before your time. I left a village, I find a town – I left a beadle, I find a mayor and corporation – I left a pump, I find a statue to a borough member. The inn is a 'Palace Hotel Company' – the alms-house a county jail – the pound is a police station, and the common a colony of semi-detached bungalows! Everything changed, including myself – everything new, except myself – ha, ha!

JENNY: I shall be glad to offer you any assistance in my power, I should be a good guide, for I have lived here thirty-two years!

SPREADBROW: Thirty-two years! Is it possible? Then surely I ought to know you? (*He feels for his glasses.*) My name is Spreadbrow — Sir Henry Spreadbrow!

JENNY: Spreadbrow! (*putting on spectacles*) Is it possible? Why, my very dear old friend (*offering both her hands*) don't you recollect me?

SPREADBROW: (*He puts on his double eye-glass, takes both her hands.*) God bless me! — Is it possible? — And this is really you! — You don't say so! Dear me, dear me! Well, well, well! I assure you I am delighted, most unaffectedly delighted, to renew our friendship! (*Shaking hands again, they sit under tree and look at each other curiously.*) Not changed a bit! My dear Jane, you really must allow me. (*They shake hands again.*) And now tell me, how is Mr Braybrook?

JENNY: (*rather surprised*) Oh, Mr Braybrook is very well; I expect him home presently; he will be very glad to see you, for he has often heard me speak of you.

SPREADBROW: Has he indeed? It will give me the greatest — the very greatest possible pleasure, believe me (*very emphatically*) to make his acquaintance.

JENNY: (*still surprised at his emphatic manner*) I'm sure he will be delighted.

SPREADBROW: Now tell me all about yourself. Any family?

JENNY: (*puzzled*) I beg your pardon?

SPREADBROW: Any family?

JENNY: Mr Braybrook?

SPREADBROW: Well — yes.

JENNY: Mr Braybrook is a bachelor.

SPREADBROW: A bachelor? Then let me understand — am I not speaking to Mrs Braybrook?

JENNY: No, indeed you are not! Ha, ha! (*much amused*) Mr Braybrook is my nephew; the place belongs to him now.

SPREADBROW: Oh! Then, my dear Jane, may I ask who you are?

JENNY: I am not married.

SPREADBROW: Not married!

JENNY: No; I keep house for my nephew.

SPREADBROW: Why, you don't mean to sit there and look me in the face and tell me, after thirty years, that you are still Jane Northbrook?

JENNY: (*rather hurt at the mistake*) Northcott.

SPREADBROW: Northcott, of course. I beg your pardon — I should have said Northcott. And you are not Mrs Braybrook? You are not even married! Why, what were they about — what were they about? Not married! Well, now, do you know, I am very sorry to hear that. I am really more sorry and disappointed than I can tell you. (*She looks surprised and rather hurt.*) You'd have made an admirable wife, Jane, and an admirable mother. I can't tell you how sorry I am to find that you are still Jane Northbrook — I should say, Northcott.

JENNY: The same in name — much changed in everything else (*sighing*).

SPREADBROW: Changed? Not a bit — I won't hear of it. I knew you the moment I saw you! We are neither of us changed. Mellowed perhaps — a little mellowed, but what of that? Who shall say that the blossom is pleasanter to look upon than the fruit? Not I for one, Jane — not I for one.

JENNY: Time has dealt very kindly with us, but we're old folks now, Henry Spreadbrow. (*Rises.*)

SPREADBROW: I won't allow it, Jane — I won't hear of it. (*Rises.*) What constitutes youth? A head of hair? Not at all; I was as bald as an egg at five-and-twenty — babies are always bald. Eyesight? Some people are born blind. Years? Years are an arbitrary impertinence. Am I an old man or you an old woman, because the earth contrives to hurry round the sun in three hundred and sixty-five days? Why, Saturn can't do it in thirty years. If I had been born on Saturn I should be two years old, ma'am — a public nuisance in petticoats. Let us be thankful that I was not born on Saturn. No — no, as long as I can ride to cover twice a week, walk my five-and-twenty miles without turning a hair, go to bed at twelve, get up at six, turn into a cold tub and like it, I'm a boy, Jane — a boy — a boy!

JENNY: And you are still unmarried?

SPREADBROW: I? Oh dear, yes — very much so. No time to think of marriage. Plenty of opportunity, mind, but no leisure to avail myself of it. I've had a bustling time of it, I assure you, Jane, working hard at the Bar and on the Bench, with some success — with some success; (*Sits again.*) and now that I've done my work, I throw myself back in my easy-chair, fold my hands, cross my legs, and prepare to enjoy myself. Life is before me, and I'm going to begin it. Ha, ha! And so we are really Jane Northcott still?

JENNY: Still Jane Northcott.

SPREADBROW: I'm indignant to hear it — I assure you that I am positively indignant to hear it. You would have made some fellow so infernally happy; (*Rises.*) I'm sorry for that fellow's sake — I don't know him, but still I am sorry. Ah, I wish I had remained in England. I do wish, for the very first time since I left it, that I had remained in England.

JENNY: Indeed! And why?

SPREADBROW: Why? Because I should have done my best to remove that reproach from society. I should indeed, Jane! Ha, ha! After all, it don't much matter, for you wouldn't have had me. Oh yes! You had no idea of it; but, do you know, I've a great mind to tell you — I *will* tell you. Do you know, I was in love with you at one time. Boy and girl, you know — boy and girl. Ha, ha! *You*'d no idea of it, but I was!

JENNY: (*in wonder*) Oh yes; I knew it very well.

SPREADBROW: (*much astonished*) You knew it? You knew that I was attached to you?

JENNY: Why, of course I did!

SPREADBROW: Did you, indeed! Bless me, you don't say so. Now that's amazingly curious. Leave a woman alone to find *that* out! It's instinctive, positively instinctive. Now, my dear Jane, I'm a very close student of human nature, and in pursuit of that study I should like above all things to know by what signs you detected my secret admiration for you. (*Takes her hand.*)

JENNY: Why, bless the man! There was no mystery in the matter! You told me all about it!

SPREADBROW: I told you all about it?

JENNY: Certainly you did — here, in this garden.

SPREADBROW: That I admired you — loved you?

JENNY: Most assuredly! Surely you've not forgotten it. (*He drops her hand.*) *I* haven't.

SPREADBROW: I remember that I had the impertinence to be very fond of you. I forgot that I had the impertinence to tell you so. I remember it now. I made a fool of myself. I remember it by that. I told you that I adored you, didn't I? — that you were as essential to me as the air I breathed — that it was impossible to support existence without you — that your name should be the most hallowed of earthly words, and so forth. Ha, ha! My dear Jane, before I'd been a week on board I was saying the same thing to a middle-aged governess whose name has entirely escaped me. (*She has exhibited signs of pleasure during the earlier part of this speech, and disappointment at the last two lines.*) What fools we make of ourselves!

JENNY: And of others!

SPREADBROW: Oh, I meant it, Jane; I meant every word I said to you.

JENNY: And the governess?

SPREADBROW: And the governess! I would have married you, Jane.

JENNY: And the governess?

SPREADBROW: And the governess! I'd have married her, if she had accepted me — but she didn't. Perhaps it was as well — she was a widow with five children — I cursed my destiny at the time, but I've forgiven it since. I talked of blowing out my brains. I'm glad I didn't do it, as I've found them useful in my profession. Ha, ha! (*Looking round;* JENNY *stands watching him.*)* The place has changed a good deal since my time — improved — improved — we've all three improved. I don't quite like this tree, though — it's in the way. What is it? A kind of beech, isn't it?

JENNY: No, it's a sycamore.

SPREADBROW: Ha! I don't understand English trees — but it's a curious place for a big tree like this, just outside the drawing-room window. Isn't it in the way?

JENNY: It *is* rather in the way.

SPREADBROW: I don't like a tree before a window, it checks the current of fresh air — don't you find that?

JENNY: It *does* check the current of fresh air.

SPREADBROW: Then the leaves blow into the house in autumn, and that's a nuisance — and besides, it impedes the view.

JENNY: It is certainly open to these objections.

SPREADBROW: Then cut it down, my dear Jane. Why don't you cut it down?

JENNY: Cut it down! I wouldn't cut it down for worlds. That tree is identified in my mind with many happy recollections.

SPREADBROW: Remarkable the influence exercised by associations over a woman's mind. Observe — you take a house, mainly because it commands a beautiful view. You apportion the rooms principally with reference to that

---

*French adds: '*Her back to audience.*'

view. You lay out your garden at great expense to harmonize with that view, and, having brought that view into the very best of all possible conditions for the full enjoyment of it, you allow a gigantic and wholly irrelevant tree to block it all out for the sake of the sentimental ghost of some dead and gone sentimental reality! Take my advice and have it down. If I had had anything to do with it, you would never have planted it. I shouldn't have allowed it!

JENNY: You had so much to do with it that it was planted there at your suggestion.

SPREADBROW: At mine? Never saw it before in my life.

JENNY: We planted it together thirty years ago – the day you sailed for India.

SPREADBROW: It appears to me that that was a very eventful day in my career. We planted it together! I have no recollection of having ever planted a gigantic sycamore anywhere. And we did it together? Why, it would take a dozen men to move it.

JENNY: It was a sapling then – you cut it for me.

SPREADBROW: (*suddenly and with energy*) From the old sycamore in the old garden at Hampstead! Why, I remember; I went to London expressly to get it for you. (*laughing – sitting on her left*) And the next day I called to say goodbye, and I found you planting it, and I helped; and as I was helping I found an opportunity to seize your hand. (*Does so.*) I grasped it – pressed it to my lips – (*Does so.*) – and said, 'My dear, dear Jenny' (*He drops her hand suddenly.*) and so forth. Never mind *what* I said – but I meant it – I meant it! (*Laughs heartily – she joins him, but her laughter is evidently forced – eventually she shows signs of tears, which he doesn't notice.*) It all comes back with a distinctness which is absolutely photographic. I begged you to give me a flower – you gave me one – a sprig of geranium.

JENNY: Mignonette.

SPREADBROW: *Was* it mignonette? I think you're right – it was mignonette. I seized it – pressed it to my trembling lips – placed it next my fluttering heart, and swore that come what might I would never, never part with it! – I wonder what I did with that flower! – And then I took one from my buttonhole – begged you to take it – you took it, and – ha, ha, ha! – you threw it down carelessly on the table, and thought no more about it, you heartless creature – ha, ha, ha! Oh, I was very angry! I remember it perfectly; it was a camellia.

JENNY: (*half crying aside*) Not a camellia, I think.

SPREADBROW: Yes, a camellia, a large white camellia.

JENNY: I don't think it was a camellia; I rather think it was a rose.

SPREADBROW: Nonsense, Jane – come, come, you hardly looked at it, miserable little flirt that you were; and you pretend, after thirty years, to stake your recollection of the circumstance against mine? No, no, Jane, take my word for it, it was a camellia.

JENNY: I'm sure it was a rose!

SPREADBROW: No, I'm sure it was a camellia.

JENNY: (*in tears*) Indeed – indeed, it was a rose. (*Produces a withered rose from a pocket-book – he is very much impressed – looks at it and at her, and seems much affected.*)

SPREADBROW: Why, Jane, my dear Jane, you don't mean to say that this is the very flower?

JENNY: That is the very flower! (*rising*)

SPREADBROW: Strange! You seemed to attach no value to it when I gave it to you, you threw it away as something utterly insignificant; and when I leave, you pick it up, and keep it for thirty years! (*rising*) My dear Jane, how like a woman!

JENNY: And you seized the flower I gave you – pressed it to your lips, and swore that wherever your good or ill fortune might carry you, you would never part with it; and – and you quite forgot what became of it! My dear Harry, how like a man!

SPREADBROW: I was deceived, my dear Jane – deceived! I had no idea that you attached so much value to my flower.

JENNY: We were both deceived, Henry Spreadbrow.

SPREADBROW: Then is it possible that in treating me as you did, Jane, you were acting a part?

JENNY: We were both acting parts – but the play is over, and there's an end of it. (*with assumed cheerfulness*) Let us talk of something else.

SPREADBROW: No, no, Janet,* the play is *not* over – we will talk of nothing else – the play is not nearly over. (*Music in orchestra, 'John Anderson my Jo'.*) My dear Jane – (*rising and taking her hand*) my very dear Jane – believe me, for I speak from my hardened old heart, so far from the play being over, the serious interest is only just beginning. (*He kisses her hand – they walk towards the house.*)

---

*French has: 'Jane'.

PRINCESS TOTO*

An entirely new and original English comic opera

First produced in London at the Royal Strand Theatre on 2 October 1876 with the following cast:

KING PORTICO	Mr Harry Cox
ZAPETER, his prime minister	Mr W.S. Penley
JAMILEK, his grand chamberlain	Mr Charles Otley
PRINCE CARAMEL	Mr J.G. Taylor
COUNT FLOSS ⎱ members of Prince	Mr W. Blatchley
BARON JACQUIER ⎰ Caramel's suite	Mr Knight
PRINCE DORO, betrothed to Princess Toto	Mons. Marius
GIOVANNI, an old beggar	Mr F. Cotterell
PAOLINI ⎱ beggars	Mr H. Seymour
VERGILLO ⎰	Mr T. Cherry
JELLY	Miss Lottie Venne
TAPIOCA	Miss Lizzie Coote
SAGO	Miss Gwynne Williams
VERMICELLI	Miss M. Jamieson
DEVINE, Princess Toto's favourite page	Miss La Feuillade
PRINCESS TOTO	Miss Kate Santley

Courtiers and court ladies, pages, brigands, Red Indians

ACT I: the gardens of King Portico's palace.
ACT II: mountain home of the brigand chief.
ACT III: an island in the Pacific Ocean.

Scenery by Mr H.P. Hall
The opera produced under the personal direction of the authors.

---

*Text used: Lord Chamberlain's licensed copy (53168L), collated with Metzler libretto (M5657) (?1880). Passages included in licensed copy but omitted from Metzler are placed in square brackets [ ]. See also appendix, p. 132.

IV *Princess Toto*. Photograph of W.S. Penley as Zapeter in the original London
production

Revived at the Opera Comique, London, on 15 October 1881 with the following cast:

KING PORTICO	Mr Richard Temple
ZAPETER	Mr Robert Brough
JAMILEK	Mr George Temple
PRINCE DORO	Mr G. Loredan
PRINCE CARAMEL	Mr Alfred Bishop
COUNT FLOSS	Mr J. Ettinson
BARON JACQUIER	Mr E. Stepan
PRISONER	Mr H. Chambers
PRINCESS TOTO	Miss Annette Albu
JELLY	Miss C. Maitland
FOLLETTE	Miss E. Vane

Chorus of courtiers, brigands, and Red Indians.

ACT I: gardens of King Portico's palace.
ACT II: a rocky pass.
ACT III: a tropical island.
SCENE: Nowhere   TIME: Never

Scenery by Mr W. Hann
The opera produced under the personal direction of the composer and Mr R. Barker.

ACT I

Gardens of KING PORTICO's *palace.* ZAPETER, JAMILEK, COURTIERS, *etc.,* *discovered. All are very prim and precise in appearance.*

CHORUS
This is a court in which you'll find
The most respectable society;
To every fault we all are blind,
Except to fault of impropriety.
We pride ourselves upon our taste,
It is indeed our only vanity;
And when in false positions placed
It almost drives us to insanity.
This is a court, etc.
(*Flourish. Enter* KING PORTICO.)

KING: Is there no sign of Prince Caramel?

ZAPETER: None, my liege.

KING: This is a bad beginning. His marriage with our daughter was to have taken place the day before yesterday; for two days and a half everything has been in readiness, and we are getting tired of waiting; besides, the people are becoming impatient, and when we appear among them we shall be received with derisive remarks. It's a very bad beginning. It's a slight. It will serve to make us appear ridiculous in the eyes of the surrounding nations. I will give him five minutes more, and then — Is everything ready?

JAMILEK: Everything, sire.

KING: The musicians are here?

JAMILEK: They are all here, sire.

KING: I trust the cornet-players have been instructed not to puff out their cheeks when they blow; nothing is more ridiculous than to see a man expressing a tender sentiment with cheeks like dumplings. The singers — I hope they will be careful not to open their mouths too wide; it's a very common fault with singers. [The pew-opener — she is not a ridiculous old person at whom the crowd are likely to laugh, I hope? A laugh would be fatal. The gentlemen of the press, too, I hope you have seen that they have had their hair cut, and that they are neatly shaved?]

ZAPETER: All this has been attended to.

KING: Very good. There will be no cheering, of course. Nothing is more vulgar than enthusiasm. I shall make but one speech, and that will be received in respectful silence.

ZAPETER: Your speeches, sire, are always so received.

KING: I have remarked it. Well, I think we have provided against mishaps, as far as we are able to do. There is nothing left but to trust that nothing will occur to make us ridiculous in the eyes of surrounding countries. [Let the procession be formed that all may be in readiness.]

(*Repeat of chorus, and exeunt* JAMILEK *and the ladies and gentle-men of the court singing,* 'This is a court in which you'll find'.)

KING: Zapeter, between ourselves, it's a most extraordinary thing that young man doesn't come. Three days late for his wedding. It's inexcusable.

ZAPETER: It will be deplorable if anything has occurred to change his mind.

KING: Deplorable! It will be more than deplorable — it will be disastrous! It is no news to you that the unparalleled eccentricities of my daughter, Toto, have caused me the greatest uneasiness; for they have drawn down ridicule upon us, and made us absurd in the eyes of surrounding nations. It therefore became necessary, as we value our own self-respect, to get her married at once. Prince Doro, to whom she was betrothed in infancy, unfortunately died, and as Prince Caramel immediately offered to supply his place I closed with him at once. He is a highly respectable young prince, but he is certainly unpunctual. Three days late! Dear, dear, dear! I trust it won't get about; I am most anxious about this. Great heavens! — if he should not come at all — or, worse still, if he should come ridiculously dressed. There is madness in the thought!

ZAPETER: My liege, in the excess of our grief and disappointment I believe we should all go stark staring mad.

KING: Do you really think you would? Then I trust you will be careful to go mad with dignity, and even in your severest paroxysms preserve your sense of self-respect.

(*Re-enter* JAMILEK.)

JAMILEK: Sire, a gentleman is at the gate, and desires to speak with your Majesty alone.

KING: Alone! This is a very strange request.

JAMILEK: The gentleman, sire, is a stranger.

ZAPETER: It may be that he brings news of Prince Caramel.

KING: Very likely; but why should he not speak openly?

ZAPETER: Perhaps he brings news that it would be undignified to publish.

KING: Such as —

ZAPETER: Such as that his Highness has the measles, or the mumps. A royal wedding postponed on account of the bridegroom's mumps! Oh! If it should get into the papers!

KING: I should die of confusion; the whole universe would be laughing at us. Admit him by all means; and if the news is such as I can listen to without loss of dignity, I will hear what he has to say.

(*Exeunt* KING *and* ZAPETER.)

(*Enter* PRINCE DORO.)

DORO: At last, after many perils by land and sea, I have arrived at my destination, and the particular fortune in store for me will soon be revealed. What a singular one is mine! Betrothed at the immature age of one to a lovely princess of twelve months, whom, owing to a confoundedly annoying series of circumstances, I have never seen since! Who can wonder at my anxiety to know what kind of young lady she has blossomed into?

SONG. – DORO

Oh bride of mine, Oh baby wife,
    In cradledom demurely plighted,
Has time dealt kindly with thy life,
    Since thou and I were first united?
Art thou as fair, and yet as fond
    As in that stage of preparation?
Ah! Since those days the wizard's wand
    Has worked some wondrous transformation.
        Oh bride of mine, whose smiles or tears
        Will season all my hopes and fears,
        How art thou changed in eighteen years!

Art thou a cold, imperious maid?
    Or canst thou stoop to homely duty?
A scornful Juno, proud and staid?
    A Hebe blushing in her beauty?
Hast thou a brain with lore opprest?
    With science in its ev'ry section?
Or is thy learning in thy breast?
    Thine only art – to win affection?
        Oh bride of mine, etc.

(*Re-enter* KING PORTICO.)

KING: I believe you wished to see the King?

DORO: Am I right in supposing this to be the royal palace?

KING: This is a – in short, one of them. It is not the best of them; but the others are under repair. [(*aside*) I trust he is not sneering at our Sunday Palace.]

DORO: Sir, I salute you with every sentiment of the profoundest respect.

KING: (*aside*) Now I wonder if he meant that!

DORO: You would perhaps like to know who I am. It is but natural. I, sir, have the honour to be betrothed to your daughter. I have had that honour for many years past, but circumstances have prevented me from making use of the fact. I have been wrecked on a savage shore, and I found myself compelled to dwell among the natives for ten years. Eventually, i made my escape, and the first thing I did was to hasten hither to see if my little Toto loved me still.

KING: (*weeping*) It is an affecting story; but I don't know you. You won't pretend you are Prince Caramel?

DORO: Certainly not; I am Prince Doro.

KING: How extremely awkward!

DORO: I am not usually considered so.

KING: Pardon me, I don't mean that. Don't be angry; but it was generally supposed that you were – in short, dead; and, not to put too fine a point upon it, the Princess is going to marry another Prince – a nice, well-behaved young man – plays the flute, does worsted work, wears galoshes [attends spelling-bees].*

---

*Metzler adds: 'He's a highly respectable young man.'

It's a highly respectable court too; they all play the flute and all wear galoshes
— a very nice court! Plenty of quiet fun, and no excess.

DORO: And where is this exemplary youth?

KING: That's what I want to know; we're waiting for him. We can't think why he
hasn't come. It — it's a slight. It will put us in an absurd light. I — I — I am
very angry — very angry indeed.

DORO: Well, upon my honour, this is extremely pleasant!

KING: It's extremely kind and extremely pleasant of you to look at it in that way;
and, between ourselves — between ourselves, I say — I don't think you've lost
much.

DORO: Not lost much! Why she promised to be as beautiful as the day.

KING: Oh! She's more beautiful than some days — the day before yesterday, for
instance. Yes, she's a very fine woman: but — well — she is rather difficult to
deal with. [The fact is — between ourselves — my daughter is a woman. This
will go no farther?

DORO: On my honour. But you astonish me.

KING: Yes, I thought I should.] Toto, bless her! is extremely wilful and obstinate,
and ridiculously impulsive and romantic. Her head is filled with foolish ideas
about gypsies, robbers, actors, pirates, paving commissioners, Red Indians,
and outlandish people of that sort. Just now it's the brigand Barberini, the
scourge of the neighbourhood. She can think and talk of nothing else — wears
a lock of his wig round her neck. You have no idea how she compromises me.
Then she has no memory — no memory whatever; forgets events that are not
ten minutes old. Acts, too, on the spur of the moment, eats, drinks, sleeps, on
the spur of the moment — gets up on the spur of the moment — sits down on
the spur of the moment. And this causes a great deal of unnecessary pain and
inconvenience.

[DORO: To the Princess?

KING: No, to the court.] I assure you, it's a fortunate thing for you that you are
dead.

DORO: But I can scarcely be said to be dead.

KING: Oh yes, you are, indeed! You think you're not, but you are. We had it on
the best authority; you were eaten by savages. You can't get over that, you
know.

DORO: But I assure —

KING: Really, I can't permit the subject to be reopened. It comes to this. Either
you are dead, or *I* am placed in a very awkward and ridiculous position. You
see my difficulty.

DORO: Perfectly. I also see my own. Am I to understand that I've travelled night
and day from the shores of Patagonia for nothing?

KING: Of course, I can't say how much it has cost you, but you are lucky if you've
travelled all that way for nothing; you've nothing to complain of. After all,
you'll see the wedding festivities, you know; you're in time for that. Your
name will be in the papers. What more can you want?

DORO: What more? Why, my life is a blank from this moment, I loved her the first
day I saw her. I can see her now, lying in her nurse's arms, and toying with an
india-rubber ring. Is she much changed?

KING: Yes, you'll find her grown. Fickle, like all women, she has wearied of her india-rubber ring. As for her personal appearance, you can judge for yourself, for here she comes.
> (KING *and* DORO *retire.*)
> (*Enter* BRIDESMAIDS *and* PRINCESS TOTO, *followed by* JELLY.)

CHORUS OF BRIDESMAIDS

> Of our opinions to impart
> Some notion let's endeavour:
> May she be mistress of her heart,
> And he her slave for ever.

TOTO: Dressed at last! How do I look, Jelly?

JELLY: Lovely, your Highness!

TOTO: Let me see! What did I put on this dress for, Jelly?

JELLY: To be married in, your Highness.

TOTO: Of course; I forgot. It's an awful thing to be married!

JELLY: It's still more awful not being married, your Highness!

TOTO: Do you find that, Jelly?

JELLY: I do, your Highness.

TOTO: Well, I suppose you're right. It's certainly very pleasant to think that somebody who loves you better than anybody else in the whole world, and who is going to love you like that, only more so, all his life, and isn't going to care a button for anyone else as long as he lives, is coming all the way from ever-so-far [to marry you]* because he feels he can't get on any longer without you.

[BALLAD. – TOTO

> Like an arrow from its quiver
> Comes my love this very day.
> On the ever-running river
> Speeds my love upon his way.
> Comes to give a lover's greeting –
> Comes to press me to his heart.
> Those who meet with such a meeting
> Surely never, never part.
>> Over spotted meadows fleeting,
>> Over hill and over lea,
>> Flushed with joyous hope of meeting,
>> Comes my love to marry me.
>
> I the while, my love awaiting,
> Sit in silence, prim and coy:
> Yet my heart is palpitating

---

*Metzler has: 'like an arrow from its quiver'.

> And I can't conceal my joy.
> Though I droop my eyes demurely,
> Though my hands I primly fold,
> Yet my beating heart will surely
> Tell the truth that they withhold.
> Tell the truth that gaily fleeting
> Over hill and over lea,
> Flushed with joyous hope of meeting,
> Comes my love to marry me.]
> (KING *comes down stage.*)

TOTO: Why, papa, you look annoyed. Don't you like the song?*

KING: Yes, [it's an agreeable song, and] I like the sentiment [of it]; but it won't do, my child, it don't fit the situation. He is not coming like an arrow from its quiver; he's dawdling, my child, dawdling.

TOTO: Who's dawdling?

KING: Why, Prince Caramel's dawdling.

TOTO: And who is Prince Caramel, I wonder? I know the name, too. I've heard it somewhere. Jelly, what do I know about Prince Caramel?

JELLY: He's the gentleman your Highness is going to be married to.

TOTO: Of course; I remember. Today, isn't it?

JELLY: This very day! I've just been dressing you for the purpose.

TOTO: To be sure you have. Now, what an old goose you must be to have forgotten that!

KING: Pardon me, we did not forget it; and we are not an old goose.

TOTO: Well, if I'm to be married, let's get it over!

KING: But the bridegroom! We must wait for the bridegroom.

TOTO: Wait for the bridegroom? Nonsense! Who cares about the bridegroom at a wedding? Nobody thinks about him. The bride monopolizes all the interest; and if she is ready we'll begin. She is ready, isn't she?

JELLY: Quite ready, your Highness!

TOTO: Then send her here; I should like to see her. (JELLY *hands a looking-glass.*) What's this? Oh! Of course, I'm the bride. You silly old man, you forgot I was the bride. Ah! It's lucky I've my wits about me, or I don't know what would become of you all.

KING: But the bridegroom! He's insignificant, I admit, but so is the organ-blower in church, yet the organist can't get on without him. You admit the parallel?

TOTO: Entirely; but as anybody can blow an organ, so anyone can be a bridegroom. This gentleman, for instance – who is he? (*indicating* DORO)

DORO: I am the unhappy prince, who has been cruelly jilted. False girl, I am the miserable Doro.

TOTO: Doro? I know that name – Jelly, what do I know about the miserable Doro?

JELLY: He's the gentleman your Highness was betrothed to before Prince Caramel; the gentleman who died.

---

*Metzler has: 'sentiment'.

TOTO: I remember. I loved you, Doro, and to this day when I think of your unhappy end, I can't restrain my tears. You — you were devoured by cannibals:
they ate you up (*sobbing*). Did — did — did it hurt?

DORO: Cruel girl, you concern yourself with the torture of a devoured body, but
you have little sympathy for the agony of a crushed soul. Learn, faithless one,
that I was not eaten — that I escaped — and that I stand before you.

TOTO: My own, own husband (*embracing him*).

DORO: You love me then?

TOTO: Love you? If you had any idea how slowly the last three days have passed
without you, you would not ask that question. (*to* JELLY) Come, we must
be off.

(*Re-enter* ZAPETER.)

JELLY: Off! Off where?

TOTO: Off where? What a memory you have! Why off to church, to be sure.
They've entirely forgotten that this is my wedding day. Oh! It's enough to
vex a saint, it is.

DORO: But why are we to go to church?

TOTO: Why? Why, to be married, of course — I've waited three days. Isn't that
enough?

ZAPETER: Oh, but your Highness, this is not —

KING: (*aside*) Hush! Silence! She has mixed up her lovers. (*aloud to* DORO) Fall
in with her views.

ZAPETER: But, sire, reflect, Prince Caramel may arrive at any moment, and if he
should lose his temper — a very likely contingency under the circumstances —
and interrupt the ceremony, you would be placed in a very ridiculous and
absurd position. Everyone would laugh at you.

KING: Oh, would they? Very good. We will take precautions against that. You will
remain here, and receive Prince Caramel; you will explain the case to him
diplomatically — you will so frame your explanation that he shall receive it in
perfect good humour; indeed, he shall rather like it than otherwise. And if he
gets angry, or says or does anything to make us appear ridiculous in the eyes
of surrounding nations, we shall hold you responsible for it; you understand?

ENSEMBLE. —

TOTO, DORO, ZAPETER *and* KING

DORO: Come, let us hasten, love, to make us one,
           And on your finger I will place a token;

(*aside*)   This is a thing that's very often done,
           For promises are made but to be broken.

TOTO: I mean to be his wife this very day,
           And you should have been here some days before, oh!

(*aside*)   I have resolved to give my heart away,
           And if to anyone, why not to Doro?

KING (*aside*)   ZAPETER (*aside*)

We cannot wait;   They cannot wait;

If he is late   If he is late

It's his affair,	It's my affair,
And he must bear	And I must bear
Without offence	For my offence
The consequence	The consequence
Of being late;	Of being late;
We cannot wait,	They cannot wait
It's his affair	It's my affair,
And he must bear, etc.	And he must bear, etc.

ALL

DORO, TOTO *and* KING   ZAPETER

So let us away to the wedding,	So now they are off to the wedding,
Away to the wedding today,	Off, off to the wedding today,
No minuet measure be treading,	While I many tears shall be shedding,
But merrily trip it away.	But there'll be the dickens to pay.

(*All but* ZAPETER *dance off.*)

ZAPETER: This is a pleasant position for a diplomatist. I have to explain, diplomatically, to the Prince, that the bride he is coming to marry is at present being married to somebody else, and the news must be broken so diplomatically that he shall rather like it than otherwise. (*Trumpet heard without.*) Unless I am very much mistaken, there he is. He has arrived at last. Oh! Spirit of diplomacy — angel or devil — whichever you are — assist me in this emergency. (*Exit.*)

(*Enter* COUNT FLOSS, PRINCE CARAMEL *and* JACQUIER [*preceded by fife and drum*]. *The* PRINCE *is engaged on a pair of worsted work slippers.* JACQUIER *is knitting, and* FLOSS *is tatting. They are very mild and simple young men.*)

MARCH

With princely state
   With fife and drum
Some three days late
   We come, we come!
When such as we come out in state,
What if *we be some three days late*!

CARAMEL: Three days late! It's not much, and even now my wedding present is not finished! [(*showing slipper*)]
JACQUIER: Nor mine!
FLOSS: Nor mine!
CARAMEL: Late as we are, they don't seem to be ready for us. The town is empty; not a soul to be seen! Not a guard of honour, no sentries, no band, no people! It's most extraordinary!

(*Re-enter* ZAPETER.)

JACQUIER: (*seeing* ZAPETER) Ha! here is a person at last! Sir, will you kindly inform us whom we have the honour of addressing?

ZAPETER: (*aside*) A skilful diplomatist never commits himself to a statement. (*aloud*) You ask me who I am? Who shall say? Know thyself, said the philosopher; and he was right. (*aside*) Neatly parried.

CARAMEL: The Princess, I trust, is well?

ZAPETER: Well and ill are relative terms. Of three individuals — A, B and C — A may be singularly robust as compared with C, but a confirmed invalid as compared with B. These are momentous questions. (*aside*) Well fenced.

FLOSS: Is her Highness engaged?

ZAPETER: It may be that she is engaged. It may even be that she is married. (*aside*) The thin edge of the wedge!

CARAMEL: I do not understand you. Her Highness is a single lady.

ZAPETER: Single and double are relative terms of people. Of three people, A, B and C, B may be single as compared with A, but double as compared with C. Some people are more single than others; some people, on the other hand, are more double than others. A wedding! What is it? A ceremony! Why stand upon ceremony? The Princess desires that there may be no ceremony between you. (*aside*) The ice is broken.

CARAMEL: Oh, sir, I am a plain man who does not understand wily talk. That your words are wise, I feel sure, for I cannot make head or tail of them. It seems to me that you wish to express some idea. If you would kindly translate it into words of two syllables and under, I think I should succeed in grasping it more readily.

ZAPETER: (*aside*) Brought to bay. It is not possible to express oneself diplomatically in two syllables. (*aloud*) Sir, the Princess waited for you until she could wait no longer.

CARAMEL: Yes, I follow you.

ZAPETER: So, another potentate —

CARAMEL: That's three syllables.

ZAPETER: True: I apologize.

JACQUIER: That's four!

ZAPETER: I really beg your pardon.

[JACQUIER: Oh, but it is. A — po — lo — gize.

ZAPETER: Yes, I mean to say that I'm sorry, I regret it. A prince having offered — Prince Doro — she accepted.

FLOSS: Three.

ZAPETER: (*correcting himself*) Closed with him.] They are being married now. (*aside*) Ruined; he winces.

CARAMEL: But, goodness me! You don't mean to say that I'm jilted?

ZAPETER: I didn't mean to say it, but you made me. If you had let me run on in polysyllables.

[CARAMEL: There you go again.]

ZAPETER: I would have broken it more delicately; but you would have it in two syllables, and I'm a ruined diplomatist.

FLOSS: But is there no way?

ZAPETER: None, they're at the church now [; the first part of the wedding takes place today, the second part tomorrow].

CARAMEL: We will go to the church, and protest.

ZAPETER: (*in great terror*) No, no, don't do that, for mercy's sake; I shall lose my head if you do.

CARAMEL: But what am I to do? You can't expect that I am going to submit quietly to such an insult. I can bear a good deal, but I can't stand that.

FLOSS *and* JACQUIER: We can't stand that, you know.

ZAPETER: Stop! An idea occurs to me. Work upon her emotions; trade on her impulses; make capital out of her eccentricities. The Princess has no memory; and acts always on the spur of the moment. Just now she can talk and think of nothing but the brigand Barberini. Her romantic mind is fascinated by the account she has heard of his personal beauty and his picturesque exploits. Disguise yourself as the brigand, catch her alone after the ceremony, declare yourself, she will forget all about her recent marriage, she will propose to join you, yield an unwilling assent — off you go with her.

CARAMEL: But where?

ZAPETER: To the Rocky Pass. Send your friends and relations on ahead disguised as the brigand's band; keep up the illusion for a day or two; then, when she is thoroughly tired of robber life, undeceive her, have a clergyman in readiness, and marry her straight off. (*aside*) I ought to be ashamed of myself.

QUARTET. —

PRINCE CARAMEL, FLOSS, JACQUIER *and* ZAPETER

CARAMEL: My hand upon it — 'tis agreed!
             I'll do the deed!

FLOSS *and* JACQUIER: He'll do the deed!

CARAMEL: In masquerade as brigand chief,
             I'll play the thief!

FLOSS *and* JACQUIER: He'll play the thief!

ZAPETER: Then come with me, and do not doubt;
             I'll rig you out!

THE OTHERS: He'll rig us out!

ZAPETER: Look fierce, and stamp to make a show;
             And stamp just so — just so!

ENSEMBLE

        In this disguise
            From knowing eyes
        We shall be quite secure;
            A brigand dress
                This quaint Princess
        Successfully will lure!
        (*Exeunt omnes.*)
        (*Enter wedding procession with* KING, PRINCE DORO, PRINCESS TOTO *etc.* COURT *all dancing.*)

[CHORUS*

Yes, here we come back from the wedding,
    And all has gone smoothly today;
The populace tears have been shedding
    In a most satisfactory way.]
(*They dance off, leaving* TOTO *and* DORO.)

DORO: At last we are alone together! Alone for the first time in our lives!

TOTO: It's very pleasant. I wonder if I shall like you!

DORO: I think you'll like me; I'm very popular.

TOTO: Good-tempered?

DORO: Angelic.

TOTO: Because I think I ought to have a good-tempered husband. I think I am the sort of girl who would irritate a touchy man. You see my temper is uncertain; and I'm impetuous, and impulsive, and my memory is very bad.

DORO: Very bad?

TOTO: Very bad indeed. Do you know — but you'll be angry if I tell you.

DORO: Not a bit.

TOTO: Well, then, do you know that on my way back from church I've been twice on the point of asking you if you were going to make a long stay with us?

DORO: No?

TOTO: It's a fact — and just now I was all but enquiring of Jelly whether you were married or single. I quite forgot we'd just been married; that's bad, isn't it?

DORO: Yes, I should try and recollect that, if I were you. It might give rise to unpleasantness if you forget it often. What are you doing?

TOTO: (*who is tying a knot in her pocket-handkerchief*) That is to remind me that I'm a married lady; as long as that's there I shall never forget it.

DORO: But in the course of time the pocket-handkerchief will go to the wash, and what will you do then?

TOTO: What a clever man you are! Of course it will, I never thought of that. Then, bless me! (*showing another knot*) I shall forget this too — and this is ten times more important than the other.

DORO: And what may that knot be for?

TOTO: I shan't tell you — it's a secret.

DORO: But there must be no secrets between us; we are man and wife now, and you must tell me everything.

DUET. — DORO *and* TOTO

Oh tell me now, by plighted vow,
    And tell me, tell me truly,
What cunning plot lies in that knot,
    That you have tied so newly?
Does it recall some public ball

---

*See appendix, p. 133.

          To which you want inviting?
          Or is it to encourage you
             Some letter to be writing?
          My jealous mind no rest will find
             My eyes will know no sleeping,
          Till I extract the mystic fact
             It holds within its keeping.
          Oh, let that mystic fact be known
             To me alone, to me alone.

TOTO: No, no; that secret shall be known
             To me alone, to me alone.
          Yes, I'll confide why this was tied —
             Forgive my thoughtless chatter.
          It is designed to call to mind
             A most important matter.
          I'll tell you now, although I vow
             We're not one till tomorrow,
          This knot was tied by me, your bride,
             To tell me that —
          To tell me that —
          To tell me that —
          To tell me that —
             Oh grief, oh rage, oh sorrow!
          My fatal memory knows no laws,
             My head is filled with cotton,
          I cannot tell you, dear, because,
             Alas, I've quite forgotten;
          That secret never can be known,
             Not even unto me alone.

DORO: (*angrily*) Until that fact to me is known
             I'll live alone — I'll live alone. (*Exit furiously.*)

TOTO: Poor fellow, I'm sorry he's so angry, but what can I do? I've entirely for-
    gotten what it refers to. Next time I want to remember something, I shall tie
    two knots — one to remind me that I want to remember something, and the
    other to remind me what it is I want to remember.

          (*Re-enter JELLY in great excitement.*)

JELLY: Oh! Your Highness, such news. As I was looking through the great iron
    gates of the palace just now, what should I see but three great fierce-looking
    men in sugar-loaf hats trimmed with ribbons, great mysterious-looking cloaks
    on their shoulders, and guns and daggers and pistols stuck all over them.

TOTO: (*delighted*) They must be brigands — how delightful! And what did you do?

JELLY: Do! I saw at a glance that all was lost, so I ran back to the palace for the
    key, unlocked the gates, and threw myself into their arms, exclaiming 'Resist-
    ance is useless: I am your prisoner, carry me off to your mountain home.'

TOTO: Noble-hearted girl! And what did they do?

JELLY: Why, they said I was a bold-faced thing, and ought to be ashamed of
    myself. The tall one gave me a tract.

TOTO: Eccentric creatures! Did you hear their names?

JELLY: Let me see, the tall one was called Barbar — Barber —

TOTO: (*excited*) Not Rini? Don't say it was Rini.

JELLY: Rini it was Barberini.

TOTO: It is their blood-stained and desperate chief.

JELLY: He was working a pair of slippers. He said they were for you.

TOTO: For me? Send him here at once, don't lose a moment. (*Exit* JELLY.) At last I shall see the romantic monster who is the dread of the whole country. What can he want with me? — Perhaps to carry me off — How dreadful but how picturesque!

> (*Enter* PRINCE CARAMEL *disguised as a brigand. He is followed by* JELLY, *and looks very mean and pitiful.*)

CARAMEL: My heart is in my mouth, but I have committed myself to it, and must go on with it. I have sent Floss and Jacquier to tell my court to disguise themselves as brigands, and await me in the Rocky Pass.

TOTO: (*coming forward*) Are you really Barberini?

CARAMEL: I am really Barberini. Ain't you frightened?

TOTO: Not a bit.

CARAMEL: But I look terrible, don't I?

TOTO: Not so terrible as I expected. I thought there would be more of this sort of thing about you (*striding fiercely about*).

CARAMEL: Oh, I'm like that sometimes. (*Strides about stage.*)

TOTO: That's more like it. Go on — oh, it's lovely. Isn't it, Jelly?

JELLY: It's beautiful — so noble, so picturesque [and oh, so beautiful].

CARAMEL: (*who has been stamping all this time*) Do you wish me to keep this up? It's rather fatiguing.

TOTO: No, not now that I see you can do it, if you like. Come and sit down, and tell me all about yourself.

CARAMEL: With pleasure. [(*They sit.* JELLY *takes up carbine and looks into it.*)] Don't touch that, my dear; never play with firearms, an accident so soon happens. Put it down, there's a good girl.

TOTO: Do what the gentleman tells you, Jelly. And so you are really the ferocious monster I've heard so much about? You don't look so very dreadful either.

CARAMEL: Oh, that's my nasty cunning; it disarms people and puts them off their guard. [(JELLY *has taken up carbine.*)] Now do leave that gun alone.

TOTO: And do you really hide behind trees, and pot at travellers as they ride by, and take them prisoners, and make them write for ransom, and send them home a little bit at a time if the ransom don't come?

CARAMEL: All this we do, and much more. We are devils of fellows!

TOTO: And then at night do you sit round your fires in a cavern, and count your disgraceful gains? And you sing choruses, and have bands of bayadères to dance before you?

CARAMEL: Yes, and we play for tremendous stakes too! We think nothing of threepenny points we devils don't! [(*To* JELLY, *who has taken up the gun again.*)] Now, once for all, if that girl don't put down that firearm, I shall go!

TOTO: Jelly, you're making the gentleman nervous. Do be quiet! And where are
    you going now?

CARAMEL: I am on my way to join my band in my home. We have a little dance
    tonight. All the respectable brigands for miles around will be there.

TOTO: And you'll dance in the moonlight, I dare say?

CARAMEL: Yes, the wild quadrille, the maddening Sir Roger de Coverley. Bless
    you, we devils don't care what we dance!

TOTO: (*suddenly*) I'll go with you!

JELLY: But your Highness —

TOTO: I'll go with him, and so will you! Now don't stop to argue the point. When
    my mind's made up, all the talk in the world won't change it.

JELLY: But think for one moment —

TOTO: I've no occasion to think! I'm my own mistress, and I can do what I like.
    That's the beauty of being single! We'll come for a week just to see how we
    like it. You have some elderly ladies there to make it respectable?

CARAMEL: Lots of elderly ladies! Bless you, we devils don't care how elderly they
    are!

TOTO: Then that decides me. I'll come. The life will suit me exactly. The dress is
    picturesque, the occupation is healthy, I've plenty of pluck, and absolutely
    nothing to detain me here. What do you say?

CARAMEL: My hand on it. (*aside*) She's mine. (*Whistles — the stage is filled with*
    BRIGANDS.)

      FINALE. —

      TOTO, JELLY, CARAMEL, JACQUIER *and* CHORUS

TOTO: A hat and a bright little feather,
          A gun on my shoulder — so;
      A dagger in scabbard of leather,
          And a pistol for a foe.
      Like a daring mountain ranger
          From rock to rock I'll bound;
      In the foremost ranks of danger
          Your Toto will be found.

[TRIO: Like a daring mountain ranger *etc.*

TOTO: (*suddenly*) Who goes there?

CARAMEL: ⎫
JELLY: ⎬ (*alarmed*) Who goes where?

TOTO: (*pointing*) Why, there.

      A man on a pony a-straddle,
          Hurrying home to his bed.
      Bang — and he drops from his saddle,
          Dead as the lead in his bed.
      (*aside*)   Who shall it be?
                           Let me see (*considering*).

      (*aside — suddenly*)

He's a bagman from Emmanuel
On an expedition annual,
Or he represents the names
Of Howell and of James;
   With jewels o'erladen
   For highly bred maiden
His wallet and things are bursting with rings.
   A diamond locket
   In each waistcoat pocket,
His coat-tails distended with emeralds rare,
And rubies and diamonds everywhere.
   This kind of prey
   Will come my way
   Three times a day,
   Three times a day.]

ALL: Then away to the mountain brow,
   With rifle and six-shooter;
The life of lives, I vow,
   Is the life of a freebooter.
(*As they are going the act drop falls.*)

ACT II

A picturesque mountain pass. JACQUIER, FLOSS *and other members of*
CARAMEL's *court are discovered disguised as brigands; they are engaged, when the
curtain rises, in waiting on a very ragged old beggar, whom they have taken prisoner.
They are supplying him with wine and other good things, and* JELLY *is superin-
tending his comforts. A party of female brigands dance before the old man at
intervals, and all are vying with each other in ministering to him.*

CHORUS

Cheer up, old man — pluck up a heart;
Cheer up, old man — soon you'll depart;
Cheer up, old man — give us a smile;
Cheer up, old man — 'tis but for a while.

SOLO. – JELLY

If he's feeling weak or fainty,
Run and fetch a tonic dainty;
If from want of food he drops,
Feed him up with mutton chops.

---

bagman: a commercial traveller ('somewhat depreciatory', *OED*).
Emmanuel: perhaps a reference to an Evangelical branch of the Anglican Church.
Howell and James: apparently a well-known jeweller's.

ALL: With mutton chops.
[JACQUIER: Here's Chateau-Margaux; pray mention
              If Lafitte you would prefer.
        None can pay too much attention
              To a poor old prisoner.]
        (*Dance.*)

CHORUS

        Poor old man,
Poor unhappy party,
      If you can,
Make a dinner hearty.
      Come, cheer up,
You shall go tomorrow;
      In this cup
Try to drown your sorrow.
Cheer up, old man, pluck up a heart, etc.
(*At the end of chorus* PRISONER *falls into a drunken sleep.*)
[FEMALE BRIGANDS *fan him.*]

JACQUIER: Poor old gentleman, he seems quite comfortable now.

FLOSS: Yes, he has forgotten all his troubles for the moment. How peacefully he slumbers!

[JACQUIER: It's an awful thing, Floss, to reflect how one act of deception leads to another, and how often that which begins in harmless folly ends in downright crime. We began by pretending to be brigands in order to enable our dear Prince to recover possession of his promised bride. Well, there's no harm in that. But being brigands we've got to act like brigands, and that's where the harm comes in. The Princess Toto has unfortunately taken a liking to the life, and insists on our committing all sorts of atrocities from which our tastes revolt.

FLOSS: I wish it were all over. I'm a respectable man and I've a wife and family, and I want to go home.

JACQUIER: Well, as soon as the Princess consents to marry Caramel, he will explain the deception we have practised on her, and then we shall all go home. And the sooner the better, for I've had three days of this, and I'm heartily sick of it. But hush — here comes her waiting-maid; we must keep up appearances before her.

        (*Enter* JELLY.)

JELLY: Good morning, Jacquier.

JACQUIER: Good morning, Jelly. Well, you've had three days among the brigands. How d'you like the life?

JELLY: Oh, it's lovely. Nothing to do all day but to sing and dance, and eat and sleep, and do your hair, and keep company. It shows what a hard time we poor servants have when I tell you that I've been six years in service, and this is the only place I ever had that exactly suits me.

FLOSS: I'm glad you like it, Jelly. We're a noble set of fellows, ain't we?

JELLY: Well, n — no, I don't agree with you there, I'm rather disappointed in you. You don't do the dashing things I expected of you.

JACQUIER: (*hurt*) Dashing things, Jelly?

JELLY: Yes. Attacking travelling carriages, shooting gendarmes, and all that sort of thing. (*Sees* PRISONER.) Who's that?

JACQUIER: (*with some pride*) That, Jelly, is a prisoner. The last one. He came in last night.

JELLY: Why, he's tipsy!

JACQUIER: No, he's not, he's drunk.

JELLY: What has made him drunk?

JACQUIER: I can't imagine, unless it's the champagne.

JELLY: Champagne?

JACQUIER: Yes, perhaps he's not used to champagne.

JELLY: I should think not. Why, he's a beggar.]

*FLOSS: (*pityingly*) Poor old boy!

JELLY: What strange brigands you are! You take a penniless little boy, or a ragged old woman, and you feed them up and treat them so kindly that you've the greatest difficulty in inducing them to return to their friends; and when they do return, they give such a glowing account of your kindness, that the whole village comes in instalments to give themselves up to you. How many have you got now?

FLOSS: We've thirty-seven.

JELLY: And instead of cutting them up, and sending them home in little bits, they feed on the fat of the land, while you wait on them, and hope they are pretty comfortable.

(*During the last few lines* CARAMEL *has entered.*)

CARAMEL: Well, you know, Jelly, prisoners are fellow-creatures after all, and they have their feelings like you and me. If we take them we are bound to look after them; you know the rites of hospitality must be respected.

JELLY: (*sarcastically*) Do you expect to get much ransom out of him?

CARAMEL: That gentleman's mother is going to send five hundred thousand francs for him this very afternoon. (PRISONER *wakes.*) He wakes. (*All interested.*) Have you had a nice dinner, my good old friend?

PRISONER: Pretty good; the mutton was rather tough.

CARAMEL: Tough, was it? (*to* FLOSS) Now that's your fault. (*to* PRISONER) You see we've had such a rush of prisoners today, that our larder was exhausted; but it shall not occur again. Did you sleep pretty comfortably last night?

PRISONER: Pretty well. I should like another blanket; it gets chilly towards morning.

CARAMEL: You are quite right, it does get chilly towards morning; I feel it myself when I'm standing sentry over you to keep the wild beasts away. Jelly, see that the gentleman has another blanket. (*to* PRISONER) Go with Jelly, there's a good man.

---

*Metzler allocates this to Jacquier.

JELLY: Five hundred thousand francs! His mother must be very fond of him. If he were my son, I'd give five hundred thousand francs to get rid of him.

(*Exit* JELLY* *with* PRISONER.)

CARAMEL: Poor fellow! It goes to my heart to detain him; but when you're a desperado, you must act like a desperado. If I were to obey the natural impulses of my heart, Toto would detect the imposture in a moment.

(*Enter* SAGO.)†

SAGO: Prince Caramel.

CARAMEL: Hush! Barberini! The blood-thirsty Barberini if you please.

SAGO: I beg your pardon: Barberini, I've bad news for you.

CARAMEL: Bad news! Are the police upon us?

SAGO: No, but two more peasants have come to yield themselves prisoners.

CARAMEL: Two more? How tiresome. We shall be eaten out of house and home. Where are they?

(SAGO‡ *beckons; enter two ragged and dirty* PRISONERS *led by a* BRIGAND.)

CARAMEL: (*aside*) Humph! – Not much to be got out of them. (*aloud*) Well, gentlemen, what can we do for you?

SECOND PRISONER: We've come to surrender.

CARAMEL: But nobody asked you to surrender.

SECOND PRISONER: No, but we feel resistance would be useless; we are your prisoners, and we are very hungry.

PRISONERS: Very hungry.

CARAMEL: It's extremely tiresome, but there's no help for it. If you are a desperado, you must behave like a desperado. I dine in half an hour, and they must dine with me. (*to* FLOSS) Take them away and give them a nice suit of clothes – I won't have them at my table in those rags – and here's an order for blankets, counterpanes, and feather beds. Do you prefer a feather bed, or a mattress?

PRISONERS: Feather beds is what we've been mostly used to.

CARAMEL: Yes; so I should think. Perhaps you'd like a warm bath, gentlemen, before dinner?

PRISONERS: No, we don't seem to care much about a warm bath.

CARAMEL: But, indeed, I think you'd better. You've no idea how refreshing a warm bath is now and then. [(*to* JACQUIER) Tell Jelly to see that they have a warm bath. Or stop – Floss had better see about that.]

§SECOND PRISONER: But I don't want a warm bath.

CARAMEL: (*ferociously*) Ha! Rebellion! The Brigand Barberini has spoken! Away with them, they *shall* be washed!

(*Exeunt* [SAGO *and*] PRISONERS, *followed by* FLOSS.)

[FLOSS: (*yawning*) Oh dear, oh dear, I'm getting very tired of this.]

JACQUIER: Is there no sign of the Princess relenting?

---

* Metzler has: '*and* FLOSS'.
† Metzler has: '*Re-enter* FLOSS' and allocates Sago's speeches to Floss.
‡ Metzler has 'FLOSS'.
§ Metzler has: 'PRISONERS'.

CARAMEL: My dear friends, your patience and devotion are about to be crowned with success. Congratulate me — I have at length persuaded her to consent to an immediate marriage. In half an hour we shall be made one [. The friar I brought with me has orders to prepare at once for the wedding,] and tomorrow I shall break the truth to her that we are gentlemen of character, wealth, and position, that instead of a brigand's wife she is the bride of one of the wealthiest potentates in the world.

ALL: Hurrah!

CARAMEL: So go, and make your preparations for an early departure; at six o'clock tomorrow we start.

     (*Exeunt* BRIGANDS.)*

CARAMEL: At last, at last! Oh Toto, what crimes I have committed for you! What risks I have run for you! (*Enter* TOTO.) My darling, you look depressed, you have not repented your promise?

TOTO: No, but it's a terrible step to take; I've often thought over it, and wondered why a girl can't be happy without deserting the people who, for the last twenty years of her life, have proved themselves to be her very best friends, [and casting her lot with that of the man of whose real character in nine cases out of ten she knows nothing whatsoever. Yes,] I often think of it. I once dreamed I *was* married.

CARAMEL: Nonsense!

TOTO: Yes, to a beautiful young Prince named Doro.

CARAMEL: (*hurriedly*) Oh! It was only a dream.

TOTO: (*sighing*) Yes, I know it was only a dream. He was a great deal too handsome to be true. One's only married to really handsome men in dreams.

CARAMEL: (*hurt*) That's rather a reckless thing to say, Toto.

TOTO: It's quite true.

CARAMEL: It may be true, but it's not pretty to say so.

[TOTO: We went off to church, and there was papa, looking very correct, and all the court looking very correct, and there was Jelly, and all of them looking very correct. And we were regularly married by a very correct clergyman and an extremely correct clerk, and a very correct pew-opener, and a highly correct beadle kept off a most correct crowd of spectators. And then I came back, and I sang and danced, and then — I don't remember anything more. Ah, it was very nice, I've often tried to dream that dream again.

CARAMEL: Yes, but you mustn't try to dream of him now, Toto.

TOTO: Why not? He's in a kind of way my husband. I married him in my sleep, you know.

CARAMEL: But you're going to marry me when you're awake, you know.

TOTO: Yes, you'll be my husband while I'm awake, and he'll be my husband when I'm asleep. Surely that's reasonable.

CARAMEL: But marriages in one's sleep don't count for anything.

TOTO: Don't they? Then there can be no harm in trying to make them.]

---

*See appendix, p. 133.

SONG. – TOTO

I have two worlds – I live two lives –
    One here, and one elsewhere;
In both of them men marry wives,
    And love them here and there.
This world that rolls about the sun
    With sin and sorrow teems;
The other, and the fairer one,
    Is called the world of dreams.

In that sweet land you rule the roast,
    Whatever rank you bear,
For, come what may, you are the most
    Important person there.
Whatever you may wish come true,
    You always win your stake,
And, should misfortune threaten you,
    You've only got to wake.

Oh, if we, who are wide awake,
    And very shrewd and deep,
Could wipe out every sad mistake
    By falling fast asleep;
If from our folly we were freed
    Whene'er a nap we take,
How very, very few indeed
    Would ever keep awake!

(*Enter* [SAGO,] BRIGANDS, BRIDESMAIDS *etc.* [*All the*
BRIGANDS *imitating trumpets,* 'Tan – ra – ra – ra, Tan –ra –ra –
ra'.])

*SAGO: Everything is prepared for the wedding; the clergyman is ready, and the
bridesmaids are ready, and we are only awaiting your pleasure.

COUPLETS

TOTO: At last I shall marry my own,
             For I love Barberini alone;
             It cannot too widely be known
             That at last I shall marry my own.
             Let everybody be gay,
             For I'm to be married today.

CARAMEL: The brigand has chosen a bride,
             In a minute the knot will be tied;
             To be with a brigand allied,

---

*Metzler allocates this speech to Jelly.

Is a very fine thing for a bride.
Let everybody be gay,
For I'm to be married today.

JELLY: I wish that my turn it would come,
But all of these brigands are dumb,
I'd pay down a pretty large sum
If it only would make my turn come.
Let everybody be gay,
For they're to be married today.

[FLOSS: I wish that this bubble would bust.
I'm sick of it, own it I must.
When once they are married, I trust
This jolly old bubble will bust.
Let everybody be gay
For they're to be married today.]
(*General dance and exeunt.*)
(*Enter* DORO.)

DORO: This must be the spot which was indicated to me as the halting-place of the brigand Barberini; but I see no sign of his presence. So, Prince Doro, your fortunes are about to take a decided turn for the worse; you are about to enlist yourself in the ranks of one of the most unscrupulous ruffians of modern times. You're a nice young man, Prince Doro, to declare war against your fellow-man, and in such disreputable society. Declare war against my fellow-man? Nothing of the kind, my fellow-man has declared war against me. Who induced me to fall in love with Toto? My fellow-man. Who married me to her? My fellow-man. And who bolted with her ten minutes after marriage? My fellow-man. My fellow-man has thrown down the glove, and in joining Barberini's band I only take up the challenge. Will he have me? Yes, I'm young and strong, and brave, and I don't care twopence for my life – in fact I want to die, and if a man who wants to die won't make a good brigand, who will? Oh! I dare say it's very shocking, but I'm tired of life, and desperate; besides, there are plenty of brigands in broadcloth who hold up their heads in society, and I don't see that a scoundrel's any the worse for being picturesque.

SONG. – DORO

There are brigands in every station,
    And robbers in every rank;
Some plunder the wealth of a nation,
    Some modestly pillage a bank;
Some brigands are bubble directors,
    And others may wear a fez hat;
They're out of the reach of inspectors,
    But they're none the less brigands for that.

Oh, did you know all that I know,
    Your eyes would start out of their sockets;

> You'd better take care of your pockets
> If you only knew half that I know.
>
> There are brigands well known as stock-jobbers,
>   Who safely may follow this bent,
> While other respectable robbers
>   Lend money at eighty per cent;
> Then think of the swindlers and plotters,
>   The forgers and robbers of banks,
> The murderers, thieves, and garotters
>   Now walking about in your ranks.
>
> Oh, did you know, etc. (*Exit.*)*
> (*Re-enter* CARAMEL *and* TOTO.)

TOTO: Married at last.

CARAMEL: Yes, securely married at last.

TOTO: Dear husband!

CARAMEL: Dear wife!

TOTO: To think that my dream is realized, and that I'm a real live brigand queen at last. I've longed all my life to be a brigand queen.

CARAMEL: Yes, it's a delightful life — so comfortable.

TOTO: So unconventional.

CARAMEL: So snug.

TOTO: So romantic.

CARAMEL: So respectable.

TOTO: So — so honest.

CARAMEL: Yes, 'so-so' honest.

TOTO: Then there's such good feeling between you all. You all hang together so well; that's the best of it.

CARAMEL: Yes, we *shall* all hang together, and that's the worst of it.

TOTO: The life suits me down to the ground. I shall live and die a brigand queen.

CARAMEL: Quite so. But what a joke it would be if — if, I say — it turned out that we were not real brigands, but only respectable people who were playing at brigands! I say, if that were to take place, what a joke! Oh Lord, what a joke it would be!

TOTO: (*severely*) You have a very grim idea of a joke.

CARAMEL: Grim?

TOTO: Yes, grim, not to say ghastly.

CARAMEL: Why, what would you do?

TOTO: Do? What would I do if I thought you had deceived me? Let me think; — in the first place I would shoot you.

CARAMEL: Shoot me?

TOTO: Dead.

CARAMEL: You're joking.

TOTO: Am I? Try.

---

*Metzler adds: '*Shout outside.*'

CARAMEL: But I only said 'if'.

TOTO: I know you did; but 'if' is quite enough. I am much obliged to you for the suggestion. It will be extremely useful to me in my profession.

CARAMEL: How, useful?

TOTO: Why, thus. When I want to nerve myself to a deed of unusual daring, when I want to screw myself up to a pitch of remorseless fury, when I want to throw off the woman and assume the tigress, I shall only have to imagine for a moment that I have been made the victim of a practical joke. Do you understand?

CARAMEL: I think I understand.

TOTO: *Thoroughly?*

CARAMEL: Thoroughly. I was only joking.

TOTO: I am glad of it. (*Exit.*)

CARAMEL: Whew! Here's a pretty piece of business. Who'd have thought she had so much devil in her? And how is all this to end? I shall have to carry this sort of thing on to the end of my life; I'm committed to it. We shall get into nice hot water with the police; I know we shall. Gracious goodness! If we should be taken up; she's always urging me to stop mail-coaches, and secure wealthy travellers. We shall catch a Tartar some day, as sure as a gun.

    (*Re-enter* DORO.)

CARAMEL: (*seeing him*) We are lost; the police are upon us.

DORO: Are you the ferocious Barberini?

CARAMEL: (*in terror*) I am, but I have repented of all my crimes, and in a fit of remorse I was just going to deliver myself up to justice as you came in.

DORO: I am sorry for that, for I came for the purpose of joining your band.

CARAMEL: Then you're not the police?

DORO: Not at all.

CARAMEL: (*fiercely*) And yet you have dared, audacious mortal, to beard the ferocious Barberini in his den? Are ye not aware that none but the police are ever admitted into this lair? Are ye not terrified at the probable consequences of your presumption?

DORO: Not a bit. You will no doubt be delighted to admit so promising a recruit to your band. I'm a dare-devil fellow, and whenever you have an expedition of unusual danger on hand, I only ask that you will place me at its head.

CARAMEL: You seem to have a pretty good opinion of yourself, you do.

DORO: No, I'm a reckless, desperate man. This is not courage, it is despair. I want to die.

CARAMEL: If I can assist you in any way — (*Offers him pistol.*)

DORO: You can. Appoint me your lieutenant.

CARAMEL: I think you're a very pushing young man.

DORO: Then you refuse to admit me into your ranks?

CARAMEL: Yes, we've no opening for you at present. If any vacancy should occur, leave your address, and we'll let you know.

DORO: Very good. Then, in the meantime, I suppose I must consider myself your prisoner. Take me; I surrender.

CARAMEL: Now look here! We don't want any more prisoners. We've more than we can manage already. Go away. We've nothing for you. You are a very pushing young man.

(*Re-enter* TOTO.)

TOTO: Stop; what is all this about?

DORO: (*aside*) Why, if I'm neither mad, nor asleep, this is my Toto.

CARAMEL: This, Toto, is a forward young man, who wants to join our band. I've told him we have no vacancy, and he had better join his friends.

TOTO: You told him that?

CARAMEL: Yes.

TOTO: You told that fine young man you didn't want him?

CARAMEL: That is what I told him.

TOTO: Then you're a donkey. Come here, young man.

DORO: She don't recognize me. She has forgotten her husband.

TOTO: I like your appearance. It pleases me. You're smart and active — I like your face; I fancy I have seen it before.

DORO: (*aside*) She fancies she has seen it before! And this is the wife to whom I was married only three days since.

TOTO: You seem to have all the qualities that should make an excellent brigand; I am Queen of the band, and I hereby admit you a member of it.

CARAMEL: But, Toto, my darling, reflect —

TOTO: Silence! (*to* DORO) Behave well, show yourself worthy of promotion, and you shall have it! (*aside*) I cannot think where I have seen that young man's face before.

TRIO. — TOTO, DORO *and* CARAMEL

TOTO: So take my hand, we are agreed;
             A brigand you will be indeed;
             It is a life you will adore.
(*aside*)   I'm sure I've seen his face before.

DORO: Three days ago the knot was tied
             Which constituted her my bride;
             Yet when we meet she isn't sure,
             But 'thinks she's seen my face before'.

CARAMEL: This conduct comes within the range
             Of that which is considered strange;
             She likes him well, and, what is more,
             She 'thinks she's seen his face before'.

ENSEMBLE

(DORO *and* CARAMEL *sing these lines mutatis mutandis.*)

TOTO: Oh matter perplexing,
             Annoying, and vexing,
             All over the world I'll explore —

> I'll travel, and travel,
> This knot to unravel,
> And learn where I've met him before.
> [No bothering worry,
> No family flurry
> Turns out such a terrible bore,
> As when you see faces
> Forgetting the places
> In which you have met before.]
>   (*Exit* CARAMEL.)

TOTO: I'll tell you what it is, my husband must be mad to reject such a promising recruit. [Have a cigarette?] You're just the sort of man we want up here, for between ourselves, our brigands are not up to much. They're a very weedy lot; I have always great difficulty in spurring them up to anything like a deed of daring. Little girls sent out with halfpence to fetch milk; old ladies with their omnibus fares in their gloves; cans hanging on area railings, and so on. Such deeds as these — there's no disguising it — are not worthy of Barberini's hand. (*aside*) I can't think where I have seen his face before.

DORO: Oh! Toto, Toto, have you forgotten me so completely? Learn that I who stand before you am no other than the cheated and discarded Doro.

TOTO: Doro? I know that name.

DORO: Know that name? Perhaps you do. It is that of your husband.

TOTO: (*puzzled*) My husband? No, his name is Barber — Stay, I know, you're my dream husband! Of course you are; how stupid of me, to be sure! Then let me see — I must be asleep, and this is a dream.

DORO: A dream?

TOTO: Yes, I know it's a dream by you. Look here, I have two husbands.

DORO: (*aghast*) What?

TOTO: Two husbands. One when I'm awake — he's real; and one when I'm dreaming — he's sham. You're the sham one, you're an illusion. (*feeling his arm*) Yes, you seem real, but you're not. [You'll vanish presently; by the by, you can tell me something I want to know: what becomes of you when I wake? I hope you don't go and marry anybody else? I wish you were the real one and Barberini the sham one. I love you better than Barberini, though he's nice too.]

DORO: If you've taken leave of your senses, allow me to bring them back to you. I am your real husband; real live flesh and blood. You're as wide awake as ever you were in your life, and that's not saying much.

TOTO: Then do you mean to say that — that I did *not* dream that we were married [by a correct clergyman, in a correct church, with a respectable beadle, and an Orthodox pew-opener, and all that]?

DORO: Most certainly not! We were actually married, and immediately afterwards you vanished.

TOTO: (*crying*) Oh dear, oh dear, I am so sorry! I — I quite forgot all about it. I — I remember it now. Oh dear, oh dear, I don't know what I shall do. You'll ne — ne — never f — f — f — forgive me, I know you won't. I've been a very naughty, ungrateful, forgetful girl, and I ought to be ashamed of myself. Oh, forgive me; do, do forgive me — I won't go and marry anyone any more.

DORO: Forgive you! When you eloped with another man within ten minutes of your marriage?

TOTO: It was p — p — p — platonic. It was wrong of me, I know; but I acted on the spur of the moment.

DORO: It is impossible to accept that excuse.

TOTO: But if I forgot, what was I to do? I suppose you forget sometimes. You're not absolutely infallible, I suppose.

DORO: It is useless.

TOTO: Now, my own, own dearly-loved — darling, darling — I forget your name for the moment.

DORO: Doro!

TOTO: Exactly, Doro! Now my darling Doro, don't, oh, don't blight my young life; don't ruin my hope of happiness; don't surround my whole existence in gloom for a mere act of childish forgetfulness, for I love you dear — dear — dear —

DORO: Doro.*

TOTO: I was going to say 'Doro', only you take one up so. Indeed, indeed, I love you very fondly; and if you'll only forgive me, I'll be such a good little wife to you, and never cause you any sorrow any more (*sobbing*). Oh dear, oh dear, what shall I do?

DORO: Poor little girl, she does seem very fond of me. Well, after all, it was only an act of forgetfulness. She forgot she was married. A good many highly respectable people make the same mistake. Besides, when a woman begins to cry, what is a man to do? (*aloud*) There, Toto, I forgive you this once; but don't, oh, don't you ever, ever do such a thing again as long as you live.

TOTO: My darling husband!

DUET. — TOTO *and* DORO

DORO: My own, own love, my gentle wife,
               Devoted partner of my life,
               How sad a future would it be,
               If I were passed away from thee!

TOTO: My own, own love, my husband dear,
               In all I say I am sincere;
               While in my bosom beats a heart
               We twain will never, never part.

DORO: Oh gentle wife,
TOTO: Oh husband dear,
DORO: My love, my life,
TOTO: I am sincere.

---

*Metzler adds: 'Take a card. (*Gives card.*)'

DORO:	Oh maid divine,
TOTO:	Oh loving heart,
DORO:	Oh life of mine,
TOTO:	We'll never part.

(*Exeunt together.*)

(*As they go off the* KING *enters with* ZAPETER *and* JAMILEK *from the bridge. They are disguised as Red Indians, and carry toma- hawks, etc.* [*They enter with a quaint hopping step, singing at the same time.*])

TRIO. – KING, ZAPETER *and* JAMILEK

With skip and hop,
   With jerky jump,
We come down plop,
   And come down plump;
We are installed
   In Indian rig,
Our name is called
   Hop – pe – de – gig.

   Hoppedegig, Hoppedegig,
   Hoppedegig are we,
   Hoppedegig, Hoppedegig,
   From an isle beyond the sea,
   Hoppedegig, Hoppedegig,
   You think our colour's paint.
   Hoppedegig, Hoppedegig,
   I do not say it ain't.

With feathers, paint, and patches
   And a tom, tom, tom,
That with our colour matches
   With a tom, tom, tom,
We'll sing unmeaning snatches
   With a tom, tom, tom,
Till we are under hatches
   In a tom, tom, tom.
      With skip and hop, etc.

KING: (*who preserves a stately and dignified air, notwithstanding his disguise*) At last we are in the brigands' lair, and before many moments I shall have an opportunity of testing our scheme to take back my thoughtless daughter to my arms. Zapeter, it is to your diplomatic brain that this experiment is due. It was you, my trusty and well-beloved cousin, who suggested that we should take advantage of her taste for novelty, and disguise ourselves as Red Indians, in the hope that the peculiarity of our appearance and the quaintness of our attitudes might fascinate her volatile mind – Zapeter, I cannot thank you too affectionately for the suggestion.

JAMILEK: But should the lynx-eyed maiden see through our disguise, and detect
    the imposition that we have practised on her?

KING: Oh, heavens! The laugh would then be turned against us. If ever it should
    get abroad that I, King Portico, have stooped to disguise myself in this
    mountebank's dress, to shave my head and paint my face, I should expire
    with confusion. If tidings of this unutterable degradation were to reach the
    ears of surrounding nations, I should never hold up my head again. (*suddenly*)
    Zapeter, it is to your shifty and tortuous brain that this device, this monstrous
    device is due. If it should fail, before heaven, your head shall pay the penalty.

ZAPETER: Fear nothing. The wary paleface has diligently studied the works of
    Fenimore Cooper, and they have made him downy. He is familiar with the
    methods of expression of his red brother and the wary paleface courts investi-
    gation; his tread is the tread of the wild cat, his eye is the eye of the hawk, his
    jump is the jump of the opossum [, and his nose is the nose of the Jew]. Why
    should he tremble? The Unmitigated Blackbird has spoken. Wagh!

KING: And you, Jamilek, do you feel yourself equal to sustaining the character
    you have assumed?

JAMILEK: (*speaking in Hiawathan metre*)
> Oh thou proud and mighty monarch;
> Monarch of a loyal people,
> Monarch of a thousand cities,
> Monarch of a spacious country
> Dotted with unnumbered villas,
> Villas standing in a garden,
> Villas of both brick and stucco,
> Villas with commodious stabling,
> Stabling for a pair of horses,
> Stabling with a man's room over,
> If you ask me if I'm equal
> To sustain the part of Red Man
> So as to defy detection?
> I would answer, I would tell you,
> If the being quite familiar
> With the metre and construction
> Of the poem 'Hiawatha'
> Is enough to qualify me,
> Apprehend no kind of danger!
> For I'd give to Paw-puk-ke-wis,
> Paw-puk-ke-wis the great boaster,
> Or the lovely Mi-ne-ha-ha,
> Six to four and beat 'em easy.

KING: My true and trusty Jamilek, as for myself, fortified with the assurance that
    in assuming my present garb I have made myself sufficiently ridiculous, I will
    not further stultify myself by affecting a method of expression as artificial as
    it is inconvenient. I have stooped to this, I will stoop no lower.
> (TOTO *is heard singing without loudly.* ZAPETER *listens with his
> ear close to the ground.*)

KING: What do you hear? (KING *and* JAMILEK *are eager for a reply.*)

ZAPETER: Softly, and the Red Man will interpret. His ears are long and his
patience proverbial (*listening while* TOTO *sings very loudly*). It is the sound
of a voice — as it articulates words, it is a human voice. (KING *and* JAMILEK
surprised at ZAPETER'*s keenness of ear.*) It is fresh and bell-like, and therefore it is a woman's voice — a young woman's voice — behold! (TOTO *runs
on singing.*) Said I not well? Wagh.

KING: It is our Toto.

(KING, ZAPETER *and* JAMILEK *strike attitudes.*)

TOTO: Why, bless my heart! Who are these? They're the funniest people I ever saw
in the whole course of my life.

KING: (*aside*) Funny? Have I lived to be considered funny? Oh! The humiliation of
it! And in this tom-fool's dress — and before my own daughter, too. (*to*
JAMILEK) Tell her who we are, for upon my soul I forget.

JAMILEK: (*to* TOTO)

> Blushing maiden of the paleface,
> If you ask me to what nation,
> To what aggregate of people,
> We've the honour of belonging,
> I will answer, I will tell you!
> This is little Wappewango,
> Which in language of the paleface
> Means the consequential vulture;
> This is Pooby-Jubbegabo,
> Or the Abernethy Biscuit,
> I am Hicky-hawky-pawky,
> The Unmitigated Blackbird.
> (*They all strike attitudes; the* KING *quickly recovering himself and
> becoming dignified.*)

KING: That I should have lived to hear myself described as an Abernethy Biscuit.
'Abernethy Biscuit'. Oh, it is hard — it is hard.

TOTO: And do you always paint your face?

KING: (*aside*) To have to admit it to my own child. (*aloud*) Yes, always. It — it —
it is a sign of distinction. (*Skips, then resumes dignity — aside*) A sign of distinction! Bah! It is the sign of a mountebank.

TOTO: And where are you going?

KING: To — to the island of Brandee-pawnee. There are our wigwams, and our
squaws.
[(*Sings from* 'Old King Cole'.) 'Every wigwam has a little squaw, and a very
fine squaw is she.' Wagh! (*Skips, then resumes his dignity — aside*) Oh,
Zapeter. You shall pay heavily for this.] *

Abernethy Biscuit: 'a kind of hard biscuit flavoured with caraway seeds' (*OED*).
*Metzler has:
  KING: Wagh!
  JAMILEK: Wagh!
  ZAPETER: Wagh!

TOTO: And how do you intend to get there?

KING: A vessel is awaiting us at the nearest port.

TOTO: And are you quite primitive, and unconventional, and all that?

KING: Primitive? Unconventional? Look here! (*They skip absurdly about the stage.*) Don't you call that unconventional? (*aside*) Oh, degradation!

TOTO: That sort of thing is just what I've been seeking for years in vain. I have been educated in a court where such innocent gambols would be punished with instant death. I'll go with you!

ALL: (*affecting surprise*) What?

TOTO: I'll go with you; I'm tired of being a brigand, and there's nothing to detain me here — at least, I don't think so. (*reflecting*) No, I don't recollect anything. No, nothing. Come along; I'm delighted at the idea. I shall wear feathers, and paint, and perhaps marry one of the tribe, and be a squaw. I've often wished I was married. I once dreamt I was married to a beautiful prince named — named — let me see — Doro. But that was only a dream. Come, if I'm to be a squaw, the sooner I'm a squaw, the better.

FINALE

TOTO:
    Away, away to the Indian isle,
      Where the poo-poo sings in the trees,
    Where nature wears an eternal smile,
      And the palm trees bend to the breeze.

ALL: Away, away, etc.

KING, ZAPETER, JAMILEK: (*aside*)
      Within our wile,
      In first-rate style
    Our Toto is entrapped
      We softly smile,
      Although our guile
    May get our knuckles rapped.

ALL: Away, away, etc.

(*Re-enter* CARAMEL, JACQUIER, FLOSS, JELLY, *and all the* BRIGANDS. *They see* TOTO *and others on bridge at back.*)

CARAMEL: (*recitativo*) Who goes there? I charge you stop!

KING: (*aside*) The brigands, hold me or I drop.

CARAMEL: What are you doing, Toto, what, oh! what?

TOTO: With these Red Indians I have cast my lot.

TOTO *and* INDIANS: Hoppedegig, hoppedegig,
    Hoppedegig are we,
    Hoppedegig, hoppedegig,
    From an isle beyond the sea.
    Hoppedegig, hoppedegig,
    You think our colour's paint,
    Hoppedegig, hoppedegig,
    I do not say it ain't.

[BRIGANDS: Oh joy — oh rapture,

Our Toto's capture
Will set us free.
Away misgiving
For we'll be living
Respectablee.]

CARAMEL: (*furious*) Among you brigands is there one

Who knows the way to load a gun?
I freely promise half-a-crown
To anyone who'll bring them down.

ALL THE BRIGANDS: Among us brigands is there one, etc.

*CARAMEL: (*in despair*) Not one, not one

Can load a gun;
Not one, not one,
Can load a gun.

JELLY: You take a ball and powder,

Which you ram to make it louder;
If your enemy you'd cripple,
Place a cap upon the nipple;
Take aim, and pull the trigger,
And he'll cut a pretty figure;
If you hit him in the head,
He will fall dead, dead.

ALL: Hurrah! Hurrah!

This one, this one
Can load a gun.

MALE BRIGANDS: Let us follow,

FEMALE BRIGANDS: Let us follow,

MALE BRIGANDS: Let us follow,

FEMALE BRIGANDS: Let us follow

ALL THE BRIGANDS: Follow, follow.

(*But they don't follow.*)

KING, TOTO, ZAPETER *and* JAMILEK: If you stir a step, upon my word you'll

rue it.

BRIGANDS: Follow, follow, etc.

(*But they don't follow.*)

CARAMEL: It's all very well to cry follow,

But why the dickens don't you do it?

ENSEMBLE

CARAMEL *and* JELLY: Oh rage! Oh fury! Oh despair!

I stamp my feet, I tear my hair;
But never fear
My little dear;

---

*Metzler allocates these lines to King, Zapeter, and Jamilek.

I'll bring her back again, I swear.
ALL THE OTHERS: With joy, with rapture, and with glee,
　　　　　We are as glad as we can be.
　　　　　　　All this will end,
　　　　　　　And we shall spend
　　　　　Our future lives respectablee.
　　　　　(*Dance of joy for* BRIGANDS. CARAMEL *and* JELLY *furious.*
　　　　　TOTO *and* RED INDIANS *triumphant.*)

ACT III

A tropical island. The court of KING PORTICO *are discovered dressed as Red
Indians.* [*During the opening chorus* ZAPETER *dances a war-dance of a grotesque
description.*]

CHORUS

Bang the merry tom-tom, sing the merry song,
　　Wear a merry Indian smile,
Pleasantly the merry moments fly along,
　　On the merry Indian isle.

SOLO. – FOLLETTE

　　　　Coriander seeds,
　　　　Glass and metal beads,
　　　　Pretty little bells,
　　　　Feathers, too, and shells.
These be merry playthings of the merry throng,
Bang the merry tom-tom, sing the merry song,
Pleasantly the merry moments fly along
　　　On the merry Indian isle.

ZAPETER: Whew! That's hot work; but what's worth doing at all is worth doing
　　well. When you're a Red Indian you must do as Red Indians do; and a Red
　　Indian tribe without a war-dance were a degrading spectacle indeed.
[CATHAY: I like this out-of-door life.] * What a contrast to the ceremony and for-
　　mality of our pompous court at home.
[DEVINE: Yes, fancy the King's state of mind if he caught us smoking cigarettes in
　　the palace. Now here we can smoke the pipe of peace under the royal nose, if
　　we like, because it's an Indian habit.]
FOLLETTE: For my part, I don't like living in the open air, and I should like to get
　　home at once. Brown paint don't become me.
ZAPETER: Local colour, my dear, nothing more.
FOLLETTE: Local colour is all very well, but a girl's complexion is her complexion.

---

*Metzler allocates this to Follette.

ZAPETER: (*dancing*) Not always.* [Brown suits you very well. You're just what a
    meerschaum should be after three days' smoking; you're colouring beautifully.
CATHAY: (*kissing her*) And you've a lovely mouthpiece.
FOLLETTE: I wish you wouldn't do that. I'm always telling you of it.
DEVINE: But, Zapeter, don't it occur to you that we are taking rather a round-
    about way to lure the Princess back to civilization?
ZAPETER: No doubt, my dear, but we must be diplomatic.]
FOLLETTE: But her father has got her away from the brigand! Why don't he
    reveal himself and put an end to it all?
[ZAPETER: Diplomacy, my dear. You don't understand these things.]
FOLLETTE: Instead of that, he makes us all disguise ourselves as Red Indians, and
    encamp on a desert rock ten miles from anywhere.
ZAPETER: All this is diplomacy. (*Dances down stage.*)
        (*Enter* KING PORTICO *as Red Indian. He sees* ZAPETER *dancing*
        ridiculously. He is much shocked.)
KING: Zapeter, Zapeter, what are you doing?
ZAPETER: Sire, I am practising the war-dance of the tribe.
KING: It cuts me to the heart to see you, a man of high position and education – a
    minister, a grave, earnest gentleman – compelled to resort to such buffoonery.
ZAPETER: Sire, so great is our love to you, so earnest our desire that you and
    yours may be more happy, that we care little what personal humiliation we
    may undergo. (*Dances.*)
KING: My faithful friend! It now remains to be answered how we shall break the
    news to the Princess, that we have deceived her. Oh, Zapeter, I know her way-
    ward temper well, and it will be necessary to proceed with the utmost caution.
    I dread the consequences of telling her that she must return with us to our
    court.
ZAPETER: But why return to your court at all?
KING: Eh?
ZAPETER: Why not live here for ever? You look a Red Indian! Why not be a Red
    Indian? As for your kingdom, great as would be the pain of quitting you for
    ever, I would even return, and rule in your place; such, sire, is the love I bear
    you.
KING: My faithful and self-denying Zapeter, it is wisely and kindly purposed – we
    will think of it! But, soft, she approaches.
        (*They all resume dance and chorus as* TOTO *enters*[, *dressed as an*
        Indian princess. ZAPETER *dances at her.*]. *At end of chorus all*
        exeunt except KING, TOTO, *and* ZAPETER. [ZAPETER *continues*
        to dance at her.])
KING: Ha! Hum! The brow of the ha – paleface young woman is clouded. Is any-
    thing wrong?
TOTO: Yes, I'm bitterly disappointed – and that's the truth. It has been the aim of
    my life to throw off the trammels of conventionality, and to revel in the
    society of barbaric man in all his primeval magnificence. I thought I had

---

*Metzler adds: 'my dear, not always'.

found it in the brigand's lair, but the brigand, imposing at a distance, turned out, on close inspection, to be a thing of petty fears, insignificant jealousies, and undeveloped intelligence. I thought I had found it amongst the Red Indians, but the Red Indians eat caviare, and shave with a Mappin's razor. His very tomahawk has the Birmingham stamp on it.

KING: And yet we are considered a very fair representative tribe.

TOTO: (*contemptuously*) A Red Indian with a double eye-glass.

KING: The fact is, that the hawk-eyed Red Man is getting on in years, and his eyesight isn't what it was. There was a time when he could see the wind, when he had — a — no difficulty in following the flight of a bullet, when he was known as — as — Zapeter, what was I known as before my eyesight went?

ZAPETER: You were known, sire, as 'Pish-tush-pooh-bah', or the Oxy-hydrogen Microscope.

KING: Exactly — a — that is what I was known as.

TOTO: Yes, I dare say you were all you say, but civilization has set its stamp upon you, and you interest me no more. True, you are called 'Chumpee Chookee', the 'Abernethy Biscuit', that sounds very well; but for anything primeval there is about you, your name might be Watkins, and you might keep a penny ice shop in the Borough Road. Why, your very dinners are civilized; boiled mutton and caper sauce. Why don't the Red Man go and hunt the wild buffalo like a Red Man?

KING: Because, to be quite plain with you, I do not think the Red Man would succeed in capturing that animal. If the Red Man depended for his meals on the wild buffaloes he might happen to secure, the Red Man would go supperless to his — what do you call it?

TOTO: Wigwam.

KING: Wigwam — thank you, that is the word I wanted.

TOTO: But it's very easy! You've only got to disguise yourself in a buffalo's skin, and when you see a herd approaching, go up to them on all fours, bellowing like a bull. Now, do go and catch a wild buffalo.

KING: Never, never; now understand me, Toto, I will not do it.

TOTO: This is rebellion. (*Retires up stage.*)

KING: Very likely. I can't help it, I will *not* catch wild buffalo.

ZAPETER: (*aside to* KING) Sire, I think if I were you I should humour her.

KING: Zapeter, I will not do it. I have stooped to so much since I came here. I have painted my face like a clown in a pantomime, I have danced ridiculous war-dances, I have dressed myself in unpleasant skins that tickle dreadfully, but go on all fours bellowing like a bull [— I will *not*; now understand me], I will *not* do it.

[TOTO: Well, I declare, I wish I'd never left the brigands. (*Comes over.*) I was very happy there, although I didn't know it. One never knows when one's well off. It's like the old story of the King of the Pigs.

Mappin: Mappin and Webb, cutlery manufacturers.
Borough Road: working-class district in South London.

KING: The King of the Pigs? The Red Man cannot recollect that he ever heard of
   that potentate.
TOTO: Then I'll tell you all about him.

SONG. – TOTO

The King of the Pigs was a good piggee,
But he was as lean as lean could be,
And he feared what his subjects all would say
In the Cattle Show week, on the opening day.
He tried all kinds of fattening fare
Till he gave it up in a blank despair,
And at last determined one fine day
To make his mark in a different way.

Said he, with a sigh: 'The world is right,
A very fat pig *is* a lovely sight,
And the judges properly give the prize
To the pig that can't see out of his eyes.
But the judges are men of liberal views,
And it's not unlikely they might choose
To forgive my want of adipose
If I came to the show in a Roman nose.'

This original notion pleased him much –
The King was a King, and behaved as such;
And he tried all night, and he tried all day
To bend his nose in the Roman way.
He tied it down with a piece of string,
And he hung great weights to his royal ring
Till his natural snout – the story goes –
Was more or less like a Roman nose.

It was high at the bridge, and the tip drooped down,
And it lent itself to a noble frown.
He could sneer also if he felt inclined,
For the nostrils both were well defined.
There was general joy when the news got wing,
For his subjects all adored their King,
And every pig walked on tip toes
When he found his King had a Roman nose.

But his sad ambition proved his ban.
He was sold at once to a peep-show man.
His foolish dream of glory fed.
He was shown to the mob at a penny a head:
'Walk up, walk up, here's the spotted child,
A knock-kneed giant, an Indian wild,

A dwarf but two-foot-six in his hose,
And a real live pig with a Roman nose.'

MORAL (*All rise.*)

Now let this tale impress on you,
For every word is strictly true
And cannot be too widely known,
That golden rule, 'Let well alone'.
When to astonish friends and foes,
You ill-advisedly propose
To gild pure gold, or paint the rose,
Remember the pig with a Roman nose.
(*Exeunt* TOTO *and Chorus.*)]

JAMILEK: (*who has been looking out at back*) Sire, a boat is approaching the shore, and there are five strangers on board. What in the world shall we do?

KING: A boat with five strangers? Great heavens! If they should happen to know me I should be a standing object of ridicule to the end of my days. We must conceal ourselves at once. Where can we lie hid?

JAMILEK: Sire, there is a thicket of prickly cactus within a few hundred yards. In that we might conceal ourselves till they depart.*

KING: Thanks, thanks, my trusty Jamilek. Your ingenious suggestions are always at hand in cases of emergency. Bless you, Jamilek! I do not altogether like lying down in prickly cactus, but there is no time to hesitate. To think that King Portico should have to stoop to such an expedient. Oh, Jamilek, if ever it should become known that I had stooped to conceal myself in a bed of prickly cactus, your head shall pay the penalty.
(*Exeunt.*)
(*Enter* DORO, CARAMEL, JACQUIER, FLOSS *and* JELLY, *rowing in an open boat at back.*)

BARCAROLLE

When you're afloat
In an open boat,
    With nobody there to tow,
You ply your oar
Till you reach the shore,
    And that is all we know.
When you're afloat in a sailing boat
Which is much too big to row,
        You spread your sail
        To an evening gale,
And that is all we know.
(DORO, CARAMEL *and* JELLY *disembark,* FLOSS *and* JACQUIER *row off.*)

---

*Metzler adds:
  TOTO: Prickly cactus! Oh, how horrid!

CARAMEL: At last, after a week's weary tossing in an open boat on a rough sea, we have arrived at our destination.

DORO: Yes, this is no doubt the island which was indicated to us as that to which the ship sailed that conveyed the beautiful Toto from her unhappy husband's arms.

CARAMEL: My kind friend.

DORO: My devoted ally.

JELLY: (*crying*) My poor mistress! She was very kind to me. [(*Exit boat.*)]

CARAMEL: Oh, she was a lovely woman!

DORO: Lovely indeed; to this moment the tears come into my eyes when I think of her.

CARAMEL: My dear friend! (*aside to* JELLY) This man's sympathy for my loss is inexplicable. He could not have regretted her more if he had been married to her himself. (*Retires up stage.*)

DORO: (*aside to* JELLY) Jelly, this good fellow's interest in my bereavement touches me here — here, Jelly. Such single-hearted sorrow for the misfortunes of a comparative stranger is simply phenomenal. My more than a brother!

JELLY: Now, this is very affecting. Each of these young men thinks that the other is helping him to discover his wife. They've been too sea-sick to compare notes, and when the truth comes out that Toto has married both of them, there'll be a row. (*Exit.*)

[DORO: (*coming down stage*) What a wife she would have made.

CARAMEL: You may say that.]

DORO: (*suddenly*) Caramel, I will never desist until I have discovered Toto.

CARAMEL: I am afraid you are giving yourself a great deal of trouble.

DORO: Trouble! What is trouble when such an end is in view?

CARAMEL: Well, you are the kindest-hearted fellow I ever met.

DORO: Kindest-hearted? No, it is upon you the epithet should be conferred. I cannot tell you how I honour you for your efforts to discover her.* (*Exit.*)

        (*Re-enter* TOTO.)

TOTO: Why, whom in the world have we here?

CARAMEL: At last, at last I've found her (*clasping her in his arms*). Toto, Toto, where have you been all this time, and what have you been doing?

TOTO: (*in his arms*) I know your face somewhere.

CARAMEL: To quit me as you did, within an hour of your marriage, and then to give me this hunt after you — oh, Toto, it's too bad.

TOTO: Stop a bit; let us understand each other. You are — let me see —

CARAMEL: I am Prince Caramel, known to you as Barberini.

TOTO: Barberini! I know that name. (*suddenly*) It's the brigand.

CARAMEL: (*hurt*) Yes, it's the brigand.

TOTO: Let me see — didn't I marry you [or something]?

CARAMEL: Yes, you did marry me, and you left me immediately afterwards with

---

*Metzler adds: 'Caramel, it is noble — noble.'

a parcel of Red Indians, and I've followed you ever since! And now I've found you, what have you got to say for yourself?

TOTO: That I'm very, very sorry. I remember it all now [There was a highly correct clergyman, and a beadle and a pew-opener.

CARAMEL: (*annoyed*) There was no beadle and no clergyman. We were married by a friar in the mountains.

TOTO: Of course, the other was a dream. I remember all about it, but my going away was a mere lapse of memory.] The Indians came, and they amused me, and when they asked me to join them I forgot all about you, and I went. But I'm very sorry, and I love you very dearly, and I won't run away any more. Oh dear, oh dear! If you only knew how I loved you, you'd forgive me directly.

CARAMEL: (*annoyed*) Well − I − now don't cry, I can't bear to see anyone cry. If you'll promise to return with me and never forget you've been married any more, why I'll try and forgive you.

TOTO: And never tease me about it again?

CARAMEL: No, the matter shall be buried and forgotten.

TOTO: Then I'm forgiven?

CARAMEL: Yes. (*Kisses her.*)

TOTO: (*in his arms*) Quite?

CARAMEL: Quite.

SONG. − TOTO (*First verse sung to* CARAMEL)

I'm a simple little maid,
    A garden growing wild;
I cannot be demure and staid −
    I'm but a wayward child.
My simple heart knows no deceit,
    It loves but thee alone,
And while I live that heart will beat
    For thee, my own − my own.
[Oh have no fear, oh love of mine,
My simple heart is ever thine.]

(*At the end of the first verse* CARAMEL *turns up stage and goes off slowly as* DORO *enters.* DORO *comes down stage and* TOTO *sings second verse to him, not noticing that any change has taken place.*)

While borne from thee o'er many a mile
    Of cold and stormy sea,
Although my lips have worn a smile
    My heart has ached for thee.
If many a year had passed away
    And time had left his sign,
And thou and I were old and grey,
    My heart would still be thine.
[Oh have no fear, oh love of mine,
My simple heart is ever thine.

ENSEMBLE. –

TOTO	DORO
Oh have no fear *etc.*	To call me 'dear' and 'love of mine',
	Thy fickle heart shall ne'er be mine.]

(*At the end of the song he repulses her.*)

TOTO: There, now you're cross again.

DORO: Cross? I should think so, to leave me as you did, with a set of strangers. I'll never forgive you, never – never –

TOTO: Why, you promised you would never refer to it again!

DORO: I promised you that?

TOTO: Certainly! Now, do drop the subject, and don't refer to it again.

DORO: Well, you're the coolest young lady I've met for some time.

TOTO: (*coaxingly*) Now, Barberini –

DORO: Barberini? I beg to inform you that my name is Doro.

TOTO: Doro, is it? Then why did you tell me your name was Barberini?

DORO: I never told you so.

TOTO: Then I'm mixing you up with someone else.

DORO: I object to that process.

TOTO: There is a brigand, Barberini, isn't there?

DORO: There is just now, but if you mix him up with me, there won't be a brigand Barberini very long.

TOTO: I'll try and keep you distinct, but it's very confusing. Let me see, [I was married to you by a friar in the mountains.

DORO: By a friar in the mountains? Not at all, we were married in a church. There was a clergyman, a beadle, and a pew-opener, and your father gave you away.

TOTO: So I said just now, but you contradicted me.

DORO: Never.

TOTO: I shall never get this right. You see, I married one man in reality and one man in a dream. Now which are you?

DORO: I am the real man.

TOTO: Then look here,] you wear that (*tying a handkerchief round his arm*) and then I shall know you.

DORO: It shall never quit me while I have life. (*Kisses her.*)

(*Enter* CARAMEL, *who comes down to the place* DORO *occupied.*)

TOTO: (*speaking to* CARAMEL) Why, you've taken it off already. Oh, you men, there's no trusting you.

CARAMEL: I don't think I quite understand.

DORO: Now you're mixing us up again.

TOTO: True. Caramel, get away, you're a dream.

CARAMEL: A dream!

TOTO: A hideous dream.

DORO: A nightmare.

CARAMEL: But –

TOTO: Go away, I tell you. Don't come near me. If you speak another word I'll wake, and then where will you be?

CARAMEL: False, fickle, perjured girl! I renounce you for ever! There is one lowlier in station, but lovelier in personal appearance, who tended me during the protracted agonies of the voyage, and to whom my heart will ever turn with sympathetic yearnings. I go to her.* (*Exit.*)

[TOTO: Oh, Doro, I begin to regret that I ever left home. I can't help thinking that young girls should never leave their father's roof with a band of brigands, without first obtaining their father's permission. Mine was not a very wise man, perhaps, but he loved his daughter devotedly.]

       (*Re-enter the* KING, *one half of his face is quite white; he keeps the painted side towards* TOTO.)

KING: The crisis is at hand. The rain came as I was sleeping sweetly in the prickly cactus, and I forgot to bring the walnut-juice with me. There isn't a drop in the island. [If I can't contrive to keep the painted side of my face towards her, all must be discovered. With a little ingenuity I may contrive to keep up the deception for a few hours, but I cannot hope to be permanently successful.

TOTO: (*coming down stage with* DORO) Allow me to introduce my husband who has come here in search of me. Prince Doro, this is 'Choakee-Choakee', the 'Abernethy Biscuit'.

KING: (*aside*) This is extremely awkward. (*As* DORO *is on his white side, the* KING *conceals that side of his face with his drapery.*)

DORO: I have come to claim my bride. I hope there will be no difficulty?

KING: (*aloud*) None whatever. (*aside*) If they could only be induced to keep on the same side of me, all might be well. (*aloud*) In this country, it is customary for married people never to leave each other's side for a moment.

DORO: It is not customary in my country, but I am quite willing. (*Crosses to* TOTO.)

KING: (*aside*) A piece of diplomacy worthy of Zapeter!]

       (*Enter* CARAMEL *and* JELLY. *They come down to the white side of the* KING.)

[KING: Tut, tut, this is worse than ever; who would have thought of finding these people here?]

JELLY: Why, that's never your Majesty?

TOTO: Jelly! My dear Jelly, I am delighted to see you. Let me introduce you to our Ruler.

JELLY: Bless you, I've known his Majesty since I was born! [(*aside*) Poor thing, she's quite forgotten I've seen him every day for six years.]

CARAMEL: If you please, I had the honour of being betrothed to the Princess, but finding that she loves somebody else —

JELLY: Why, he's going to marry me!

TOTO: Why, Jelly, you're never going to marry that! Why, he's a dream!

       (*Re-enter* JAMILEK, ZAPETER, *and* COURT.)

KING: Zapeter, how is this? You have removed your complexions! This is indelicate.

[JELLY: Why, if it isn't the Prime Minister and all his court.

TOTO: I know all your faces somewhere; haven't I seen them before?]

---

*Metzler adds: ' — My own Jelly!'

ZAPETER: Sire, it is no use! The last shower was too much for us, and there is no colouring matter on the island.

TOTO: [(*sees* KING*'s full face*)] Why, what in the world have you been doing to yourself? Surely this side of your face is familiar to me?

KING: I am your poor father who practised a deception on you to bring you back to his arms.

TOTO: My father. (*Is about to embrace him, but shrinks from painted side of his face.*) No, the other side, please!

KING: And you forgive me?

TOTO: I have been very wilful and perverse and wayward, [and I have given you a good deal of trouble and made you appear very ridiculous. (KING *deeply hurt*) No, I don't mean that, but I'm very sorry and we'll all return to the court at once.

KING: But first promise me one thing — that come what may, nothing shall ever induce you to reveal the fool I made of myself to regain possession of you. If it got about that I had consented to waive my rank and go about in the disguise of an Abernethy Biscuit, I should never hold up my head again.

TOTO: Then that's settled;] and now that I have a husband to look after me, I won't give you any more trouble, as he will be always at hand to pull me up whenever I attempt to act on the spur of the moment.

FINALE. —

TOTO *and* CHORUS
At last I shall marry my own,
For I love my dear Doro alone;
It cannot too widely be known,
At last I shall marry my own.
Let everybody be gay,
For we're to be married today.

APPENDIX

The libretto and vocal score published by Metzler are undated but have been assigned to the years 1880–1, since the version printed seems to represent that staged at the Opera Comique in October 1881. However, the piano score of Sullivan's Incidental Music to *Henry VIII*, also published by Metzler in 1879 or 1880, contains an advertisement for the libretto and vocal score of *Princess Toto*, suggesting a date not later than 1880 for the latter.

The Lord Chamberlain's licensed copy of the libretto was submitted in time for the first performance of the pre-London tour in 1876; it was endorsed 'Theatre Royal, Northampton' (evidently an error for Nottingham) and issued on 21 June 1876. As has been pointed out by Terence Rees in the *Gilbert and Sullivan Journal* vol. X, no. 16 (1979), the first performance was given on 24 June, and not as recorded in Nicoll and elsewhere on 1 July.

The Lord Chamberlain's script includes passages of dialogue, two complete lyrics, and several portions of other lyrics not in the Metzler libretto. Since Gilbert is known to have transferred his rights in the work after its first London run, opening at the Strand on 2 October 1876, and specifically disclaimed responsibility for the Opera Comique revival, the Lord Chamberlain's text alone carries the author's *imprimatur*, although it is highly probable that some of the changes recorded in Metzler were made by Gilbert, or at least with his approval, for the Strand production. For instance, the playbill omits any reference to a character, Cathay, allocated dialogue at the start of act III in the Lord Chamberlain's script.

The vocal score largely conforms to the lyrics as printed in Metzler and most of the portions included in the Lord Chamberlain's script but omitted by Metzler are also absent from the vocal score. On the other hand Toto's solo, 'The pig with a Roman nose', included in the Lord Chamberlain's script but omitted from Metzler, is printed as an additional number in the vocal score, which also provides an alternative setting of Toto's and Doro's duet 'My own, own love' (act II, p. 117).

Two numbers omitted from the Lord Chamberlain's script but printed in Metzler are included in the vocal score. Instead of the Chorus 'Yes, here we come back from the wedding' (act I, p. 102) Toto sings this 'vocal waltz':

> Banish sorrow till tomorrow,
>   Let me not rejoice alone;
> Rob from pleasure all its treasure,
>   For my love is all my own.
>
> Banish reason for a season,
>   Place King Folly on his throne,
> Fairest flowers deck the hours,
>   For my love is all my own.
>
> Men tell of vows that droop and perish,
>   Ere yet the spring of life is past;
> Within my heart thy love I'll cherish:
>   While it beats that love will last.

While in act II, instead of the Lord Chamberlain's script insisting on *'Exeunt*

BRIGANDS' (p. 110), both Metzler and the vocal score supply the following chorus:

MALE BRIGANDS
We are nobles all, though in brigands' disguise,
All men of peace, though armed to the eyes;
Forced to masquerade in ferocious attire —
Not the sort of thing that we nobles admire.

FEMALE BRIGANDS
We are ladies all, and of gentle degree,
Picturesque in our dress, perhaps you'll agree;
Forced to masquerade in this brigand attire —
It's not the sort of thing that we ladies admire —
    For oh! this masquerade is
    To hard upon ladies;
    No more, forsooth, we'll brigands be,
    But end our lives respectably.

Toto's solo, 'Like an arrow' (act I, p. 96), omitted from Metzler, is included (although in a much abridged form) in the vocal score. Other, smaller discrepancies between Metzler and the vocal score include

Finale act II, p. 121, vocal score reads:
Away, away, to the Indian Isles
    That dot Pacific seas, (for 'Where the poo-poo sings in the trees')
Where nature wears eternal smiles
    And the palm trees woo the breeze. (for 'bend to the breeze')

Finale act II, p. 121, vocal score reads:
CARAMEL: What are you doing, Toto, what, oh what?
TOTO: With these Red Indians I have cast my lot.
          I leave you brigands, so pursue me not

followed by a reprise of 'With feathers, paint and patches' instead of the repeat of 'Hoppedegig', although by way of compensation a snatch of 'Hoppedegig' is allotted to Jamilek in the opening chorus act III.

Lastly the vocal score supplies its own finale act III (not in the Lord Chamberlain's script or Metzler):

TOTO
So pardon pray, you may depend
Of all my follies here's an end.
From further error I'll be free,
I've a husband now to think for me.

If ever I go wrong again
Or make mistakes, it's very plain
The whole responsibilitee
Will rest with him and not with me!
ALL
The whole responsibilitee will rest with him!

The whole responsibilitee for the text of *Princess Toto*, however, rests with a number of 'hims'.

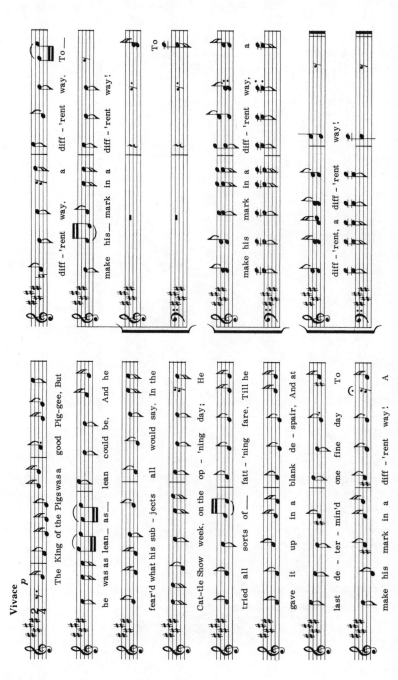

V *Princess Toto*. Extract from the vocal score (Metzler, c. 1879) in which 'The pig with a Roman nose' was published as part of the appendix

135

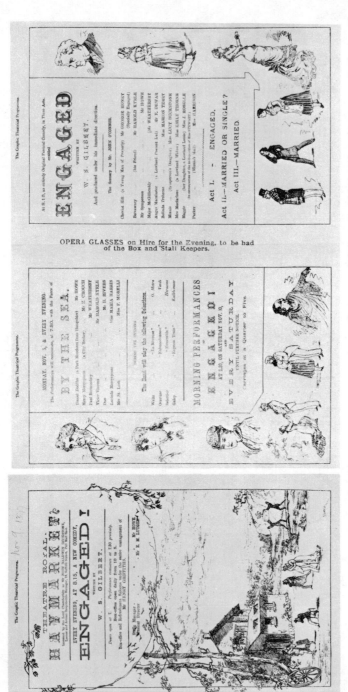

VI *a* and *b* *Engaged*. This 'Graphic Theatrical Programme' was issued during the original run, and depicts act I, together with sketches of the principal characters

ENGAGED*

An entirely original farcical comedy

First produced at the Theatre Royal, Haymarket, London, on 3 October 1877, with the following cast:

CHEVIOT HILL, a young man of property	Mr George Honey
BELVAWNEY, his friend	Mr Harold Kyrle
MR SYMPERSON	Mr Howe
ANGUS MACALISTER, a Lowland peasant lad	Mr Dewar
MAJOR McGILLICUDDY	Mr Weathersby
BELINDA TREHERNE	Miss Marion Terry
MINNIE, Symperson's daughter	Miss Lucy Buckstone
MRS MACFARLANE, a Lowland widow	Miss Emily Thorne
MAGGIE, her daughter, a Lowland lassie	Miss Julia Stewart
PARKER, Minnie's maid	Miss Julia Roselle
[Two friends of McGILLICUDDY]	

ACT I: ENGAGED. Garden of a cottage, near Gretna. (On the border, between England and Scotland.)
ACT II: MARRIED OR SINGLE? Drawing-room in Symperson's house in London.
ACT III: MARRIED. The same.

Three months' interval is supposed to elapse between acts I and II.
Three days' interval is supposed to elapse between acts II and III.

Scenery by Mr John O'Connor.

---

*Text used: *Original Plays*, second series (1881, reissued 1909), collated with French's acting edition no. 1748.

ACT I

The garden of a humble but picturesque cottage, near Gretna, on the border be-
tween England and Scotland. The whole scene is suggestive of rustic prosperity and
content. MAGGIE MACFARLANE, *a pretty country girl, is discovered spinning at*
a wheel, and singing as she spins. ANGUS MACALISTER, *a good-looking peasant*
lad, appears at back, and creeps softly down to MAGGIE *as she sings and spins,*
and places his hands over her eyes.

ANGUS: Wha is it?

MAGGIE: Oh, Angus, ye frightened me sae! (*He releases her.*) And see there — the
flax is a' knotted and scribbled — and I'll do naething wi' it!

ANGUS: Meg! My Meg! My ain bonnie Meg!

MAGGIE: Angus, why, lad, what's wrang wi' 'ee? Thou hast tear drops in thy
bonnie blue een.

ANGUS: Dinna heed them, Meg. It comes fra glowerin' at thy bright beauty.
Glowerin' at thee is like glowerin' at the noon-day sun!

MAGGIE: Angus, thou'rt talking fulishly. I'm but a puir brown hill-side lassie. I
dinna like to hear sic things from a straight honest lad like thee. It's the way
the dandy toun-folk speak to me, and it does na come rightly from the lips of
a simple man.

ANGUS: Forgive me, Meg, for I speak honestly to ye. Angus Macalister is not the
man to deal in squeaming compliments. Meg, I love thee dearly, as thou well
knowest. I'm but a puir lad, and I've little but twa braw arms and a straight
hairt to live by, but I've saved a wee bit siller — I've a braw housie and a
scrappie of gude garden-land — and it's a' for thee, lassie, if thou'll gie me thy
true and tender little hairt!

MAGGIE: Angus, I'll be fair and straight wi' 'ee. Thou askest me for my hairt. Why,
Angus, thou'rt tall, and fair, and brave. Thou'st a gude, honest face, and a
gude, honest hairt, which is mair precious than a' the gold on earth! No man
has a word to say against Angus Macalister — no, nor any woman neither.
Thou hast strong arms to work wi', and a strong hairt to help thee work. And
wha am I that I should say that a' these blessings are not enough for me? If
thou, gude, brave, honest man, will be troubled wi' sic a puir little, humble
mousie as Maggie Macfarlane, why, she'll just be the proudest and happiest
lassie in a' Dumfries!

ANGUS: My ain darling! (*They embrace.*)

(*Enter* MRS MACFARLANE *from cottage.*)

MRS MAC: Why, Angus — Maggie, what's a' this!

ANGUS: Mistress Macfarlane, dinna be fasht wi' me; dinna think worse o' me than
I deserve. I've loved your lass honestly these fifteen years, but never plucked
up the hairt to tell her so until noo; and when she answered fairly, it wasna in
human nature to do aught else but hold her to my hairt and place one kiss on
her bonnie cheek.

MRS MAC: Angus, say nae mair. My hairt is sair at losing my only bairn; but I'm

---

Gretna: Gretna Green, a village much patronized for its 'instant' marriage ceremonies.

nae fasht wi' 'ee. Thou'rt a gude lad, and it's been the hope of my widowed auld heart to see you twain one. Thou'lt treat her kindly — I ken that weel. Thou'rt a prosperous, kirk-going man, and my Mag should be a happy lass indeed. Bless thee, Angus; bless thee!

ANGUS: (*wiping his eyes*) Dinna heed the water in my ee' — it will come when I'm ower glad. Yes, I'm a fairly prosperous man. What wi' farmin' a bit land, and gillieing odd times, and a bit o' poachin' now and again; and what wi' my illicit whusky still — and throwin' trains off the line, that the poor distracted passengers may come to my cot, I've mair ways than one of making an honest living — and I'll work them a' nicht and day for my bonnie Meg!

MRS MAC: D'ye ken, Angus, I sometimes think that thou'rt losing some o' thine auld skill at upsetting railway trains. Thou hast not done sic a thing these sax weeks, and the cottage stands sairly in need of sic chance custom as the poor delayed passengers may bring.

MAGGIE: Nay, mither, thou wrangest him. Even noo, this very day, has he not placed twa bonnie braw sleepers across the up-line, ready for the express from Glaisgie, which is due in twa minutes or so?

MRS MAC: Gude lad! Gude thoughtfu' lad! But I hope the unfortunate passengers will na' be much hurt, puir unconscious bodies!

ANGUS: Fear nought, mither. Lang experience has taught me to do my work deftly. The train will run off the line, and the traffic will just be blocked for half a day, but I'll warrant ye that, wi' a' this, nae mon, woman, or child amang them will get sae much as a bruised head or a broken nose.

MAGGIE: My ain tender-hearted Angus! He wadna hurt sae much as a blatherin' buzzin' bluebottle flee!

ANGUS: Nae, Meg, not if takin' care and thought could help the poor dumb thing! (*wiping his eyes*) There, see, lass (*looking off*), the train's at a standstill, and there's nae harm done. I'll just go and tell the puir distraught passengers that they may rest them here, in thy cot, gin they will, till the line is cleared again. Mither, get thy rooms ready, and put brose i' the pot, for mebbe they'll be hungry, puir souls. Farewell, Meg; I'll be back ere lang, and if I don't bring 'ee a full half-dozen o' well-paying passengers, thou may'st just wed the red-headed exciseman! (*Exit.*)

MAGGIE: Oh, mither, mither, I'm ower happy! I've nae deserved sic a good fortune as to be the wife o' yon brave and honest lad!

MRS MAC: Meg, thine auld mither's hairt is sair at the thought o' losing ye, for hitherto she's just been a' the world to 'ee; but now thou'lt cleave to thine Angus, and thou'lt learn to love him better than thy puir auld mither! But it mun be — it mun be!

MAGGIE: Nay, mither, say not that. A gude girl loves her husband wi' one love and her mother wi' anither. They are not alike, but neither is greater or less than the ither, and they dwell together in peace and unity. That is how a gude girl loves.

---

brose: 'a dish made by pouring boiling water (or milk) on oatmeal (or oatcake) seasoned with salt and butter' (*OED*).

MRS MAC: And thou art a gude girl, Meg?

MAGGIE: I am a varra gude girl indeed, mither — a varra, varra gude girl!

MRS MAC: I'm right sure o' that. Well, the puir belated passengers will be here directly, and it is our duty to provide for them sic puir hospitality as our humble roof will afford. It shall never be said o' Janie Macfarlane that she ever turned the weary traveller fainting from her door!

MAGGIE: My ain gentle-hearted mither!

        (*Exeunt together into cottage.*)

        (*Enter* ANGUS *with* BELVAWNEY *and* MISS TREHERNE. *She is in travelling costume, and both are much agitated and alarmed.*)

ANGUS: Step in, sir — step in, and sit ye doun for a wee. I'll just send Mistress Macfarlane to ye. She's a gude auld bodie, and will see to your comforts as if she was your ain mither.

BELV: Thank you, my worthy lad, for your kindness at this trying moment.

ANGUS: Ah, sir, wadna any mon do as muckle? A dry shelter, a bannock and a pan o' parritch is a' we can offer ye, but sic as it is ye're hairtily welcome.

BELV: It is well — we thank you.

ANGUS: For wha wadna help the unfortunate?

BELV: (*occupied with* MISS TREHERNE) Exactly — everyone would.

ANGUS: Or feed the hungry?

BELV: No doubt.

ANGUS: It just brings the tear drop to my ee' to think —

BELV: (*leading him off*) My friend, we would be alone, this maiden and I. Farewell! (*Exit* ANGUS, *into cottage.*) Belinda — my own — my life! Compose yourself. It was in truth a weird and gruesome accident. The line is blocked — your parasol is broken, and your butterscotch trampled in the dust, but no serious harm is done. Come, be cheerful. We are safe — quite safe.

MISS TRE: Safe! Ah, Belvawney, my own Belvawney — there is, I fear, no safety for us so long as we are liable to be overtaken by that fearful Major to whom I was to have been married this morning!

BELV: Major McGillicuddy? I confess I do not feel comfortable when I think of Major McGillicuddy.

MISS TRE: You know his barbaric nature, and how madly jealous he is. If he should find that I have eloped with you, he will most surely shoot us both!

BELV: It is an uneasy prospect. (*suddenly*) Belinda, do you love me?

MISS TRE: With an impetuous passion that I shall carry with me to the tomb!

BELV: Then be mine tomorrow! We are not far from Gretna, and the thing can be done without delay. Once married, the arm of the law will protect us from this fearful man, and we can defy him to do his worst.

MISS TRE: Belvawney, all this is quite true. I love you madly, passionately; I care to live but in your heart, I breathe but for your love; yet, before I actually consent to take the irrevocable step that will place me on the pinnacle of my fondest hopes, you must give me some definite idea of your pecuniary position. I am not mercenary, heaven knows; but business is business, and I confess I should like a little definite information about the settlements.

BELV: I often think that it is deeply to be deplored that these grovelling questions of money should alloy the tenderest and most hallowed sentiments that inspire our imperfect natures.

MISS TRE: It is unfortunate, no doubt, but at the same time it is absolutely necessary.

BELV: Belinda, I will be frank with you. My income is £1000 a year, which I hold on certain conditions. You know my friend Cheviot Hill, who is travelling to London in the same train with us, but in the third class?

MISS TRE: I believe I know the man you mean.

BELV: Cheviot, who is a young man of large property, but extremely close-fisted, is cursed with a strangely amatory disposition, as you will admit when I tell you that he has contracted a habit of proposing marriage, as a matter of course, to every woman he meets. His haughty father (who comes of a very old family — the Cheviot Hills had settled in this part of the world centuries before the Conquest) is compelled by his health to reside in Madeira. Knowing that I exercise an all but supernatural influence over his son, and fearing that his affectionate disposition would lead him to contract an undesirable marriage, the old gentleman allows me £1000 a year so long as Cheviot shall live single, but at his death or marriage the money goes over to Cheviot's uncle Symperson, who is now travelling to town with him.

MISS TRE: Then so long as your influence over him lasts, so long only will you retain your income?

BELV: That is, I am sorry to say, the state of the case.

MISS TRE: (*after a pause*) Belvawney, I love you with an imperishable ardour which mocks the power of words. If I were to begin to tell you now of the force of my indomitable passion for you, the tomb would close over me before I could exhaust the entrancing subject. But, as I said before, business is business, and unless I can see some distinct probability that your income will be permanent, I shall have no alternative but to weep my heart out in all the anguish of maiden solitude — uncared for, unloved, and alone! (*Exit into cottage.*)

BELV: There goes a noble-hearted girl, indeed! Oh, for the gift of Cheviot's airy badinage — oh, for his skill in weaving a net about the hearts of women! If I could but induce her to marry me at once before the dreadful Major learns our flight! Why not? We are in Scotland. Methinks I've heard two loving hearts can wed, in this strange country, by merely making declaration to that effect. I will think out some cunning scheme to lure her into marriage unawares.

(*Enter* MAGGIE, *from cottage.*)

MAGGIE: Will ye walk in and rest a wee, Maister Belvawney? There's a room ready for ye, kind sir, and ye're heartily welcome to it.

BELV: It is well. Stop! Come hither, maiden.

MAGGIE: Oh, sir! you do not mean any harm towards a puir, innocent, unprotected cottage lassie?

BELV: Harm! No: of course, I don't. What do you mean?

Cheviot Hills: a range marking the border between England and Scotland.

MAGGIE: I'm but a puir, humble mountain girl; but let me tell you, sir, that my character's just as dear to me as the richest and proudest lady's in the land. Before I consent to approach ye, swear to me that you mean me no harm.

BELV: Harm? Of course, I don't. Don't be a little fool. Come here.

MAGGIE: There is something in his manner that reassures me. It is not that of the airy trifler with innocent hairts. (*aloud*) What wad ye wi' puir, harmless Maggie Macfarlane, gude sir?

BELV: Can you tell me what constitutes a Scotch marriage?

MAGGIE: Oh, sir, it's nae use asking me that; for my hairt is not my ain to give. I'm betrothed to the best and noblest lad in a' the bonnie Borderland. Oh, sir, I canna be your bride!

BELV: My girl, you mistake. I do not want you for my bride. Can't you answer a simple question? What constitutes a Scotch marriage?

MAGGIE: Ye've just to say before twa witnesses, 'Maggie Macfarlane is my wife'; and I've just to say, 'Maister Belvawney is my husband', and nae mon can set us asunder. But, sir, I canna be your bride; for I am betrothed to the best and noblest —

BELV: I congratulate you. You can go.

MAGGIE: Yes, sir. (*Exit into cottage.*)

BELV: It is a simple process; simple but yet how beautiful! One thing is certain — Cheviot may marry any day, despite my precautions, and then I shall be penniless. He may die, and equally I shall be penniless. Belinda has £500 a year; it is not much, but it would, at least, save me from starvation. (*Exit.*)

> (*Enter* SYMPERSON *and* CHEVIOT HILL *over bridge. They both show signs of damage — their hats are beaten in and their clothes disordered through the accident.*)

SYMP: Well, here we are at last —

CHEVIOT: Yes; here we are at last, and a pretty state I'm in, to be sure.

SYMP: My dear nephew, you would travel third class, and this is the consequence. After all, there's not much harm done.

CHEVIOT: Not much harm? What d'ye call that? (*showing his hat*) Ten and nine-pence at one operation! My gloves split — one and four! My coat ruined — eighteen and six! It's a coarse and brutal nature that recognizes no harm that don't involve loss of blood. I'm reduced by this accident from a thinking, feeling, reflecting human being, to a moral pulp — a mash — a poultice. Damme, sir, that's what I am! I'm a poultice!

SYMP: Cheviot, my dear boy, at the moment of the accident you were speaking to me on a very interesting subject.

CHEVIOT: Was I? I forget what it was. The accident has knocked it clean out of my head.

SYMP: You were saying that you were a man of good position and fortune; that you derived £2000 a year from your bank; that you thought it was time you settled. You then reminded me that I should come into Belvawney's £1000 a year on your marriage, and I'm not sure, but I rather think you mentioned, casually, that my daughter Minnie is an Angel of Light.

CHEVIOT: True, and just then we went off the line. To resume — Uncle Symperson,

ᶍ your daughter Minnie is an Angel of Light, a perfect being, as innocent as a
   new-laid egg.

SYMP: Minnie is, indeed, all that you have described her.

CHEVIOT: Uncle, I'm a man of few words. I feel and I speak. I love that girl,
   madly, passionately, irresistibly. She is my whole life, my whole soul and
   body, my Past, my Present, and my To Come. I have thought for none but
   her; she fills my mind, sleeping and waking; she is the essence of every hope —
   the tree upon which the fruit of my heart is growing — my own To Come!

SYMP: (*who has sunk overpowered on to stool during this speech*) Cheviot, my
   dear boy, excuse a father's tears. I won't beat about the bush. You have
   anticipated my devoutest wish. Cheviot, my dear boy, take her, she is yours!

CHEVIOT: I have often heard of rapture, but I never knew what it was till now.
   Uncle Symperson, bearing in mind the fact that your income will date from
   the day of the wedding, when may this be?

SYMP: My boy, the sooner the better! Delicacy would prompt me to give Belvawney a reasonable notice of the impending loss of his income, but should I,
   for such a mere selfish reason as that, rob my child of one hour of the happiness that you are about to confer upon her? No! Duty to my child is para-
   mount!

CHEVIOT: On one condition, however, I must insist. This must be kept from
   Belvawney's knowledge. You know the strange, mysterious influence that his
   dreadful eyes exercise over me.

SYMP: I have remarked it with astonishment.

CHEVIOT: They are much inflamed just now, and he has to wear green spectacles.
   While this lasts I am a free agent, but under treatment they may recover. In
   that case, if he knew that I contemplated matrimony, he would use them to
   prevent my doing so — and I cannot resist them — I cannot resist them!
   Therefore, I say, until I am safely and securely tied up, Belvawney must know
   nothing about it.

SYMP: Trust me, Cheviot, he shall know nothing about it from *me*. (*aside*) A
   thousand a year! I have endeavoured, but in vain, to woo Fortune for fifty-six
   years, but she smiles upon me at last! — She smiles upon me at last! (*Exit
   into cottage.*)

CHEVIOT: At length my hopes are to be crowned! Oh, my own — my own — the
   hope of my heart — my love — my life!
   (*Enter* BELVAWNEY, *who has overheard these words.*)

BELV: Cheviot! Whom are you apostrophizing in those terms? You've been at it
   again, I see!

CHEVIOT: Belvawney, that apostrophe was private; I decline to admit you to my
   confidence.

BELV: Cheviot, what is the reason of this strange tone of defiance? A week ago I
   had but to express a wish, to have it obeyed as a matter of course.

CHEVIOT: Belvawney, it may not be denied that there was a time when, owing to
   the remarkable influence exercised over me by your extraordinary eyes, you
   could do with me as you would. It would be affectation to deny it; your
   eyes withered my will; they paralyzed my volition. They were strange and

lurid eyes, and I bowed to them. Those eyes were my Fate — my Destiny — my unerring Must — my inevitable Shall. That time has gone — for ever!

BELV: Alas for the days that are past and the good that came and went with them!

CHEVIOT: Weep for them if you will. I cannot weep with you, for I loved them not. But, as you say, they are past. The light that lit up those eyes is extinct — their fire has died out — their soul has fled. They are no longer eyes, they are poached eggs. I have not yet sunk so low as to be the slave of two poached eggs.

BELV: Have mercy. If any girl has succeeded in enslaving you — and I know how easily you are enslaved — dismiss her from your thoughts; have no more to say to her; and I will — yes, I will bless you with my latest breath!

CHEVIOT: Whether a blessing conferred with one's latest breath is a superior article to one conferred in robust health we need not stop to inquire. I decline, as I said before, to admit you to my confidence on any terms whatever. Begone! (*Exit* BELVAWNEY.) Dismiss from my thoughts the only woman I ever loved! Have no more to say to the tree upon which the fruit of my heart is growing! No, Belvawney, I cannot cut off my tree as if it were gas or water. I do not treat women like that. Some men do, but I don't. I am not that sort of man. I respect women; I love women. They are good; they are pure; they are beautiful; at least, many of them are. (*Enter* MAGGIE *from cottage; he is much fascinated.*) This one, for example, is very beautiful indeed!

MAGGIE: If ye'll just walk in, sir, ye'll find a bannock and a pan o' parritch waitin' for ye on the table.

CHEVIOT: This is one of the loveliest women I ever met in the whole course of my life!

MAGGIE: (*aside*) What's he glowerin' at? (*aloud*) Oh, sir, ye mean no harm to the poor Lowland lassie?

CHEVIOT: Pardon me; it's very foolish. I can't account for it — but I am arrested, fascinated.

MAGGIE: Oh, gude sir, what's fascinated ye?

CHEVIOT: I don't know; there is something about you that exercises a most remarkable influence over me; it seems to weave a kind of enchantment around me. I can't think what it is. You are a good girl, I am sure. None but a good girl could so powerfully affect me. You *are* a good girl, are you not?

MAGGIE: I am a varra gude girl indeed, sir.

CHEVIOT: I was quite sure of it. (*Gets his arm round her waist.*)

MAGGIE: I am a much better girl than nineteen out of twenty in these pairts. And they are all gude girls too.

CHEVIOT: My darling! (*Kisses her.*)

MAGGIE: Oh, kind sir, what's that for?

CHEVIOT: It is your reward for being a good girl.

MAGGIE: Oh, sir, I didna look for sic a recompense; you are varra varra kind to puir little Maggie Macfarlane.

CHEVIOT: I cannot think what it is about you that fascinates me so remarkably.

MAGGIE: Maybe it's my beauty.

CHEVIOT: Maybe it is. It is quite possible that it may be, as you say, your beauty.

MAGGIE: I am remarkably pretty, and I've a varra neat figure.

CHEVIOT: There is a natural modesty in this guileless appreciation of your own
    perfection that is, to me, infinitely more charming than the affected ignor-
    ance of an artificial town-bred beauty.

MAGGIE: Oh, sir, can I close my een to the picture that my looking-glass holds up
    to me twenty times a day? We see the rose on the tree, and we say that it is
    fair; we see the silver moon sailing in the braw blue heavens, and we say that
    she is bright; we see the brawling stream purling over the smooth stanes i' the
    burn, and we say that it is beautiful; and shall we close our een to the fairest
    of nature's works — a pure and beautiful woman? Why, sir, it wad just be base
    ingratitude! No, it's best to tell the truth about a' things: I am a varra, varra
    beautiful girl!

CHEVIOT: Maggie Macfarlane, I'm a plain, blunt, straightforward man, and I come
    quickly to the point. I see more to love in you than I ever saw in any woman
    in all my life before. I have a large income, which I do not spend recklessly. I
    love you passionately; you are the essence of every hope; you are the tree
    upon which the fruit of my heart is growing — my Past, my Present, my
    Future — you are my own To Come. Tell me, will you be mine — will you
    join your life with mine?

            (*Enter* ANGUS, *who listens.*)

MAGGIE: Ah, kind sir, I'm sairly grieved to wound sae true and tender a love as
    yours, but ye're ower late, my love is nae my ain to give ye, it's given ower to
    the best and bravest lad in a' the bonnie Borderland!

CHEVIOT: Give me his address that I may go and curse him!

MAGGIE: (*kneels to* CHEVIOT HILL) Ah, ye must not curse him. Oh, spare him,
    spare him, for he is good and brave, and he loves me, oh, sae dearly, and I
    love him, oh, sae dearly too. Oh, sir, kind sir, have mercy on him, and do not
    — do not curse him, or I shall die! (*throwing herself at his feet*)

CHEVIOT: Will you, or will you not, oblige me by telling me where he is, that I
    may at once go and curse him?

ANGUS: (*coming forward*) He is here, sir, but dinna waste your curses on me.
    Maggie, my bairn (*raising her*) I heard the answer ye gave to this man, my true
    and gentle lassie! Ye spake well and bravely, Meg — well and bravely! Dinna
    heed the water in my ee' — it's a tear of joy and gratitude, Meg — a tear of
    joy and gratitude!

CHEVIOT: (*touched*) Poor fellow! I will *not* curse him! (*aloud*) Young man, I
    respect your honest emotion. I don't want to distress you, but I cannot help
    loving this most charming girl. Come, is it reasonable to quarrel with a man
    because he's of the same way of thinking as yourself?

ANGUS: Nay, sir, I'm nae fasht, but it just seems to drive a' the bluid back into my
    hairt when I think that my Meg is loved by anither! Oh, sir, she's a fair and
    winsome lassie, and I micht as justly be angry wi' ye for loving the blue
    heavens! She's just as far above us as they are! (*wiping his eyes and kissing her*)

CHEVIOT: (*with decision*) Pardon me, I cannot allow that.

ANGUS: Eh?

CHEVIOT: I love that girl madly — passionately — and I cannot possibly allow you
    to do that — not before my eyes, I beg. You simply torture me.

MAGGIE: (*to* ANGUS) Leave off, dear, till the puir gentleman's gone, and then ye can begin again.

CHEVIOT: Angus, listen to me. You love this girl?

ANGUS: I love her, sir, a'most as weel as I love mysel'!

CHEVIOT: Then reflect how you are standing in the way of her prosperity. I am a rich man. I have money, position, and education. I am a much more intellectual and generally agreeable companion for her than you can ever hope to be. I am full of anecdote, and all my anecdotes are in the best possible taste. I will tell you some of them some of these days, and you can judge for yourself. Maggie, if she married me, would live in a nice house in a good square. She would have wine – occasionally. She would be kept beautifully clean. Now, if you really love this girl almost as well as you love yourself, are you doing wisely or kindly in standing in the way of her getting all these good things? As to compensation – why, I've had heavy expenses of late – but if – yes, if thirty shillings –

ANGUS: (*hotly*) Sir, I'm puir in pocket, but I've a rich hairt. It is rich in a pure and overflowing love, and he that hath love hath all. You canna ken what true love is, or you wadna dare to insult a puir but honest lad by offering to buy his treasure for money.

(CHEVIOT *retires up stage.*)

MAGGIE: My ain true darling! (*They embrace.*)

CHEVIOT: Now, I'll not have it! Understand me, I'll not have it. It's simple agony to me. Angus, I respect your indignation, but you are too hasty. I do not offer to buy your treasure for money. You love her; it will naturally cause you pain to part with her, and I prescribe thirty shillings, not as a cure, but as a temporary solace. If thirty shillings is not enough, why, I don't mind making it two pounds.

ANGUS: Nae, sir, it's useless, and we ken it weel, do we not, my brave lassie? Our hearts are one as our bodies will be some day; and the man is na born, and the gold is na coined, that can set us twain asunder!

MAGGIE: Angus, dear, I'm varra proud o' sae staunch and true a love; it's like your ain true self, an' I can say nae more for it than that. But dinna act wi'out prudence and forethought, dear. In these hard times twa pound is twa pound, and I'm nae sure that ye're acting richtly in refusing sae large a sum. I love you varra dearly – ye ken that right weel – an' if ye'll be troubled wi' sic a poor little mousie I'll mak' ye a true an' loving wife, but I doubt whether, wi' a' my love, I'll ever be worth as much to ye as twa pound. Dinna act in haste, dear; tak' time to think before ye refuse this kind gentleman's offer.

ANGUS: Oh, sir, is not this rare modesty? Could ye match it amang your toun-bred fine ladies? I think not! Meg, it shall be as you say. I'll tak' the siller, but it'll be wi' a sair and broken hairt! (CHEVIOT *gives* ANGUS *money.*) Fare thee weel, my love – my childhood's – boyhood's – manhood's love! Ye're ganging fra my hairt to anither, who'll gie thee mair o' the gude things o' this world than I could ever gie 'ee, except love, an' o' that my hairt is full indeed! But it's a' for the best; ye'll be happier wi' him – and twa pound is twa pound. Meg, mak' him a gude wife, be true to him, and love him as ye loved me. Oh, Meg, my poor bruised hairt is well nigh like to break! (*Exit into cottage, in great agony.*)

MAGGIE: (*looking wistfully after him*) Puir laddie, puir laddie! Oh, I did na ken till noo how weel he loved me!

CHEVIOT: Maggie, I'm almost sorry I — poor lad, poor fellow! He has a generous heart. I am glad I did not curse him. (*aside*) This is weakness! (*aloud*) Maggie my own — ever and for always my own, we will be very happy, will we not?

MAGGIE: Oh, sir, I dinna ken, but in truth I hope so. Oh, sir, my happiness is in your hands noo; be kind to the puir cottage lassie who loves ye sae weel; my hairt is a' your ain, and if ye forsake me my lot will be a sair one indeed! (*Exit, weeping, into cottage.*)

CHEVIOT: Poor little Lowland lassie! That's my idea of a wife. No ridiculous extravagance; no expensive tastes. Knows how to dress like a lady on £5 a year; ah, and does it too! No pretence there of being blind to her own beauties; she knows that she is beautiful, and scorns to lie about it. In that respect she resembles Symperson's dear daughter, Minnie. My darling Minnie. (*Looks at miniature.*) My own darling Minnie. Minnie is fair, Maggie is dark. Maggie loves me! That excellent and perfect country creature loves me! She is to be the light of my life, my own To Come! In some respects she is even prettier than Minnie — my darling Minnie, Symperson's dear daughter, the tree upon which the fruit of my heart is growing; my Past, my Present, and my Future, my own To Come! But this tendency to reverie is growing on me; I must shake it off. (*Enter MISS TREHERNE.*) Heaven and earth, what a singularly lovely girl!

MISS TRE: A stranger! Pardon me, I will withdraw! —

CHEVIOT: A stranger indeed, in one sense, inasmuch as he never had the happiness of meeting you before — but, in that he has a heart that can sympathize with another's misfortune, he trusts he may claim to be regarded almost as a friend.

MISS TRE: May I ask, sir, to what misfortunes you allude?

CHEVIOT: I — a — do not know their precise nature, but that perception would indeed be dull, and that heart would be indeed flinty, that did not at once perceive that you are very very unhappy. Accept, madam, my deepest and most respectful sympathy.

MISS TRE: You have guessed rightly, sir! I am indeed a most unhappy woman.

CHEVIOT: I am delighted to hear it — a — I mean I feel a pleasure, a melancholy and chastened pleasure, in reflecting that, if your distress is not of a pecuniary nature, it may perchance lie in my power to alleviate your sorrow.

MISS TRE: Impossible, sir, though I thank you for your respectful sympathy.

CHEVIOT: How many women would forgo twenty years of their lives to be as beautiful as yourself, little dreaming that extraordinary loveliness can co-exist with the most poignant anguish of mind! But so, too often, we find it, do we not, dear lady?

MISS TRE: Sir! This tone of address, from a complete stranger!

CHEVIOT: Nay, be not unreasonably severe upon an impassionable and impulsive man, whose tongue is but the too faithful herald of his heart. We see the rose on the tree, and we say that it is fair, we see the bonnie brooks purling over the smooth stanes — I should say stones — in the burn, and we say that it is beautiful, and shall we close our eyes to the fairest of nature's works, a pure and beautiful woman? Why, it would be base ingratitude, indeed!

MISS TRE: I cannot deny that there is much truth in the sentiments you so beautifully express, but I am, unhappily, too well aware that, whatever advantages I may possess, personal beauty is not among their number.

CHEVIOT: How exquisitely modest is this chaste insensibility to your own singular loveliness! How infinitely more winning than the bold-faced self-appreciation of under-bred country girls!

MISS TRE: I am glad, sir, that you are pleased with my modesty. It has often been admired.

CHEVIOT: Pleased! I am more than pleased — that's a very weak word. I am enchanted. Madam, I am a man of quick impulse and energetic action. I feel and I speak — I cannot help it. Madam, be not surprised when I tell you that I cannot resist the conviction that you are the light of my future life, the essence of every hope, the tree upon which the fruit of my heart is growing — my Past, my Present, my Future, my own To Come! Do not extinguish that light, do not disperse that essence, do not blight that tree! I am well off; I'm a bachelor; I'm thirty-two; and I love you, madam, humbly, truly, trustfully, patiently. Paralyzed with admiration, I wait anxiously and yet hopefully, for your reply.

MISS TRE: Sir, that heart would indeed be cold that did not feel grateful for so much earnest, single-hearted devotion. I am deeply grieved to have to say one word to cause pain to one who expresses himself in such well-chosen terms of respectful esteem; but, alas! I have already yielded up my heart to one who, if I mistake not, is a dear personal friend of your own.

CHEVIOT: Am I to understand that you are the young lady of property whom Belvawney hopes to marry?

MISS TRE: I am, indeed, that unhappy woman!

CHEVIOT: And is it possible that you love him?

MISS TRE: With a rapture that thrills every fibre of my heart — with a devotion that enthralls my very soul! But there's some difficulty about his settlements.

CHEVIOT: A difficulty! I should think there was. Why, on my marrying, his entire income goes over to Symperson! I could reduce him to penury tomorrow. As it happens, I *am* engaged, I recollect, to Symperson's daughter; and if Belvawney dares to interpose between you and me, by George, I'll do it!

MISS TRE: Oh, spare him, sir! You say that you love me? Then, for my sake, remain single for ever — it is all I ask, it is not much. Promise me that you will never, never marry, and we will both bless you with our latest breath!

CHEVIOT: There seems to be a special importance attached to a blessing conferred with one's latest breath that I entirely fail to grasp. It seems to me to convey no definite advantage of any kind whatever.

MISS TRE: Cruel, cruel man!

(*Enter* BELVAWNEY, *in great alarm.*)

BELV: We are lost! — We are lost!

MISS TRE: What do you mean?

CHEVIOT: Who has lost you?

BELV: Major McGillicuddy discovered your flight, and followed in the next train. The line is blocked through our accident, and his train has pulled up within a few yards of our own. He is now making his way to this very cottage! What do you say to that?

MISS TRE: I agree with you, we are lost!

CHEVIOT: I disagree with you; I should say you are found.

BELV: This man is a reckless fire-eater; he is jealous of me. He will assuredly shoot us both if he sees us here together. I am no coward – but – I confess I am uneasy.

MISS TRE: (*to* CHEVIOT) Oh, sir, you have a ready wit; help us out of this difficulty, and we will both bless you –

BELV: With our latest breath!

CHEVIOT: That decides me. Madam, remain here with me. Belvawney, withdraw. (BELVAWNEY *retires*.) I will deal with this maniac alone. All I ask is, that if I find it necessary to make a statement that is not consistent with strict truth, you, madam, will unhesitatingly endorse it?

MISS TRE: I will stake my very existence on its veracity, whatever it may be.

CHEVIOT: Good. He is at hand. Belvawney, go. (*Exit* BELVAWNEY.) Now, madam, repose upon my shoulders, place your arms around me, so – is that comfortable?

MISS TRE: It is luxurious.

CHEVIOT: Good.

MISS TRE: You are sure it does not inconvenience you?

CHEVIOT: Not at all. Go back, I like it. Now we are ready for him.

>   (*Enter* McGILLICUDDY *with two friends dressed as for a wedding,
>   with white favours.* McGILLICUDDY *has pistols. All greatly excited.*)

McGILL: Where is the villain? I'll swear he is concealed somewhere. Search every tree, every bush, every geranium. Ha! They are here. Perjured woman! I've found you at last.

MISS TRE: (*to* CHEVIOT) Save me!

>   (BELVAWNEY *appears at back, listening.*)

McGILL: Who is the unsightly scoundrel with whom you have flown – the unpleasant-looking scamp whom you have dared to prefer to me? Uncurl yourself from around the plain villain at once, unless you would share his fate.

>   (MAGGIE *and* ANGUS *appear from cottage.*)

MISS TRE: Major, spare him!

CHEVIOT: Now, sir, perhaps you will be so good as to explain who the deuce you are, and what you want with this lady?

McGILL: I don't know who you may be, but I'm McGillicuddy. I am betrothed to this lady; we were to have been married this morning. I waited for her at the church from ten till four, then I began to get impatient.

CHEVIOT: I really think you must be labouring under some delusion.

McGILL: Delusion? Ha! ha! (*Two friends produce large wedding cake.*) Here's the cake!

CHEVIOT: Still I think there's a mistake somewhere. This lady is my wife.

McGILL: What! Belinda! Oh, Belinda! Tell me that this unattractive man lies; tell me that you are mine and only mine, now and for ever!

MISS TRE: I cannot say that. This gentleman is my husband!

> (McGILLICUDDY *falls sobbing on seat;* BELVAWNEY *tears his hair in despair;* MAGGIE *sobs on* ANGUS*'s shoulder.*)

ACT II

Double drawing-room in SYMPERSON*'s house. Indications that a wedding is about to take place. A plate of tarts and a bottle of wine on table. Enter* MINNIE SYMPERSON, *in wedding dress, followed by* PARKER, *her maid, holding her train.*

MINNIE: Take care, Parker — that's right. There! How do I look?

PARKER: Beautiful, miss; quite beautiful.

MINNIE: (*earnestly*) Oh, Parker, am I really beautiful? Really, *really* beautiful, you know?

PARKER: Oh, miss, there's no question about it. Oh, I do so hope you and Mr Cheviot Hill will be happy.

MINNIE: Oh, I'm sure we shall, Parker. He has often told me that I am the tree upon which the fruit of his heart is growing; and one couldn't wish to be more than *that*. And he tells me that his greatest happiness is to see me happy. So it will be my duty — my *duty*, Parker — to devote my life, my whole life, to making myself as happy as I possibly can.

> (*Enter* SYMPERSON, *dressed for wedding.*)

SYMP: So, my little lamb is ready for the sacrifice. You can go, Parker. And I am to lose my pet at last; my little dickey-bird is to be married today! Well, well, it's for her good. I must try and bear it — I must try and bear it.

MINNIE: And as my dear old papa comes into £1000 a year by it, I hope he won't allow it to distress him too much. He must try and bear up. He mustn't fret.

SYMP: My child, I will not deny that £1000 a year is a consolation. It's quite a fortune. I hardly know what I shall do with it.

MINNIE: I think, dear papa, you will spend a good deal of it on brandy, and a good deal more on billiards, and a good deal more on betting.

SYMP: It may be so: I don't say it won't. We shall see, Minnie, we shall see. These simple pleasures would certainly tend to smooth your poor old father's declining years. And my darling has not done badly either, has she?

MINNIE: No, dear papa; only fancy! Cheviot has £2000 a year from shares in the Royal Indestructible Bank.

SYMP: And don't spend £200. By the by, I'm sorry that my little bird has not contrived to induce him to settle anything on her; that, I think, was remiss in my tom-tit.

MINNIE: Dear papa, Cheviot is the very soul of honour; he's a fine, noble, manly, spirited fellow, but if he *has* a fault, it is that he is very, oh very, *very* stingy. He would rather lose his heart's blood than part with a shilling unnecessarily. He's a noble fellow, but he's like that.

SYMP: Still, I can't help feeling that if my robin had worked him judiciously —

MINNIE: Papa, dear, Cheviot is an all but perfect character, the very type of knightly chivalry; but he *has* faults, and among other things he's one of the worst tempered men I ever met in all my little life. Poor, simple, little Minnie thought the matter over very carefully in her silly childish way, and she came to the conclusion, in her foolish little noddle, that, on the whole, perhaps she could work it better after marriage, than before.

SYMP: Well, well, perhaps my wren is right. (*Rises.*)

MINNIE: Don't laugh at my silly little thoughts, dear papa, when I say I'm sure she is.

SYMP: Minnie, my dear daughter, take a father's advice, the last he will ever be entitled to give you. If you would be truly happy in the married state, be sure you have your own way in everything. Brook no contradictions. Never yield to outside pressure. Give in to no argument. Admit no appeal. However wrong you may be, maintain a firm, resolute, and determined front. These were your angel mother's principles through life, and she was a happy woman indeed. I neglected those principles, and while she lived I was a miserable wretch.

MINNIE: Papa dear, I have thought over the matter very carefully in my little baby-noddle, and I have come to the conclusion − don't laugh at me, dear papa − that it is my duty − my *duty* − to fall in with Cheviot's views in everything *before* marriage, and Cheviot's duty to fall into my views in everything *after* marriage. I think that is only fair, don't you?

SYMP: Yes, I dare say it will come to that.

MINNIE: Don't think me a very silly little goose when I say I'm sure it will. Quite, quite sure, dear papa. Quite. (*Exit.*)

SYMP: Dear child − dear child! I sometimes fancy I can see traces of her angel mother's disposition in her. Yes, I think − I *think* she will be happy. But, poor Cheviot! Oh, lor, poor Cheviot! Dear me, it won't bear thinking of!
           (*Enter* MISS TREHERNE, *unobserved. She is dressed in stately and funereal black.*)

MISS TRE: Come here, manservant. Approach. I'm not going to bite you. Can I see the fair young thing they call Minnie Symperson?

SYMP: Well, really, I can hardly say. There's nothing wrong, I hope?

MISS TRE: Nothing wrong? Oh, thoughtless, frivolous, light-hearted creature! Oh, reckless old butterfly! Nothing wrong! You've eyes in your head, a nose on your face, ears on each side of it, a brain of some sort in your skull, haven't you, butler?

SYMP: Undoubtedly, but I beg to observe I'm not the −

MISS TRE: Have you or have you not the gift of simple apprehension? Can you or can you not draw conclusions? Go to, go to, you offend me.

SYMP: (*aside*) There *is* something wrong, and it's *here* (*touching his forehead*). I'll tell her you're here. Whom shall I say?

MISS TRE: Say that one on whose devoted head the black sorrows of a long life-time have fallen, even as a funeral pall, craves a minute's interview with a dear old friend. Do you think you can recollect that message, butler?

SYMP: I'll try, but I beg, I *beg* to observe, I'm not the butler. (*aside*) This is a most surprising young person! (*Exit.*)

MISS TRE: At last I'm in my darling's home, the home of the bright blythe caroling thing that lit, as with a ray of heaven's sunlight, the murky gloom of my miserable school-days. But what do I see? Tarts? Ginger wine? There are rejoicings of some kind afoot. Alas, I am out of place here. What have I in common with tarts? Oh, I am ill-attuned to scenes of revelry! (*Takes a tart and eats it.*)

>   (*Enter* MINNIE.)

MINNIE: Belinda! (*They rush into each other's arms.*)

MISS TRE: Minnie! My own long-lost lamb! This is the first gleam of joy that has lighted my darksome course this many and many a day! And in spite of the change that time and misery have brought upon me, you knew me at once! (*eating the tart all this time*)

MINNIE: Oh, I felt sure it was you, from the message.

MISS TRE: How wondrously fair you have grown! And this dress! Why, it is surely a bridal dress! Those tarts — that wine! Surely this is not your wedding day?

MINNIE: Yes, dear, I shall be married in half-an-hour.

MISS TRE: Oh, strange chance! Oh, unheard-of coincidence! Married! And to whom?

MINNIE: Oh, to the dearest love — My cousin, Mr Cheviot Hill. Perhaps you know the name?

MISS TRE: I have heard of the Cheviot Hills, somewhere. Happy — strangely happy girl! You, at least, know your husband's name.

MINNIE: Oh yes, it's on all his pocket-handkerchiefs.

MISS TRE: It is much to know. I do not know mine.

MINNIE: Have you forgotten it?

MISS TRE: No; I never knew it. It is a dark mystery. It may not be unfathomed. It is buried in the fathomless gulf of the Eternal Past. There let it lie.

MINNIE: Oh, tell me all about it, dear.

MISS TRE: It is a lurid tale. Three months since I fled from a hated one, who was to have married me. He pursued me. I confided my distress to a young and wealthy stranger. Acting on his advice, I declared myself to be his wife; he declared himself to be my husband. We were parted immediately afterwards, and we have never met since. But this took place in Scotland; and by the law of that remarkable country we are man and wife, though I didn't know it at the time.

MINNIE: What fun!

MISS TRE: Fun! Say, rather, horror — distraction — chaos! I am rent with conflicting doubts! Perhaps he was already married; in that case, I am a bigamist. Maybe he is dead; in that case, I am a widow. Maybe he is alive; in that case, I am a wife. What am I? Am I single? Am I married? Am I a widow? Can I marry? Have I married? May I marry? Who am I? Where am I? What am I? — What is my name? What is my condition in life? If I am married, to whom am I married? If I am a widow, how came I to be a widow, and whose widow came I to be? Why am I his widow? What did he die of? Did he leave me anything? If anything, how much, and is it saddled with conditions? — Can I marry again without forfeiting it? Have I a mother-in-law? Have I a family of step-children, and if so, how many, and what are their ages, sexes, sizes, names and dispositions? These are questions that rack me night and day, and until they are settled, peace and I are not on terms!

MINNIE: Poor dear thing!

MISS TRE: But enough of my selfish sorrows. (*Goes up to table and takes a tart.*

MINNIE *is annoyed at this.*) Tell me about the noble boy who is about to
make you his. Has he any dross?

MINNIE: I don't know. (*Secretly removes tarts to another table close to door.*) I
never thought of asking — I'm such a goose. But papa knows.

MISS TRE: Have those base and servile things called settlements been satisfactorily
adjusted? (*eating*)

MINNIE: I don't know. It never occurred to me to inquire. But papa can tell you.

MISS TRE: The same artless little soul!

MINNIE: (*standing so as to conceal tarts from* MISS TREHERNE) Yes, I am quite
artless — quite, quite artless. But now that you *are* here you will stay and see
me married.

MISS TRE: I would willingly be a witness to my darling's joy, but this attire is,
perhaps, scarcely in harmony with a scene of revelry.

MINNIE: Well, dear, you're not a cheerful object, and that's the truth.

MISS TRE: And yet these charnel-house rags may serve to remind the thoughtless
banquetters that they are but mortal.

MINNIE: I don't think it will be necessary to do that, dear. Papa's sherry will make
that quite clear to them.

MISS TRE: Then I will hie me home, and array me in garments of less sombre hue.

MINNIE: I think it would be better, dear. Those are the very things for a funeral,
but this is a wedding.

MISS TRE: I see very little difference between them. But it shall be as you wish,
though I have worn nothing but black since my miserable marriage. There is
breakfast, I suppose?

MINNIE: Yes, at dear Cheviot's house.

MISS TRE: That is well. I shall return in time for it. Thank heaven I can still eat!
(*Takes a tart from table, and exit, followed by* MINNIE.)
(*Enter* CHEVIOT HILL. *He is dressed as for a wedding.*)

CHEVIOT: Here I am at last — quite flurried and hot after the usual row with the
cabman, just when I wanted to be particularly calm and self-contained. I got
the best of it, though. Dear me, this is a great day for me — a great day.
Where's Minnie, I wonder? Arraying herself for the sacrifice, no doubt. Pouf!
This is a very nervous occasion. I wonder if I'm taking a prudent step.
Marriage is a very risky thing; it's like Chancery, once in it you can't get out
of it, and the costs are enormous. There you are — fixed. Fifty years hence,
if we're both alive, there we shall both be — fixed. That's the devil of it. It's
an unreasonably long time to be responsible for another person's expenses. I
don't see the use of making it for as long as that. It seems greedy to take up
half a century of another person's attention. Besides — one never knows —
one might come across somebody else one liked better — that uncommonly
nice girl I met in Scotland, for instance. No, no, I shall be true to my Minnie
— quite true. I am quite determined that nothing shall shake my constancy to
Minnie. (*Enter* PARKER.) What a devilish pretty girl!

PARKER: (*aside*) He's a mean young man, but he ought to be good for half-a-
crown today.

CHEVIOT: Come here, my dear; a — How do I look?

PARKER: Very nice indeed, sir.

CHEVIOT: What, really?

PARKER: Really.

CHEVIOT: What, tempting, eh?

PARKER: Very tempting indeed.

CHEVIOT: Hah! The married state is an enviable state, Parker.

PARKER: *Is* it, sir? I hope it may be. It depends.

CHEVIOT: What do you mean by 'it depends'? You're a member of the Church of England, I trust? Then don't you know that in saying 'it depends' you are flying in the face of the marriage service? Don't go and throw cold water on the married state, Parker. I know what you're going to say — it's expensive. So it is, at first, very expensive, but with economy you soon retrench that. By a beautiful provision of Nature, what's enough for one is enough for two. This phenomenon points directly to the married state as our natural state.

PARKER: Oh, for that matter, sir, a tigress would get on with you. You're so liberal, so gentle, so — there's only one word for it — dove-like.

CHEVIOT: What, you've remarked that, eh? Ha! ha! But dove-like as I am, Parker, in some respects, yet (*getting his arm round her*) in other respects — (*aside*) deuced pretty girl! — in other respects I am a man, Parker, of a strangely impetuous and headstrong nature. I don't beat about the bush; I come quickly to the point. Shall I tell you a secret? There's something about you, I don't know what it is, that — in other words, you are the tree upon which — no, no, damn it, Cheviot — not today, not today.

PARKER: What a way you have with you, sir!

CHEVIOT: What, you've noticed that, have you? Ha! ha! yes, I have a way, no doubt; it's been remarked before. Whenever I see a pretty girl (and you are a very pretty girl) I can't help putting my arm like that (*putting it round her waist*). Now, pleasant as this sort of thing is, and you find it pleasant, don't you? (PARKER *nods.*) Yes, you find it pleasant — pleasant as it is, it is decidedly wrong.

PARKER: It is decidedly wrong in a married man.

CHEVIOT: It is decidedly wrong in a married man. In a married man it's abominable, and I shall be a married man in half-an-hour. So, Parker, it will become necessary to conquer this tendency, to struggle with it, and subdue it — in half-an-hour (*getting more affectionate*). Not that there's any real harm in putting your arm round a girl's waist. Highly respectable people do it, when they waltz.

PARKER: Yes, sir, but then a band's playing.

CHEVIOT: True, and when a band's playing it don't matter, but when a band is *not* playing, why it's dangerous, you see. You begin with this, and you go on from one thing to another, getting more and more affectionate, until you reach *this* stage (*kissing her*). Not that there's any real harm in kissing, either; for you see fathers and mothers, who ought to set a good example, kissing their children every day.

PARKER: Lor, sir, kissing's nothing; everybody does that.

CHEVIOT: That is your experience, is it? It tallies with my own. Take it that I am your father, you are my daughter — or take it even that I am merely your husband, and you my wife, and it would be expected of me (*kissing her*).

PARKER: But I'm not your wife, sir.

CHEVIOT: No, not yet, that's very true, and, of course, makes a difference. That's why I say I must subdue this tendency; I must struggle with it; I must conquer it — in half-an-hour.

MINNIE: (*without*) Parker, where's Mr Cheviot?

CHEVIOT: There is your mistress, my dear — she's coming. Will you excuse me? (*releasing her*) Thank you. Good day, Parker.

PARKER: (*disgusted*) Not so much as a shilling; and that man's worth thousands! (*Exit.*)

(*Enter* MINNIE.)

CHEVIOT: My darling Minnie — my own, own To Come! (*kissing her*)

MINNIE: Oh, you mustn't crush me, Cheviot, you'll spoil my dress. How do you like it?

CHEVIOT: It's lovely. It's a beautiful material.

MINNIE: Yes; dear papa's been going it.

CHEVIOT: Oh, but you're indebted to me for that beautiful dress.

MINNIE: To you! Oh, thank you — thank you!

CHEVIOT: Yes. I said to your papa, 'Now do for once let the girl have a nice dress; be liberal; buy the very best that money will procure, you'll never miss it.' So, thanks to me, he bought you a beauty. Seventeen and six a yard if it's a penny. Dear me! To think that in half-an-hour this magnificent dress will be *my* property!

MINNIE: Yes. Dear papa said that as you had offered to give the breakfast at your house, he would give me the best dress that money could procure.

CHEVIOT: Yes, I *did* offer to provide the breakfast in a reckless moment; that's so like me. It was a rash offer, but I've made it, and I've stuck to it. Oh, then, there's the cake.

MINNIE: Oh, tell me all about the cake.

CHEVIOT: It's a very pretty cake. Very little cake is eaten at a wedding breakfast, so I've ordered what's known in the trade as the three-quarter article.

MINNIE: I see; three-quarters cake, and the rest wood.

CHEVIOT: No; three-quarters wood, the rest cake. Be sure, my dear, you don't cut into the wood, for it has to be returned to the pastrycook to be filled up with cake for another occasion. *I* thought at first of ordering a seven-eighths article; but one isn't married every day — it's only once a year — I mean it's only now and then. So I said, 'Hang the expense; let's do the thing well.' And so it's three-quarters.

MINNIE: How good you are to me! We shall be very happy, shall we not?

CHEVIOT: I — I hope so — yes. I *hope* so. Playfully happy, like two little kittens.

MINNIE: That will be delightful.

CHEVIOT: Economically happy, like two sensible people.

MINNIE: Oh, we must be very economical.

CHEVIOT: No vulgar display; no pandering to a jaded appetite. A refined and economical elegance; that is what we must aim at. A simple mutton chop, nicely broiled, for you; and *two* simple mutton chops, *very* nicely broiled, for me —

MINNIE: And some flowery potatoes —

CHEVIOT: A loaf of nice household bread —

MINNIE: A stick of celery —

CHEVIOT: And a bit of cheese, and you've a dinner fit for a monarch.

MINNIE: Then how shall we spend our evenings?

CHEVIOT: We'll have pleasant little fireside games. Are you fond of fireside games?

MINNIE: Oh, they're great fun.

CHEVIOT: Then we'll play at tailoring.

MINNIE: Tailoring? I don't think I know that game.

CHEVIOT: It's a very good game. You shall be the clever little jobbing tailor, and I'll be the particular customer who brings his own materials to be made up. You shall take my measure, cut out the cloth (real cloth, you know), stitch it together, and try it on; and then I'll find fault like a real customer, and you shall alter it until it fits, and when it fits beautifully that counts one to you.

MINNIE: Delightful!

CHEVIOT: Then there's another little fireside game which is great fun. We each take a bit of paper and a pencil and try who can jot down the nicest dinner for ninepence, and the next day we have it.

MINNIE: Oh, Cheviot, what a paradise you hold open to me!

CHEVIOT: Yes. How's papa?

MINNIE: He's very well and happy. He's going to increase his establishment on the strength of the £1000 a year, and keep a manservant.

CHEVIOT: I know. I've been looking after some servants for him; they'll be here in the course of the morning. A cook, a housemaid, and a footman. I found them through an advertisement. They're country people, and will come very cheap.

MINNIE: How kind and thoughtful you are! Oh, Cheviot, I'm a very lucky girl! (*Exit.*)

CHEVIOT: Yes, I think so too, if I can only repress my tendency to think of that tall girl I met in Scotland! Cheviot, my boy, you must make an effort; you are going to be married, and the tall girl is nothing to you!
(*Enter* PARKER.)

PARKER: Please, sir, here's a gentleman to see you.

CHEVIOT: Oh, my solicitor, no doubt. Show him up.

PARKER: And please, some persons have called to see you about an advertisement.

CHEVIOT: Oh, Symperson's servants. To be sure. Show up the gentleman, and tell the others to wait.
(*Exit* PARKER.)
(*Enter* BELVAWNEY. *He looks very miserable.*)

CHEVIOT: Belvawney! This is unexpected (*much confused*).

BELV: Yes, Cheviot. At last we meet. Don't, oh don't, frown upon a heartbroken wretch.

CHEVIOT: Belvawney, I don't want to hurt your feelings, but I will not disguise from you that, not having seen you for three months, I was in hopes that I had got rid of you for ever.

BELV: Oh, Cheviot, don't say that, I am so unhappy. And you have it in your power to make me comfortable. Do this, and I will bless you with my latest breath!

CHEVIOT: It is a tempting offer; I am not proof against it. We all have our price, and that is mine. Proceed.

BELV: Miss Treherne — Belinda — whom I love so dearly, won't have anything to say to me.

CHEVIOT: It does her credit. She's a very superior girl.

BELV: It's all through you, Cheviot. She declares that the mutual declaration you made to protect her from McGillicuddy amounts to a Scotch marriage.

CHEVIOT: What!!!

BELV: She declares she is your wife. She professes to love me as fondly as ever; but a stern sense of duty to you forbids her to hold any communication with me.

CHEVIOT: Oh, but this absurd, you know!

BELV: Of course it is; but what's to be done? You left with Symperson immediately after making the declaration. As soon as she found you were gone she implored me to tell her your name and address. Of course I refused, and she quitted me, telling me that she would devote her life to finding you out.

CHEVIOT: But this is simple madness. I can't have it! This day, too, of all others! If she'd claimed me last week, or even yesterday, I wouldn't have minded, for she's a devilish fine woman; but if she were to turn up now — ! (*aloud*) Belvawney, my dear friend, tell me what to do — I'll do anything.

BELV: It seems that there's some doubt whether this cottage, which is just on the border, is in England or Scotland. If it is in England, she has no case; if it is in Scotland, I'm afraid she has. I've written to the owner of the property to ascertain, and if, in the meantime, she claims you, you must absolutely decline to recognize this marriage for a moment.

CHEVIOT: Not for one moment!

BELV: It was a mere artifice to enable her to escape from McGillicuddy.

CHEVIOT: Nothing more!

BELV: It's monstrous — perfectly monstrous — that that should constitute a marriage. It's disgraceful — it's abominable. Damme, Cheviot, it's immoral.

CHEVIOT: So it is — it's immoral. That settles it in *my* mind. It's immoral.

BELV: You're quite sure you'll be resolute, Cheviot?

CHEVIOT: Resolute? I should think so! Why, hang it all, man, I'm going to be married in twenty minutes to Minnie Symperson!

BELV: What!

CHEVIOT: (*confused at having let this out*) Didn't I tell you? I believe you're right; I did *not* tell you. It escaped me. Oh, yes, this is my wedding day.

BELV: Cheviot, you're joking — you don't mean this! Why, I shall lose £1000 a year by it, every penny I have in the world! Oh, it can't be — it's nonsense.

CHEVIOT: What do you mean by nonsense? The married state is an honourable estate, I believe? A man is not looked upon as utterly lost to all sense of decency because he's got married, I'm given to understand! People have been married before this, and have not been irretrievably tabooed in consequence, unless I'm grossly misinformed? Then what the dickens do you mean by saying 'nonsense' when I tell you that I'm going to be married?

BELV: Cheviot, be careful how you take this step. Beware how you involve an innocent and helpless girl in social destruction.

CHEVIOT: What do you mean, sir?

BELV: You cannot marry; you are a married man.

CHEVIOT: Come, come, Belvawney, this is trifling.

BELV: You are married to Miss Treherne. I was present, and can depose to the fact.

CHEVIOT: Oh, you're not serious.

BELV: Never more serious in my life.

CHEVIOT: But, as you very properly said just now, it was a mere artifice — we didn't mean anything. It would be monstrous to regard that as a marriage. Damme, Belvawney, it would be immoral!

BELV: I may deplore the state of the law, but I cannot stand tamely by and see it deliberately violated before my eyes.

CHEVIOT: (*wildly*) But, Belvawney, my dear friend, reflect; everything is prepared for my marriage, at a great expense. I love Minnie deeply, devotedly. She is the actual tree upon which the fruit of my heart is growing. There's no mistake about it. She is my own To Come. I love her madly — rapturously. (*going on his knees to* BELVAWNEY) I have prepared a wedding breakfast at great expense to do her honour. I have ordered four flys for the wedding party. I have taken two second-class Cook's tourists' tickets for Ilfracombe, Devon, Exeter, Cornwall, Westward Ho! and Bideford Bay. The whole thing has cost me some twenty or twenty-five pounds, and all this will be wasted — utterly wasted — if you interfere. Oh, Belvawney, dear Belvawney, let the recollection of our long and dear friendship operate to prevent your shipwrecking my future life (*sobbing hysterically*).

BELV: I have a duty to do. I must do it.

CHEVIOT: But reflect, dear Belvawney; if I am married to Miss Treherne, you lose your income as much as if I married Minnie Symperson.

BELV: No doubt, if you could prove your marriage to Miss Treherne. But you can't — (*with melodramatic intensity*)

CHEVIOT: Those eyes!

BELV: You don't know where she is — (*with fiendish exultation*)

CHEVIOT: Oh, those eyes!

BELV: The cottage has been pulled down, the cottagers have emigrated to Patagonia —

CHEVIOT: Oh, those eyes!

BELV: I'm the only witness left. *I* can prove your marriage, if I like; but you can't. Ha! ha! ha! ha! (*with Satanic laugh*) It's a most painful and unfortunate situation for you; and, believe me, dear Cheviot, you have my deepest and most respectful sympathy. (*Exit.*)

CHEVIOT: This is appalling; simply appalling! The cup of happiness dashed from my lips just as I was about to drink a life-long draught. The ladder kicked from under my feet just as I was about to pick the fruit of my heart from the tree upon which it has been growing so long. I'm a married man! More than that, my honeymoon's past, and I never knew it! Stop a moment, though. The bride can't be found; the cottage is pulled down, and the cottagers have

---

Ilfracombe, Westward Ho!, Bideford Bay: seaside resorts in North Devon popular with Victorian holidaymakers.

emigrated; what proof is there that such a marriage ever took place? There's only Belvawney, and Belvawney isn't a proof. Corroborated by the three cottagers, his word might be worth something; uncorroborated, it is worthless. I'll risk it. He can do nothing; the bride is nowhere; the cottagers are in Patagonia, and —

> (*At this moment* MRS MACFARLANE, MAGGIE, *and* ANGUS *appear at the back. They stand bobbing and curtsying in rustic fashion to* CHEVIOT, *whom they do not recognize. He stares aghast at them for a moment, then staggers back to the sofa.*)

CHEVIOT: The man, the woman, and the girl, by all that's infernal!

MRS MAC: Gude day, sir. We've just ca'd to see ye about the advertisement (*producing paper*).

CHEVIOT: I don't know you — I don't know you. Go away. (*Buries his head in a newspaper, and pretends to read on sofa.*)

MAGGIE: Ah, sir, ye said that we were to ca' on ye this day at eleven o'clock, and sae we've coom a' the way fra Dumfries to see ye.

CHEVIOT: I tell you I don't know you. Go away. I'm not at all well. I'm very ill, and it's infectious.

ANGUS: We fear no illness, sir. This is Mistress Macfarlane, the gude auld mither, who'll cook the brose and boil the parritch, and sit wi' ye, and nurse ye through your illness till the sad day ye dee! (*wiping his eye*)

> (CHEVIOT *pokes a hole with his finger through newspaper, and reconnoitres unobserved.*)

MRS MAC: And this is Meg, my ain lass Meg!

CHEVIOT: (*aside*) Attractive girl, very. I remember her perfectly.

MRS MAC: And this is Angus Macalister, who's going to marry her, and who'll be mair than a son to me!

ANGUS: Oh, mither, mither, dinna say it, for ye bring the tear drop to my ee'; an' it's no canny for a strong man to be blithering and soughing like a poor weak lassie! (*wiping his eye*)

> (ANGUS *and* MRS MACFARLANE *sit.* MAGGIE *advances to hole in newspaper and peeps through.*)

MAGGIE: Oh, mither, mither! (*Staggers back into* ANGUS's *arms.*)

MRS MAC: What is it, Meg?

ANGUS: Meg, my weel lo'ed Meg, my wee wifie that is to be, tell me what's wrang wi' 'ee?

MAGGIE: Oh, mither, it's him; the noble gentleman I plighted my troth to three weary months agone! The gallant Englishman who gave Angus twa golden pound to give me up!

ANGUS: It's the coward Sassenach who well nigh broke our Meg's heart!

MRS MAC: My lass, my lass, dinna greet, maybe he'll marry ye yet.

CHEVIOT: (*desperately*) Here's another! Does anybody else want to marry me? Don't be shy. You, ma'am (*to* MRS MACFARLANE) *you're* a fine woman — perhaps *you* would like to try your luck?

MAGGIE: Ah, sir! I dinna ken your name, but your bonnie face has lived in my twa een, sleeping and waking, three weary, weary months! Oh, sir, ye should na' ha' deceived a trusting, simple Lowland lassie. 'Twas na' weel done — 'twas na' weel done! (*weeping on his shoulder; he puts his arm round her waist*)

CHEVIOT: (*softening*) My good girl, what do you wish me to do? I remember you now perfectly. I *did* admire you very much — in fact, I do still; you're a very charming girl. Let us talk this over, calmly and quietly. (MAGGIE *moves away.*) No, you needn't go; you can stop there if you like. There, there, my dear! Don't fret. (*aside*) She *is* a very charming girl. I almost wish I — I really begin to think I — no, no! Damn it, Cheviot! Not today.

MAGGIE: Oh! Mither, he told me he loved me!

CHEVIOT: So I did. The fact is, when I fell in love with you — don't go my pretty bird — I quite forgot that I was engaged. There, there! I thought at the time that you were the tree upon which the fruit of my heart was growing; but I was mistaken. Don't go; you needn't go on that account. It was another tree —

MAGGIE: Oh, mither, it was anither tree! (*weeping on CHEVIOT's shoulder*)

MRS MAC: Angus, it was anither tree! (*weeping on ANGUS's shoulder*)

ANGUS: Dinna, mither, dinna; I canna bear it! (*Weeps.*)

CHEVIOT: Yes, it was another tree — you can both remain there for the present — in point of fact, it was growing on both trees. I don't know how it is, but it seems to grow on a great many trees — a perfect orchard — and you are one of them, my dear. Come, come, don't fret, you are one of them!

(*Enter MINNIE and SYMPERSON.*)

MINNIE: Cheviot!

SYMP: What is all this?

CHEVIOT: (*rapidly referring to piece of paper given to him by MRS MACFAR-LANE, as if going over a washerwoman's bill*) 'Twenty-four pairs socks, two shirts, thirty-seven collars, one sheet, forty-four nightshirts, twenty-two flannel waistcoats, one white tie.' Ridiculous — quite ridiculous — I won't pay it.

MINNIE: Cheviot, who is this person who was found hanging on your neck? Say she is somebody — for instance, your sister or your aunt. Oh, Cheviot, say she is your aunt, I implore you!

(*The three cottagers curtsy and bow to MINNIE.*)

SYMP: Cheviot, say she is your aunt, I command you.

CHEVIOT: Oh, I beg your pardon. I didn't see you. These ladies are — are my washerwomen. Allow me to introduce them. They have come — they have come for their small account. (MAGGIE, *who has been sobbing through this, throws herself hysterically on to CHEVIOT's bosom.*) There's a discrepancy in the items — twenty-two flannel waistcoats are ridiculous, and, in short, some washerwomen are like this when they're contradicted — they can't help it — it's something in the suds: it undermines their constitution.

SYMP: (*sternly*) Cheviot, I should like to believe you, but it seems scarcely credible.

MAGGIE: Oh, sir, he's na' telling ye truly. I'm the puir Lowland lassie that he stole the hairt out of, three months ago, and promised to marry; and I love him sae weel — sae weel, and now he's married to anither!

CHEVIOT: Nothing of the kind. I —

SYMP: You are mistaken, and so is your mith — mother. He is not yet married to anith — nother.

MAGGIE: Why, sir, it took place before my very ain eyes, before us a', to a beautiful lady, three months since.

MINNIE: Cheviot, say that this is not true. Say that the beautiful lady was somebody — for instance, your aunt. Oh, say she was your aunt, I implore you!

SYMP: (*sternly*) Cheviot, say she was your aunt, I command you!

CHEVIOT: Minnie, Symperson, don't believe them — it was no marriage. I don't
even know the lady's name — I never saw her before — I've never seen her
since. It's ridiculous — I couldn't have married her without knowing it — it's
out of the question!

SYMP: Cheviot, let's know exactly where we are. I don't much care whom you
marry, so that you marry someone — that's enough for me. But please be
explicit, for this is business, and mustn't be trifled with. Tell me all about it.

CHEVIOT: (*in despair*) I cannot!

(*Enter* BELVAWNEY.)

BELV: I can.

SYMP: Belvawney!

BELV: I was present when Cheviot and a certain lady declared themselves to be
man and wife. This took place in a cottage on the border — in the presence of
these worthy people.

SYMP: That's enough for me. It's a Scotch marriage! Minnie, my child, we must
find you someone else. Cheviot's married. Belvawney, I am sorry to say, I
deprive you of your income.

BELV: I beg your pardon, not yet.

SYMP: Why not?

BELV: In the first place, it's not certain whether the cottage was in England or in
Scotland; in the second place, the bride can't be found.

SYMP: But she *shall* be found. What is her name?

BELV: That I decline to state.

SYMP: But you shall be made to state. I insist upon knowing the young lady's
name.

(*Enter* MISS TREHERNE, *in a light and cheerful dress.*)

BELV: (*amazed*) Belinda Treherne!

MISS TRE: (*rushing to* MINNIE) Minnie, my own old friend!

CHEVIOT: 'Tis she!

MISS TRE: (*turns and recognizes* CHEVIOT) My husband!

CHEVIOT: My wife!

(MISS TREHERNE *throws herself at* CHEVIOT's *feet, kissing his
hands rapturously.* BELVAWNEY *staggers back.* MINNIE *faints in
her father's arms.* MAGGIE *sobs on* ANGUS's *breast.*)

ACT III

The same as act II. BELVAWNEY *discovered with* MISS TREHERNE *and* MINNIE.
He is singing to them. MISS TREHERNE *is leaning romantically on piano.* MINNIE
is seated on a stool.

BELV: (*Sings.*) 'Says the old Obadiah to the young Obadiah,
I am drier, Obadiah, I am drier.'

CHORUS: 'I am drier.'
BELV: 'Says the young Obadiah to the old Obadiah,
               I'm on fire, Obadiah, I'm on fire.'
CHORUS: 'I'm on fire.'
MINNIE: Oh, thank you, Mr Belvawney. How sweetly pretty that is. Where can I
    get it?
MISS TRE: How marvellous is the power of melody over the soul that is fretted
    and harassed by anxiety and doubt. I can understand how valuable must have
    been the troubadours of old, in the troublous times of anarchy. Your song
    has soothed me, sir.
BELV: I am indeed glad to think that I have comforted you a little, dear ladies.
MINNIE: Dear Mr Belvawney, I don't know what we should have done without you.
    What with your sweet songs, your amusing riddles, and your clever conjuring
    tricks, the weary days of waiting have passed like a delightful dream.
MISS TRE: It is impossible to be dull in the society of one who can charm the soul
    with plaintive ballads one moment, and the next roll a rabbit and a guinea-pig
    into one.
BELV: You make me indeed happy, dear ladies. But my joy will be of brief
    duration, for Cheviot may return at any moment with the news that the fatal
    cottage was in Scotland, and then – Oh, Belinda, what is to become of me?
MISS TRE: How many issues depend on that momentous question? Has Belvawney
    a thousand a year, or is he ruined? Has your father that convenient addition
    to his income, or has he not? May Maggie marry Angus, or will her claim on
    Cheviot be satisfied? Are you to be his cherished bride, or are you destined to
    a life of solitary maidenhood? Am I Cheviot's honoured wife, or am I but a
    broken-hearted and desolate spinster? Who can tell! Who can tell! (*Crosses to*
    MINNIE.)
BELV: (*Goes to window in second drawing-room.*) Here is a cab with luggage – it is
    Cheviot! He has returned with the news! Ladies – one word before I go. One
    of you will be claimed by Cheviot, that is very clear. To that one (whichever
    it may be) I do not address myself – but to the other (whichever it may be), I
    say, I love you (whichever you are) with a fervour which I cannot describe in
    words. If you (whichever you are) will consent to cast your lot with mine, I
    will devote my life to proving that I love you and you only (whichever it may
    be) with a single-hearted and devoted passion, which precludes the possibility
    of my ever entertaining the slightest regard for any other woman in the whole
    world. I thought I would just mention it. Good morning! (*Exit.*)
MISS TRE: How beautifully he expresses himself. He is indeed a rare and radiant
    being.
MINNIE: (*nervously*) Oh, Belinda, the terrible moment is at hand.
MISS TRE: Minnie, if dear Cheviot should prove to be my husband, swear to me
    that that will not prevent your coming to stop with us – with dear Cheviot
    and me – whenever you can.
MINNIE: Indeed I will. And if it should turn out that dear Cheviot is at liberty to
    marry me, promise me that that will not prevent you looking on our house
    – on dear Cheviot's and mine – as your home.
MISS TRE: I swear it. We will be like dear, dear sisters.

(*Enter* CHEVIOT, *as from a journey, with bag and rug.*)

MISS TRE: Cheviot, tell me at once — are you my own — husband?

MINNIE: Cheviot — speak — is poor, simple little Minnie to be your bride?

CHEVIOT: Minnie, the hope of my heart, my pet fruit tree! Belinda, my Past, my Present, and my To Come! I have sorry news, sorry news.

MISS TRE: (*aside*) Sorry news! Then I am *not* his wife.

MINNIE: (*aside*) Sorry news! Then she *is* his wife.

CHEVIOT: My dear girls — my very dear girls, my journey has been fruitless — I have no information.

MISS TRE *and* MINNIE: No information!

CHEVIOT: None. The McQuibbigaskie has gone abroad!

(*Both ladies fall weeping.*)

MISS TRE: More weary waiting! More weary waiting!

MINNIE: Oh, my breaking heart; oh, my poor bruised and breaking heart!

CHEVIOT: We must be patient, dear Belinda. Minnie, my own, we must be patient. After all, is the situation so very terrible? Each of you has an even chance of becoming my wife, and in the meantime I look upon myself as engaged to both of you. I shall make no distinction. I shall love you both, fondly, and you shall both love me. My affection shall be divided equally between you, and we will be as happy as three little birds.

MISS TRE: (*wiping her eyes*) You are very kind and thoughtful, dear Cheviot.

MINNIE: I believe, in my simple little way, that you are the very best man in the whole world!

CHEVIOT: (*deprecatingly*) No, no.

MINNIE: Ah, but do let me think so: it makes me so happy to think so!

CHEVIOT: Does it? Well, well, be it so. Perhaps I am! And now tell me, how has the time passed since I left? Have my darlings been dull?

MISS TRE: We should have been dull indeed but for the airy Belvawney. The sprightly creature has done his best to make the lagging hours fly. He is an entertaining rattlesnake — I should say, rattletrap.

CHEVIOT: (*jealous*) Oh, *is* he so? Belvawney has been making the hours fly, has he? I'll make *him* fly, when I catch him!

MINNIE: His conjuring tricks are wonderful!

CHEVIOT: Confound his conjuring tricks!

MINNIE: Have you seen him bring a live hen, two hair brushes, and a pound and a half of fresh butter out of his pocket-handkerchief?

CHEVIOT: No, I have not had that advantage!

MISS TRE: It is a thrilling sight.

CHEVIOT: So I should be disposed to imagine! Pretty goings on in my absence! You seem to forget that you two girls are engaged to be married to *me*!

MISS TRE: Ah, Cheviot! Do not judge us harshly. We love you with a reckless fervour that thrills us to the very marrow — don't we, darling? But the hours crept heavily without you, and when, to lighten the gloom in which we were plunged, the kindly creature swallowed a live rabbit and brought it out, smothered in onions, from his left boot, we could not choose but smile. The good soul has promised to teach *me* the trick.

CHEVIOT: Has he? That's his confounded impudence. Now, once for all, I'll have nothing of this kind. One of you will be my wife, and until I know which, I will permit no Belvawneying of any kind whatever, or anything approaching thereto. When that is settled, the other may Belvawney until she is black in the face.

MISS TRE: And how long have we to wait before we shall know which of us may begin Belvawneying?

CHEVIOT: I can't say. It may be some time. The McQuibbigaskie has gone to Central Africa. No post can reach him, and he will not return for six years.

MISS TRE: Six years! Oh, I cannot wait six years! Why in six years I shall be eight-and-twenty!

MINNIE: Six years! Why in six years the Statute of Limitations will come in, and he can renounce us both.

MISS TRE: True; you are quite right. (*to* CHEVIOT) Cheviot, I have loved you madly, desperately, as other woman never loved other man. This poor inexperienced child, who clings to me as the ivy clings to the oak, also loves you as woman never loved before. Even that poor cottage maiden, whose rustic heart you so recklessly enslaved, worships you with a devotion that has no parallel in the annals of the heart. In return for all this unalloyed affection, all we ask of you is that you will recommend us to a respectable solicitor.

CHEVIOT: But, my dear children, reflect – I can't marry all three. I am most willing to consider myself engaged to all three, and that's as much as the law will allow. You see I do all I can. I'd marry all three of you with pleasure, if I might; but, as our laws stand at present, I'm sorry to say – I'm very sorry to say – it's out of the question. (*Exit.*)

MISS TRE: Poor fellow. He has my tenderest sympathy; but we have no alternative but to place ourselves under the protecting aegis of a jury of our countrymen!
(*Enter* SYMPERSON, *with two letters.*)

SYMP: Minnie – Miss Treherne – the post has just brought me two letters; one of them bears a Marseilles post-mark, and is, I doubt not, from the McQuibbigaskie! He must have written just before starting for Central Africa!

MINNIE: From the McQuibbigaskie? Oh, read, read!

MISS TRE: Oh, sir! How can you torture us by this delay? Have you no curiosity?

SYMP: Well, my dear, very little on this point; you see it don't much matter to me whom Cheviot marries. So that he marries someone, that's enough for me. But, however, *your* anxiety is natural, and I will gratify it. (*Opens letter and reads.*) 'Sir, – in reply to your letter, I have to inform you that Evan Cottage is certainly in England. The deeds relating to the property place this beyond all question.'

MINNIE: In England!

MISS TRE: (*sinking into a chair*) This blow is indeed a crusher. Against such a blow I cannot stand up! (*Faints.*)

MINNIE: (*on her knees*) My poor Belinda – my darling sister – love – oh forgive me – oh forgive me! Don't look like that! Speak to me, dearest – oh speak to me – speak to me.

MISS TRE: (*suddenly springing up*) Speak to you? Yes, I'll speak to you! All is *not* yet lost! True, he is not married to me, but why should he not be? I am as young as you! I am as beautiful as you! I have more money than you! I will try — oh how hard will I try!

MINNIE: Do, darling; and I wish — oh how I wish you may get him!

MISS TRE: Minnie, if you were not the dearest little friend I have in the world I could pinch you! (*Exit.*)

SYMP: (*who has been reading the other letter*) Dear me — how terrible!

MINNIE: What is terrible, dear papa?

SYMP: Belvawney writes to tell me the Indestructible Bank stopped payment yesterday, and Cheviot's shares are waste paper.

MINNIE: Well, upon my word. There's an end of *him*!

SYMP: An end of him. What do you mean? You are not going to throw him over?

MINNIE: Dear papa, I am sorry to disappoint you, but unless your tom-tit is very much mistaken, the Indestructible was not registered under the Joint-Stock Companies Act of Sixty-two, and in that case the shareholders are jointly and severally liable to the whole extent of their available capital. Poor little Minnie don't pretend to have a business head; but she's not *quite* such a little donkey as *that*, dear papa.

SYMP: You decline to marry him? Do I hear rightly?

MINNIE: I don't know, papa, whether your hearing is as good as it was, but from your excited manner, I should say you heard me perfectly. (*Exit.*)

SYMP: This is a pretty business! Done out of a thousand a year; and by my own daughter! What a terrible thing is this incessant craving after money! Upon my word, some people seem to think that they're sent into the world for no other purpose but to acquire wealth; and, by Jove, they'll sacrifice their nearest and dearest relations to get it. It's most humiliating — most humiliating!

(*Enter* CHEVIOT, *in low spirits.*)

CHEVIOT: (*throwing himself into a chair; sobs aloud*) Oh Uncle Symperson, have you heard the news?

SYMP: (*angrily*) Yes, I *have* heard the news; and a pretty man of business *you* are to invest all your property in an unregistered company!

CHEVIOT: Uncle, don't *you* turn against me! Belinda is not my wife! I'm a ruined man; and my darlings — my three darlings, whom I love with a fidelity, which, in these easy-going days, is simply Quixotic — will have nothing to say to me. Minnie, your daughter, declines to accompany me to the altar. Belinda, I feel sure will revert to Belvawney, and Maggie is at this present moment hanging round that Scotch idiot's neck, although she knows that in doing so she simply tortures me. Symperson, I never loved three girls as I loved those three — never! never! and now they'll all three slip through my fingers — I'm sure they will!

SYMP: Pooh, pooh, sir. Do you think nobody loses but you? Why, I'm done out of a thousand a year by it.

CHEVIOT: (*moodily*) For that matter, Symperson, I've a very vivid idea that you won't have to wait long for the money.

SYMP: What d'you mean? Oh — of course — I understand.

CHEVIOT: Eh?

SYMP: Mrs Macfarlane! I have thought of her myself. A very fine woman for her years; a majestic ruin, beautiful in decay. My dear boy, my very dear boy, I congratulate you.

CHEVIOT: Don't be absurd. I'm not going to marry anybody.

SYMP: Eh! Why, then how — ? I don't think I quite follow you.

CHEVIOT: There is another contingency on which you come into the money. My death.

SYMP: To be sure! I never thought of that! And, as you say, a man can die but once.

CHEVIOT: I beg your pardon. I didn't say anything of the kind — you said it; but it's true, for all that.

SYMP: I'm very sorry; but, of course, if you have made up your mind to it —

CHEVIOT: Why, when a man's lost everything, what has he to live for?

SYMP: True, true. Nothing whatever. Still —

CHEVIOT: His money gone, his credit gone, the three girls he's engaged to gone.

SYMP: I cannot deny it. It is a hopeless situation. Hopeless, quite hopeless.

CHEVIOT: His happiness wrecked, his hopes blighted; the three trees upon which the fruit of his heart was growing — all cut down. What is left but suicide?

SYMP: True, true! You're quite right. Farewell (*going*).

CHEVIOT: Symperson, you seem to think I *want* to kill myself. I don't want to do anything of the kind. I'd much rather live — upon my soul I would — if I could think of any reason for living. Symperson, can't you think of *something* to check the heroic impulse which is at this moment urging me to a tremendous act of self-destruction?

SYMP: Something! Of course I can! Say that you throw yourself into the Serpentine — which is handy. Well, it's an easy way of going out of the world, I'm told — rather pleasant than otherwise, I believe — quite an agreeable sensation, I'm given to understand. But you — you get wet through; and your — your clothes are absolutely ruined!

CHEVIOT: (*mournfully*) For that matter, I could take off my clothes before I went in.

SYMP: True, so you could. I never thought of that. You could take them off before you go in — there's no reason why you shouldn't, if you do it in the dark — and *that* objection falls to the ground. Cheviot, my lion-hearted boy, it's impossible to resist your arguments, they are absolutely convincing. (*Shakes his hand. Exit.*)

CHEVIOT: Good fellow, Symperson — I like a man who's open to conviction! But it's no use — all my attractions are gone — and I can *not* live unless I feel I'm fascinating. Still, there's one chance left — Belinda! I haven't tried her. Perhaps, after all, she loved me for myself alone! It isn't likely — but it's barely possible.

(*Enter* BELVAWNEY, *who has overheard these words.*)

BELV: Out of the question; you are too late! I represented to her that you are never likely to induce anyone to marry you now that you are penniless. She felt that my income was secure, and she gave me her hand and her heart.

CHEVIOT: Then all is lost; my last chance is gone, and the irrevocable die is cast! Be happy with her, Belvawney; be happy with her!

BELV: Happy! You shall dine with us after our honeymoon and judge for yourself.

CHEVIOT: No, I shall not do that; long before you return I shall be beyond the reach of dinners.

BELV: I understand — you are going abroad. Well, I don't think you could do better than try another country.

CHEVIOT: (*tragically*) Belvawney, I'm going to try another world! (*drawing a pistol from his pocket*)

BELV: (*alarmed*) What do you mean?

CHEVIOT: In two minutes I die!

BELV: You're joking, of course?

CHEVIOT: Do I look like a man who jokes? Is my frame of mind one in which a man indulges in trivialities?

BELV: (*in great terror*) But my dear Cheviot, reflect —

CHEVIOT: Why should it concern you? You will be happy with Belinda. You will not be well off, but Symperson will, and I dare say he will give you a meal now and then. It will not be a nice meal, but still it will be a meal.

BELV: Cheviot, you mustn't do this; pray reflect; there are interests of magnitude depending on your existence.

CHEVIOT: My mind is made up (*cocking the pistol*).

BELV: (*wildly*) But I shall be ruined!

CHEVIOT: There is Belinda's fortune.

BELV: She won't have me if I'm ruined! Dear Cheviot, don't do it — it's culpable — it's wrong!

CHEVIOT: Life is valueless to me without Belinda (*pointing the pistol to his head*).

BELV: (*desperately*) You shall have Belinda; she is much — very much to me, but she is not everything. Your life is very dear to me; and when I think of our old friendship — ! Cheviot, you shall have anything you like, if you'll only consent to live!

CHEVIOT: If I thought you were in earnest; but no — no (*putting pistol to head*).

BELV: In earnest? Of course I'm in earnest! Why what's the use of Belinda to me if I'm ruined? Why she wouldn't look at me.

CHEVIOT: But perhaps if I'm ruined, she wouldn't look at *me*.

BELV: Cheviot, I'll confess all, if you'll only live. You — you are *not* ruined!

CHEVIOT: Not ruined?

BELV: Not ruined. I — I invented the statement.

CHEVIOT: (*in great delight*) You invented the statement? My dear friend! My very dear friend! I'm very much obliged to you! Oh, thank you, thank you a thousand times! Oh, Belvawney, you have made me very, very happy! (*sobbing on his shoulder, then suddenly springing up*) But what the devil did you mean by circulating such a report about me? How dare you do it, sir? Answer me that, sir.

BELV: I did it to gain Belinda's love. I knew that the unselfish creature loved you for your wealth alone.

CHEVIOT: It was a liberty, sir; it was a liberty. To put it mildly, it was a liberty.

BELV: It was. You're quite right — that's the word for it — it was a liberty. But I'll go and undeceive her at once. (*Exit.*)

CHEVIOT: Well, as I've recovered my fortune, and with it my tree, I'm about the happiest fellow in the world. My money, my mistress, and my mistress's money, all my own. I believe I could go mad with joy!

> (*Enter* SYMPERSON *in deep black; he walks pensively, with a white handkerchief to his mouth.*)

CHEVIOT: What's the matter?

SYMP: Hallo! You're still alive?

CHEVIOT: Alive? Yes; why, (*noticing his dress*) is anything wrong?

SYMP: No, no, my dear young friend, these clothes are symbolical; they represent my state of mind. After your terrible threat, which I cannot doubt you intend to put at once into execution —

CHEVIOT: My dear uncle, this is very touching; this unmans me. But, cheer up, dear old friend, I have good news for you.

SYMP: (*alarmed*) Good news? What do you mean?

CHEVIOT: I am about to remove the weight of sorrow which hangs so heavily at your heart. Resume your fancy check trousers — I have consented to live.

SYMP: Consented to live? Why, sir, this is confounded trifling. I don't understand this line of conduct at all; you threaten to commit suicide; your friends are dreadfully shocked at first, but eventually their minds become reconciled to the prospect of losing you, they become resigned, even cheerful; and when they have brought themselves to this Christian state of mind, you coolly inform them that you have changed your mind, and mean to live. It's not business, sir — it's not business.

CHEVIOT: But, my dear uncle, I've nothing to commit suicide for; I'm a rich man, and Belinda will, no doubt, accept me with joy and gratitude.

SYMP: Belinda will do nothing of the kind. She has just left the house with Belvawney, in a cab, and under the most affectionate circumstances.

CHEVIOT: (*alarmed*) Left with Belvawney? Where have they gone?

SYMP: I don't know. Very likely to get married.

CHEVIOT: Married?

SYMP: Yes, before the registrar.

CHEVIOT: I've been sold! I see that now! Belvawney has done me! But I'm not the kind of man who stands such treatment quietly. Belvawney has found his match. Symperson, they may get married, but they shall not be happy; I'll be revenged on them both before they're twenty-four hours older. She marries him because she thinks his income is secure. I'll show her she's wrong; I won't blow out my brains; I'll do worse.

SYMP: What?

CHEVIOT: I'll marry.

SYMP: Marry?

CHEVIOT: Anybody. I don't care who it is.

SYMP: Will Minnie do?

CHEVIOT: Minnie will do; send her here.

SYMP: In one moment, my dear boy — in one moment! (*Exit, hurriedly.*)

CHEVIOT: Belinda alone in a cab with Belvawney! It's maddening to think of it! He's got his arm round her waist at this moment, if I know anything of human nature! I can't stand it — I cannot and I will not stand it! I'll write at once to the registrar and tell him she's married. (*Sits at writing table and pre-*

pares to write.) Oh, why am I constant by disposition? Why is it that when I love a girl I can think of no other girl but that girl, whereas, when a girl loves me she seems to entertain the same degree of affection for mankind at large? I'll never be constant again; henceforth I fascinate but to deceive!

(*Enter* MINNIE.)

MINNIE: Mr Cheviot Hill, papa tells me that you wish to speak to me.

CHEVIOT: (*hurriedly – writing at table*) I do. Miss Symperson, I have no time to beat about the bush; I must come to the point at once. You rejected me a short time since – I will not pretend that I am pleased with you for rejecting me – on the contrary, I think it was in the worst taste. However, let bygones be bygones. Unforeseen circumstances render it necessary that I should marry at once, and you'll do. An early answer will be esteemed, as this is business. (*Resumes his writing.*)

MINNIE: Mr Hill, dear papa assures me that the report about the loss of your money is incorrect. I hope this may be the case, but I cannot forget that the information comes from dear papa. Now dear papa is the best and dearest papa in the whole world, but he has a lively imagination, and when he wants to accomplish his purpose, he does not hesitate to invent – I am not quite sure of the word, but I think it is 'bouncers'.

CHEVIOT: (*writing*) You are quite right, the word is bouncers. Bouncers or bangers – either will do.

MINNIE: Then forgive my little silly fancies, Mr Hill; but, before I listen to your suggestion, I must have the very clearest proof that your position is, in every way, fully assured.

CHEVIOT: Mercenary little donkey! I will not condescend to proof. I renounce her altogether. (*Rings bell.*)

(*Enter* MAGGIE *with* ANGUS *and* MRS MACFARLANE. ANGUS *has his arm round her waist.*)

CHEVIOT: (*suddenly seeing her*) Maggie, come here. Angus, do take your arm from round that girl's waist. Stand back, and don't you listen. Maggie, three months ago I told you that I loved you passionately; today I tell you that I love you as passionately as ever; I may add that I am still a rich man. Can you oblige me with a postage-stamp? (MAGGIE *gives him a stamp from her pocket – he sticks it on to his letter.*) What do you say? I must trouble you for an immediate answer, as this is not pleasure – it's business.

MAGGIE: Oh, sir, ye're ower late. Oh, Maister Cheviot, if I'd only ken'd it before! Oh, sir, I love ye right weel; the bluid o' my hairt is nae sae dear to me as thou (*sobbing on his shoulder*). Oh, Cheviot, my ain auld love! My ain auld love!

ANGUS: (*aside*) Puir lassie, it just dra's the water from my ee' to hear her. Oh, mither, mither! My hairt is just breaking. (*Sobs on* MRS MACFARLANE's *shoulder.*)

CHEVIOT: But why is it too late? You say that you love me. I offer to marry you. My station in life is at least equal to your own. What is to prevent our union?

MAGGIE: (*wiping her eyes*) Oh, sir, ye're unco guid to puir little Maggie, but ye're too late; for she's placed the matter in her solicitor's hands, and he tells her that an action for breach will just bring damages to the tune of a thousand pound. There's a laddie waiting outside noo, to serve the bonnie writ on ye! (*Turns affectionately to* ANGUS.)

CHEVIOT: (*falling sobbing on to sofa*) No one will marry me. There is a curse upon me – a curse upon me. No one will marry me – no, not one!

MRS MAC: Dinna say that, sir. There's mony a woman – nae young, soft, foolish lassie, neither; but grown women o' sober age, who'd be mair a mither than a wife to ye; and that's what ye want, puir laddie, for ye're no equal to takin' care o' yersel'.

CHEVIOT: Mrs Macfarlane, you are right. I am a man of quick impulse. I see, I feel, I speak. I – you are the tree upon which – that is to say – no, no, d–n it, I can't; I can't! One must draw the line somewhere (*turning from her with disgust*).*

> (*Enter* MISS TREHERNE *and* BELVAWNEY. *They are followed by* SYMPERSON *and* MINNIE.)

CHEVIOT: Belinda! Can I believe my eyes? You have returned to me, you have not gone off with Belvawney after all? Thank heaven, thank heaven!

MISS TRE: I thought that, as I came in, I heard you say something about a tree.

CHEVIOT: You are right. As you entered I was remarking that I am a man of quick impulse. I see, I feel, I speak. I have two thousand a year, and I love you passionately. I lay my hand, my heart, and my income, all together, at your feet!

MISS TRE: Cheviot, I love you with an irresistible fervour, that seems to parch my very existence. I love you as I never loved man before, and as I can never hope to love man again. But, in the belief that you were ruined, I went with my own adored Belvawney before the registrar, and that registrar has just made us one! (*Turns affectionately to* BELVAWNEY.)

BELV: (*Embraces* MISS TREHERNE.) Bless him for it – bless him for it!

CHEVIOT: (*deadly calm*) One word. I have not yet seen the letter that blights my earthly hopes. For form's sake, I trust I may be permitted to cast my eye over that document? As a matter of business – that's all.

BELV: Certainly. Here it is. You will find the situation of the cottage described in unmistakeable terms. (*Hands the letter to* CHEVIOT.)

CHEVIOT: (*Reads.*) 'In reply to your letter I have to inform you that Evan Cottage is certainly in England. The deeds relating to the property place this beyond all question.' Thank you; I am satisfied. (*Takes out pistol.*)

BELV: Now, sir, perhaps you will kindly release that young lady. She is my wife! (CHEVIOT*'s arm has crept mechanically round* MISS TREHERNE*'s waist.*)

MISS TRE: Oh, Cheviot! Kindly release me – I am his wife!

CHEVIOT: Crushed! Crushed! Crushed!

SYMP: (*looking over his shoulder at letter, reads*) 'Turn over.'

CHEVIOT: (*despairingly*) Why should I? What good would it do? Oh! I see. I beg your pardon! (*Turns over the page.*) Halloa! (*Rises.*)

ALL: What?

---

*French has: 'MRS MAC: But you needn't draw the line at me!'

CHEVIOT: (*Reads.*) 'P.S. – I may add that the border line runs through the property. The cottage is undoubtedly in England, though the garden is in Scotland.'

MISS TRE: And we were married in the garden!

CHEVIOT: Belinda, we were married in the garden!

> (MISS TREHERNE *leaves* BELVAWNEY, *and turns affectionately to* CHEVIOT, *who embraces her.*)

BELV: Belinda, stop a bit! Don't leave me like this!

MISS TRE: (*Crosses to* BELVAWNEY.) Belvawney, I love you with an intensity of devotion that I firmly believe will last while I live. But dear Cheviot is my husband now; he has a claim upon me which it would be impossible – nay, criminal – to resist. Farewell, Belvawney; Minnie may yet be yours! (BELVAWNEY *turns sobbing to* MINNIE, *who comforts him;* MISS TREHERNE *crosses back to* CHEVIOT.) Cheviot – my husband – my own old love – if the devotion of a lifetime can atone for the misery of the last few days, it is yours, with every wifely sentiment of pride, gratitude, admiration, and love.

CHEVIOT: (*embracing her*) My own! My own! Tender blossom of my budding hopes! Star of my life! Essence of happiness! Tree upon which the fruit of my heart is growing! My Past, my Present, my To Come!

> (*Picture.* – CHEVIOT *embracing* MISS TREHERNE. BELVAWNEY *is being comforted by* MINNIE. ANGUS *is solacing* MAGGIE, *and* MRS MACFARLANE *is reposing on* MR SYMPERSON's *bosom.*)

VII *Rosencrantz and Guildenstern.* Sketch by Moyr Smith of a performance at the Prince's Hall on 19 November 1891, published in *Black and White*, 28 November 1891. The cast was identical with that of the original production at the Vaudeville on 3 June 1891, with the exception of Henry Dana who replaced S. Herberte-Basing as Rosencrantz

ROSENCRANTZ AND GUILDENSTERN*

A tragic episode in three tableaux, founded on an old
Danish legend

First performed in public at a matinée, on behalf of the 'Serpent' Fund, at the
Vaudeville Theatre, London, on 3 June 1891, with the following cast:

KING CLAUDIUS of Denmark	Mr Alexander Watson
QUEEN GERTRUDE of Denmark	Mrs Theodore Wright
HAMLET, Queen Gertrude's son —	
betrothed to Ophelia	Mr Frank Lloyd
ROSENCRANTZ, a courtier, in love with	
Ophelia	Mr S. Herberte-Basing
GUILDENSTERN, a courtier	Mr C. Lambourne
FIRST PLAYER	Mr C. Stewart
SECOND PLAYER	Miss Bessie
OPHELIA	Miss Mary Bessie
Courtiers, pages, etc.	

Later produced at the Court Theatre, London, on 27 April 1892, with the following
cast:

KING CLAUDIUS	Mr R. Brandon Thomas
QUEEN GERTRUDE	Miss Gertrude Kingston
HAMLET	Mr Weedon Grossmith
ROSENCRANTZ	Mr Elliot
GUILDENSTERN	Mr C.P. Little
FIRST PLAYER	Mr W.L. Branscombe
SECOND PLAYER	Miss May Palfrey
POLONIUS	Mr R. Rochfort
OPHELIA	Miss Decima Moore

Scenery painted by Mr W. Callcott

The stage is under the direction of Mr Brandon Thomas

---

*Text used: *Original Plays* third series (1895, reissued 1909), collated with *Foggerty's Fairy
and Other Tales* (1890) (*FF*).

FIRST TABLEAU

Interior of KING CLAUDIUS*'s palace.* CLAUDIUS *discovered seated in a gloomy
attitude.* QUEEN GERTRUDE *on a stool at his feet, consoling him.*

QUEEN: Nay, be not sad, my lord!
KING: Sad, lovëd Queen?
           If by an effort of the will I could
           Annul the ever-present past — disperse
           The gaunt and gloomy ghosts of bygone deeds,
           Or bind them with imperishable chains
           In caverns of the past incarcerate,
           Then could I smile again — but not till then!
QUEEN: Oh, my dear lord!
           If aught there be that gives thy soul unrest,
           Tell it to me.
KING: Well-loved and faithful wife,
           Tender companion of my faltering life,
           Yes; I *can* trust thee! Listen, then, to me:
           Many years since — when but a headstrong lad —
           I wrote a five-act tragedy.
QUEEN: (*interested*)   Indeed?
KING: A play, writ by a king —
QUEEN: And *such* a king! —
KING: Finds ready market. It was read at once,
           But ere 'twas read, accepted. Then the Press
           Teemed with portentous import. Elsinore
           Was duly placarded by willing hands;
           We know that walls have ears — I gave them tongues —
           And they were eloquent with promises.
QUEEN: Even the *dead* walls?
KING: (*solemnly*)   Ay, the deader they,
           The louder they proclaimed!
QUEEN: (*appalled*)   Oh, marvellous!
KING: The day approached — all Denmark stood agape.
           Arrangements were devised at once by which
           Seats might be booked a twelvemonth in advance.
           The first night came.
QUEEN: And did the play succeed?
KING: In one sense, yes.
QUEEN: Oh, I was sure of it!
KING: A farce was given to play the people in —
           My tragedy succeeded that. That's all!
QUEEN: And how long did it run?
KING: About ten minutes.
           Ere the first act had traced one-half its course
           The curtain fell, never to rise again!
QUEEN: And did the people hiss?

KING: No — worse than that —
They laughed. Sick with the shame that covered me,
I knelt down, palsied, in my private box,
And prayed the hearsed and catacombëd dead
Might quit their vaults, and claim me for their own!
But it was not to be.

QUEEN: Oh, my good lord,
The house was surely packed!

KING: It was — by me.
My favourite courtiers crowded every place —
From floor to floor the house was peopled by
The sycophantic crew. My tragedy
Was more than even sycophants could stand!

QUEEN: Was it, my lord, so very, very bad?

KING: Not to deceive my trusting Queen, it was.

QUEEN: And when the play failed, didst thou take no steps
To set thyself right with the world?

KING: I did.
The acts were five — though by five acts too long,
I wrote an act by way of epilogue —
An act by which the penalty of death
Was meted out to all who sneered at it.
The play was not good — but the punishment
Of those that laughed at it was capital.

QUEEN: Think on't no more, my lord. Now, mark me well:
To cheer our son, whose solitary tastes
And tendency to long soliloquy
Have much alarmed us, I, unknown to thee,
Have sent for Rosencrantz and Guildenstern —
Two merry knaves, kin to Polonius,
Who will devise such revels in our court —
Such antic schemes of harmless merriment —
As shall abstract his meditative mind
From sad employment. Claudius, who can tell
But that they may divert my lord as well?
Ah, they are here!
      (*Enter* GUILDENSTERN.)

GUILD: My homage to the Queen!
      (*Enter* ROSENCRANTZ.)

ROS: (*kneeling*) In hot obedience to the royal 'hest
We have arrived, prepared to do our best.

QUEEN: We welcome you to court. Our Chamberlain
Shall see that you are suitably disposed.
Here is his daughter. She will hear your will
And see that it receives fair countenance.
      (*Exeunt* KING *and* QUEEN, *lovingly.*)
      (*Enter* OPHELIA.)

ROS: Ophelia!
    (*Both embrace her.*)
OPH: (*delighted and surprised*) Rosencrantz and Guildenstern!
    This meeting likes me much. We have not met
    Since we were babies!
ROS: The Queen hath summoned us,
    And I have come in a half-hearted hope
    That I may claim once more my baby-love!
OPH: Alas, I am betrothed!
ROS: Betrothed! To whom?
OPH: To Hamlet!
ROS: Oh, incomprehensible!
    Thou lovest Hamlet?
OPH: (*demurely*)   Nay, I said not so —
    I said we were betrothed.
GUILD: And what's he like?
OPH: Alike for no two seasons at a time.
    Sometimes he's tall — sometimes he's very short —
    Now with black hair — now with a flaxen wig —
    Sometimes an English accent — then a French —
    Then English with a strong provincial 'burr'.
    Once an American, and once a Jew —
    But Danish never, take him how you will!
    And strange to say, whate'er his tongue may be,
    Whether he's dark or flaxen — English — French —
    Though we're in Denmark, AD, ten — six — two —
    He always dresses as King James the First!
GUILD: Oh, he is surely mad!
OPH: Well, there again
    Opinion is divided. Some men hold
    That he's the sanest, far, of all sane men —
    Some that he's really sane, but shamming mad —
    Some that he's really mad, but shamming sane —
    Some that he will be mad, some that he *was* —
    Some that he couldn't be. But on the whole
    (As far as I can make out what they mean)
    The favourite theory's somewhat like this:
    Hamlet is idiotically sane
    With lucid intervals of lunacy.
ROS: We must devise some plan to stop this match!
GUILD: Stay! Many years ago, King Claudius
    Was guilty of a five-act tragedy.
    The play was damned, and none may mention it
    Under the pain of death. We might contrive
    To make him play this piece before the King,
    And take the consequences.
ROS: Impossible!

                    For every copy was destroyed.
OPH: But one —
My father's!
ROS: Eh?
OPH: In his capacity
As our Lord Chamberlain* he has *one* copy.† I
This night, when all the court is drowned in sleep,
Will creep with stealthy foot into his den
And there abstract the precious manuscript!
GUILD: The plan is well conceived.‡ But take good heed,
Your father may detect you.
OPH: Oh, dear, no.
My father spends his long official days
In reading all the rubbishing new plays.
From ten to four at work he may be found:
And then — my father sleeps exceeding sound!
              (*Picture.* — OPHELIA, ROSENCRANTZ *and* GUILDENSTERN,
              grouped.)

        SECOND TABLEAU

Enter QUEEN, *meeting* ROSENCRANTZ *and* GUILDENSTERN.
QUEEN: Have you as yet planned aught that may relieve
Our poor afflicted son's despondency?
ROS: Madam, we've lost no time. Already we
Are getting up some court theatricals
In which the Prince will play a leading part.
QUEEN: That's well-bethought — it will divert his mind.
But soft — he comes.
ROS: How gloomily he stalks,
As one o'erwhelmed with weight of anxious care.
He thrusts his hand into his bosom — thus —
Starts — looks around — then, as if reassured,
Rumples his hair and rolls his glassy eyes!
QUEEN: (*appalled*) That means — he's going to soliloquize!
Prevent this, gentlemen, by any means!
GUILD: We will, but how?
QUEEN: Anticipate his points,
And follow out his argument for him;
Thus will you cut the ground from 'neath his feet
And leave him nought to say.
ROS *and* GUILD: We will! — We will! (*They kneel.*)

---

*All bow reverentially at mention of this functionary.
† *FF* has: 'As Chamberlain', and no footnote.
‡ *FF* has: 'That's well bethought, in truth.'

QUEEN: A mother's blessing be upon you, sirs! (*Exit.*)

ROS: (*both rising*) Now, Guildenstern, apply thee to this task.
> (*Music. Enter* HAMLET. *He stalks to chair, throws himself into it.*)

HAMLET: To be — or not to be!

ROS: Yes — that's the question* —
> Whether he's bravest who will cut his throat
> Rather than suffer all —

GUILD: Or suffer all
> Rather than cut his throat?

HAMLET: (*Annoyed at interruption, says,* 'Go away — go away!'† *then resumes.*)
> To die — to sleep —

ROS: It's nothing more — Death is but sleep spun out —
> Why hesitate? (*Offers him a dagger.*)

GUILD: The only question is
> Between the choice of deaths, which death to choose. (*Offers a revolver.*)‡

HAMLET: (*in great terror*) Do take those dreadful things away. They make
> My blood run cold. Go away — go away!
>> (*They turn aside.* HAMLET *resumes.*)
> To sleep, perchance to —

ROS: Dream.
> That's very true. I never dream myself,
> But Guildenstern dreams all night long out loud.

GUILD: (*coming down and kneeling*) With blushes, sir, I do confess it true!

HAMLET: This question, gentlemen, concerns me not.
> (*Resumes.*) For who would bear the whips and scorns of time —

ROS: (*as guessing a riddle*) Who'd bear the whips and scorns? Now, let me see.
> Who'd *bear* them, eh?

GUILD: (*same business*) Who'd bear the *scorns* of time?

ROS: (*correcting him*) The *whips* and scorns.

GUILD: The whips and scorns, of course.
>> (HAMLET *about to protest.*)
> Don't tell us — let us guess — the *whips* of time?

HAMLET: Oh, sirs, this interruption likes us not.
> I pray you give it up.

ROS: My lord, we do.
> We cannot tell *who* bears these whips and scorns.

HAMLET: (*Not heeding them, resumes.*) But that the dread of something *after* death —

ROS: That's true — *post mortem* and the coroner —
> *Felo-de-se* — cross roads at twelve p.m. —
> And then the forfeited life policy —

---

*FF has: 'that's the point'.

† FF omits 'Go away — go away!'

‡ FF has: '(*Offers another.*)' [i.e. dagger].

        Exceedingly unpleasant.

HAMLET: (*really angry*)   Gentlemen,
        It must be patent to the merest dunce
        Three persons can't soliloquize at once!
           (ROSENCRANTZ *and* GUILDENSTERN *retire,* GUILDENSTERN
           goes off.)
        (*aside*) They're playing on me! Playing upon *me*
        Who am not fashioned to be played upon!
        Show them a pipe — a thing of holes and stops
        Made to be played on — and they'll shrink abashed
        And swear they have not skill on that! Now mark —
        (*aloud*) Rosencrantz! Here! (*producing a flute as* ROSENCRANTZ
        comes)
                  This is a well-toned flute;
        Play me an air upon it. Do not say
        You know not *how*! (*sneeringly*)

ROS: Nay, but I *do* know how.
        I'm rather good upon the flute — Observe —
           (*Plays eight bars of hornpipe,* then politely returns flute to*
           HAMLET.)

HAMLET: (*peevishly*)† Oh, thankye. (*aside*) Everything goes wrong!
           (*Retires, and throws himself on dais, as if buried in soliloquy.*)
           (*Enter* OPHELIA, *white with terror, holding a heavy MS.*)

OPH: Rosencrantz!

ROS: Well?

OPH: (*in a stage whisper*)   I've found the manuscript,
        But never put me to such work again!

ROS: Why, what has happened that you tremble so?

OPH: Last night I stole down from my room alone
        And sought my father's den. I entered it!
        The clock struck twelve, and then — oh, horrible! —
        From chest and cabinet there issued forth
        The mouldy spectres of five thousand plays,
        All dead and gone — and many of them damned!
        I shook with horror! They encompassed me,
        Chattering forth the scenes and parts of scenes
        Which my poor father wisely had cut out.
        Oh, horrible — oh, 'twas most horrible! (*covering her face*)

ROS: What was't they uttered?

OPH: (*severely*)   I decline to say.
        The more I heard the more convinced was I
        My father acted *most judiciously*;
        Let that suffice thee.

---

*FF has: '*Plays an elaborate "roulade"* '.
†*FF* has: '(*snatching it from him, peevishly*) Bah! Everything goes wrong!'

ROS: Give me, then, the play,
          And I'll submit it to the Prince.
OPH: (*crossing to him*)   But stay,
          Do not appear to urge him — hold him back,
          Or he'll decline to play the piece — I know him.
HAMLET: (*who has been soliloquizing under his breath*) And lose the name of
          action! (*Rises and comes down stage.*)
                                              Why, what's that?
ROS: We have been looking through some dozen plays
          To find one suited to our company.
          This is, my lord, a five-act tragedy.
          'Tis called 'Gonzago' — but it will not serve —
          'Tis very long.
HAMLET: Is there a part for *me*?
OPH: There is, my lord, a most important part —
          A mad Archbishop who becomes a Jew
          To spite his diocese.
HAMLET: That's very good!
ROS: (*turning over the pages*) Here you go mad — and then, soliloquize:
          Here you are sane again — and then you don't:
          Then, later on, you stab your aunt, because —
          Well, I can't tell you *why* you stab your aunt,
          But still — you stab her.
HAMLET: That is quite enough.
ROS: Then you become the leader of a troop
          Of Greek banditti — and soliloquize —
          After a long and undisturbed career
          Of murder (tempered by soliloquy)
          You see the sin and folly of your ways
          And offer to resume your diocese;
          But, just too late — for, terrible to tell,
          As you're repenting (in soliloquy)
          The Bench of Bishops seize you unawares
          And blow you from a gun!
               (*During this* HAMLET *has acted in pantomime the scenes described.*)
HAMLET: (*excitedly*)   That's excellent.
          That's very good indeed — we'll play this piece!
          (*taking MS. from* ROSENCRANTZ)
OPH: But, pray consider — all the other parts
          Are insignificant.
HAMLET: What matters that?
          We'll play this piece.
ROS: The plot's impossible,
          And all the dialogue bombastic stuff.
HAMLET: I tell you, sir, that we will play this piece.
          Bestir yourselves about it, and engage
          All the most fairly famed tragedians

> To play the small parts — as tragedians should.
> A mad Archbishop! Yes, that's very good!
>> (*Picture.* — HAMLET, *reading the MS. with limelight on him.*
>> ROSENCRANTZ *at entrance,* OPHELIA *at entrance.*)

THIRD TABLEAU

*March.** *Enter procession. First, two* PAGES, *who place themselves on each side of
the platform; then* ROSENCRANTZ *and* OPHELIA: *then* GUILDENSTERN *and a
LADY; then other* COURTIERS; *then* POLONIUS, *backing before the* KING *and*
QUEEN. *The* KING *sits, the* QUEEN *on his left,* OPHELIA *on his right,* ROSEN-
CRANTZ *stands above her,* GUILDENSTERN *and* POLONIUS *behind the* KING
and QUEEN: *the* COURTIERS *right and left.*

QUEEN: A fair good morrow to you, Rosencrantz.
           How march the royal revels?

ROS: Lamely, madam, lamely, like a one-legged duck. The Prince has discovered a
     strange play. He hath called it, 'A Right Reckoning Long Delayed'.

KING: And of what fashion is the Prince's play?

ROS: 'Tis an excellent poor tragedy, my lord — a thing of shreds and patches
     welded into a form that hath mass without consistency, like an ill-built villa.

QUEEN: But, sir, you should have used your best endeavours
           To wean his phantasy from such a play.

ROS: Madam, I did, and with some success, for he now seeth the absurdity of its
     tragical catastrophes, and laughs at it as freely as we do. So, albeit the poor
     author had hoped to have drawn tears of sympathy, the Prince has resolved to
     present it as a piece of pompous folly intended to excite no loftier emotion
     than laughter and surprise. Here comes the royal tragedian with his troop.
                         (*Enter* HAMLET *and* PLAYERS.)

HAMLET: Good morrow, sir. This is our company of players. They have come to
     town to do honour and add completeness to our revels.

KING: Good sirs, we welcome you to Elsinore.
           Prepare you now — we are agog to taste
           The intellectual treat in store for us.

HAMLET: We are ready, sir. But, before we begin, I would speak a word to you
     who are to play this piece. I have chosen this play in the face of sturdy oppo-
     sition from my well-esteemed friends, who were for playing a piece with less
     bombastick fury and more frolick. (*addressing* KING) But I have thought this
     a fit play to be presented by reason of that very pedantical bombast and
     windy obtrusive rhetorick that they do rightly despise. For I hold that there
     is no such antick fellow as your bombastical hero who doth so earnestly
     spout forth his folly as to make his hearers believe that he is unconscious of
     all incongruity; whereas, he who doth so mark, label, and underscore his
     antick speeches as to show that he is alive to their absurdity seemeth to utter

---

FF has: 'Room in the Palace prepared for a stage performance. Enter KING CLAUDIUS *and*
QUEEN, *meeting* ROSENCRANTZ.'

them under protest, and to take part with his audience against himself. (*turning to* PLAYERS) For which reason, I pray you, let there be no huge red noses, nor extravagant monstrous wigs, nor coarse men garbed as women, in this comi-tragedy; for such things are as much as to say, 'I am a comick fellow — I pray you laugh at me, and hold what I say to be cleverly ridiculous.' Such labelling of humour is an impertinence to your audience, for it seemeth to imply that they are unable to recognize a joke unless it be pointed out to them. I pray you avoid it.

> (*Slight applause, which* HAMLET *acknowledges.*)

1st PLAYER: Sir, we are beholden to you for your good counsels. But we would urge upon your consideration that we are accomplished players, who have spent many years in learning our profession; and we would venture to suggest that it would better befit your lordship to confine yourself to such matters as your lordship may be likely to understand. We, on our part, may have our own ideas as to the duties of heirs-apparent; but it would ill become us to air them before your lordship, who may be reasonably supposed to understand such matters more perfectly than your very humble servants.

> (*All applaud vigorously.* HAMLET *about to explode in anger.* KING *interrupts him.* HAMLET *thinks better of it, and angrily beckons* PLAYERS *to follow him. He and they exeunt.*)

KING: Come, let us take our places. Gather round
That all may see this fooling. Here's a chair
In which I shall find room to roll about
When laughter takes possession of my soul.
Now we are ready.

> (*Enter on platform a* LOVING COUPLE.* *Applause.*)

SHE: Shouldst thou prove faithless?
HE: If I do
Then let the world forget to woo (*kneeling*),
The mountaintops bow down in fears,
The midday sun dissolve in tears,
And outraged nature, pale and bent,
Fall prostrate in bewilderment!

> (*All titter through this — breaking into a laugh at the end, the* KING *enjoying it more than anyone.*)

OPH: Truly, sir, I hope he will prove faithful, lest we should all be involved in this catastrophe!

KING: (*laughing*) Much, indeed, depends upon his constancy. I am sure he hath all our prayers, gentlemen! (*to* ROSENCRANTZ) Is this play well known?

ROS: (*advancing*) It is not, my lord. (*Turns back to* OPHELIA.)

KING: Ha! I seem to have met with these lines before. Go on.

SHE: Hark, dost thou hear those trumpets and those drums?
Thy hated rival, stern Gonzago, comes!

FF has: 'The curtain rises. — Enter a Loving Couple lovingly.'

(*Exeunt* LOVING COUPLE.* *Laughter, as before.*)

QUEEN: And wherefore cometh Gonzago?

ROS: He cometh here to woo!

QUEEN: Cannot he woo without an orchestra at his elbow? A fico for such a wooing, say I!

KING: (*rather alarmed – aside to* ROSENCRANTZ) Who *is* Gonzago?

ROS: He's a mad Archbishop of Elsinore. 'Tis a most ridiculous and mirthful
character – and the more so for that the poor author had hoped to have
appalled you with his tragedical end! (*Returns to* OPHELIA.)
(*During this the* KING *has shown that he has recognized his tragedy.
He is horrified at the discovery.*)
(*Enter* HAMLET, *as Archbishop, with a robe and mitre. All laugh
and applaud except the* KING, *who is miserable.*)

HAMLET: Free from the cares of Church and State
I come to wreak my love and hate.
Love whirls me to the lofty skies –
Hate drags me where dark Pluto lies!
(*All laugh, except the* KING.)

QUEEN: Marry, but he must have a nice time of it between them! Oh, sir, this
passeth the bounds of ridicule, and to think that these lines were to have
drawn our tears!

OPH: Truly mine eyes run with tears, but they are begotten of laughter!

HAMLET: Gently, gently. Spare your ridicule, lest you have none left for the later
scenes. The tragedy is full of such windy fooling. You shall hear more anon.
There are five acts of this!
(*All groan.*)
(*Resumes.*)
For two great ends I daily fume –
The altar and the deadly tomb.
How can I live in such a state
And hold my Arch-Episcopate?

ROS: (*exhausted with laughter*) Oh, my lord – I pray you end this, or I shall die
with laughter!

QUEEN: (*ditto*) Did mortal ever hear such metrical folly! Stop it, my good lord, or
I shall assuredly do myself some injury.

OPH: (*ditto*) Oh, sir – prythee have mercy on us – we have laughed till we can
laugh no more!

HAMLET: The drollest scene is coming now. Listen.

KING: (*Rises.*) Stop! (*All start.*) Stop, I say – cast off those mummeries!
Come hither, Hamlet!

HAMLET: (*Takes off robes.*)   Why, what ails you, sir?

KING: (*with suppressed fury*) Know'st thou who wrote this play?

HAMLET: Not I indeed.
Nor do I care to know!

---

*Omitted in *FF*.

KING: *I* wrote this play —
To mention it is death, by Denmark's law!
QUEEN: (*kneeling*) Oh, spare him, for he is thine only child!
KING: No — I have two (QUEEN *horrified*) — my son — my play — both
worthless!
Both shall together perish! (*Draws dagger;* QUEEN *endeavours to
restrain him.*)
HAMLET: (*on his knees*)   Hold thine hand!
I can't bear death — I'm a philosopher!
KING: *That's true. But how shall we dispose of him?
        (*All puzzled.*)
OPH: (*suddenly*)   A thought!
There is a certain isle beyond the sea
Where dwell a cultured race — compared with whom
We are but poor brain-blind barbarians;
'Tis known as Engle-land. Oh, send him there!
If but the half I've heard of them be true
They will enshrine him on their great good hearts
And men will rise or sink in good esteem
According as they worship him, or slight him!
KING: Well, we're dull dogs in Denmark. It may be
That we've misjudged him. If such race there be
(There may be — I am not a well-read man)
They're welcome to his philosophic brain —
So, Hamlet, get thee gone — and don't come back again!
        (KING *crosses to right.* HAMLET, *who is delighted at the suggestion,
        crosses to* QUEEN *and embraces her. He then embraces* OPHELIA,
        *who receives his kiss with marked coldness. Then he turns up on to
        platform, and strikes an attitude, exclaiming, 'To Engle-land!' At the
        same moment* ROSENCRANTZ *embraces* OPHELIA. *Picture.*)

NOTE

Rosencrantz and Guildenstern was first published in *Fun* on 12, 19, and 26
December 1874, during the run of Irving's *Hamlet* (30 October 1874 to 29 June
1875). The reference to the Lyceum at the end of the original version was retained
for its appearance in *Foggerty's Fairy and Other Tales* (1890), and apparently for

---

*FF has:
  HAMLET: . . . I'm a philosopher!
  OPH: Apollo's son, Lycaeus, built a fane
              At Athens, where philosophers dispute,
              'Tis known as the 'Lyceum'. Send him there.
              He will find such a hearty welcome, sir,
              That he will stay there, goodness knows how long!
  CL[AUDIUS] : Well, be it so — and, Hamlet, get you gone!
              (*He goes to the Lyceum, where he is much esteemed.*)
              CURTAIN

the first 'public' performance in 1891. (The group then presenting it had already acted it privately, and there may have been earlier 'salon' performances.) The play's separate publication by French (1893) also retained this ending.

By the date (27 April 1892) of the piece's revival for a run at the Court Beerbohm Tree's first production of *Hamlet* (Haymarket, 21 January 1892) had achieved popular success, and the ending may have been changed accordingly. This ending was first published when the play appeared in *Original Plays*, third series, in 1895. It is tempting to attribute the odd usage 'Engle-land' in the revised ending to Tree's trace of a German accent, but the evidence, like the accent, is slight.

THE PLAYS OF W.S. GILBERT

NB Only the first London production of each title is listed.

31 October 1863	*Uncle Baby*. Lyceum.
26 December 1866	*Hush-a-Bye Baby* (with Charles Millward). Astleys.
29 December 1866	*Dulcamara*. St James's.
6 July 1867	*Robinson Crusoe* (with H.J. Byron, T. Hood, H.S. Leigh and A. Sketchley). Haymarket.
4 November 1867	*Allow Me To Explain*. Prince of Wales's.
5 December 1867	*Highly Improbable*. Royalty.
26 December 1867	*Harlequin Cock Robin and Jenny Wren*. Lyceum.
22 January 1868	*La Vivandière*. Queen's.
21 March 1868	*The Merry Zingara*. Royalty.
21 December 1868	*Robert the Devil*. Gaiety.
29 March 1869	*No Cards*. Gallery of Illustration. Music by T.G. Reed and L. Elliott. (See Jane W. Stedman, *Gilbert before Sullivan*, p. 240.)
19 June 1869	*The Pretty Druidess*. Charing Cross.
19 July 1869	*An Old Score*. Gaiety.
22 November 1869	*Ages Ago*. Gallery of Illustration. Music by F. Clay.
8 January 1870	*The Princess*. Olympic.
26 May 1870	*The Gentleman in Black*. Charing Cross. Music by F. Clay.
20 June 1870	*Our Island Home*. Gallery of Illustration. Music by T.G. Reed.
19 November 1870	*The Palace of Truth*. Haymarket.
25 January 1871	*Randall's Thumb*. Court.
30 January 1871	*A Sensation Novel*. Gallery of Illustration. Music by F. Clay.
15 April 1871	*Creatures of Impulse*. Court. Music by A. Randegger.
29 May 1871	*Great Expectations*. Court.
28 October 1871	*On Guard*. Court.
9 December 1871	*Pygmalion and Galatea*. Haymarket.
26 December 1871	*Thespis*. Gaiety. Music by Sullivan.
24 October 1872	*A Medical Man*. St George's Hall.
28 October 1872	*Happy Arcadia*. Gallery of Illustration. Music by F. Clay.
4 January 1873	*The Wicked World*. Haymarket.
3 March 1873	*The Happy Land* (with Gilbert à Beckett). Court.
18 October 1873	*The Realm of Joy*. Royalty.
15 November 1873	*The Wedding March*. Court.
3 January 1874	*Charity*. Haymarket.
17 January 1874	*Ought We To Visit Her?* Royalty.
24 January 1874	*Committed for Trial*. Globe.
4 March 1874	*The Blue-Legged Lady*. Court.
21 March 1874	*Topsy-Turvydom*. Criterion.
7 November 1874	*Sweethearts*. Prince of Wales's.
25 March 1875	*Trial by Jury*. Royalty. Music by Sullivan.

24 April 1875	*Tom Cobb.* St James's.
5 July 1875	*Eyes and No Eyes.* St George's Hall. Music by F. Pascal.
9 December 1875	*Broken Hearts.* Court.
11 September 1876	*Dan'l Druce, Blacksmith.* Haymarket.
2 October 1876	*Princess Toto.* Strand. Music by F. Clay.
3 February 1877	*On Bail.* Criterion.
3 October 1877	*Engaged.* Haymarket.
17 November 1877	*The Sorcerer.* Opera Comique. Music by Sullivan.
13 February 1878	*Ali Baba and the Forty Thieves* (with H.J. Byron). Gaiety.
25 February 1878	*The Vagabond* (title changed to *The Ne'er-do-Weel* 25 March 1878). Olympic.
25 May 1878	*HMS Pinafore.* Opera Comique. Music by Sullivan.
24 March 1879	*Gretchen.* Olympic.
3 April 1880	*The Pirates of Penzance.* Opera Comique. Music by Sullivan.
23 April 1881	*Patience.* Opera Comique. Music by Sullivan.
15 December 1881	*Foggerty's Fairy.* Criterion.
25 November 1882	*Iolanthe.* Savoy. Music by Sullivan.
5 January 1884	*Princess Ida.* Savoy. Music by Sullivan.
26 January 1884	*Comedy and Tragedy.* Lyceum.
14 March 1885	*The Mikado.* Savoy. Music by Sullivan.
22 January 1887	*Ruddigore.* Savoy. Music by Sullivan.
3 October 1888	*The Yeomen of the Guard.* Savoy. Music by Sullivan.
29 November 1888	*Brantinghame Hall.* St James's.
16 September 1889	*The Brigands.* Avenue. Music by Offenbach.
7 December 1889	*The Gondoliers.* Savoy. Music by Sullivan.
3 June 1891	*Rosencrantz and Guildenstern.* Vaudeville.
4 January 1892	*The Mountebanks.* Lyric. Music by A. Cellier.
27 July 1892	*Haste to the Wedding.* Criterion. Music by G. Grossmith.
7 October 1893	*Utopia Limited.* Savoy. Music by Sullivan.
27 October 1894	*His Excellency.* Lyric. Music by O. Carr.
7 March 1896	*The Grand Duke.* Savoy. Music by Sullivan.
18 October 1897	*The Fortune Hunter.* Queen's, Crouch End.
4 May 1904	*The Fairy's Dilemma.* Garrick.
11 December 1909	*Fallen Fairies.* Savoy. Music by E. German.
27 February 1911	*The Hooligan.* Coliseum.

SELECT BIBLIOGRAPHY

The dates of publication of Gilbert's *Original Plays* are
first series 1876; reissued 1909
second series 1881; reissued 1909
third series 1895; reissued 1909
fourth series 1911
For complete details of the first publication of Gilbert's plays, see Reginald Allen, 'William Schwenck Gilbert: An Anniversary Survey', *Theatre Notebook* vol. XV no. 4 (1961), pp. 118–28, and vol. XVI no. 1 (1962), pp. 30–1.

On Gilbert himself the following studies are useful:
Dark, Sidney and Grey, Rowland. *W.S. Gilbert, His Life and Letters*. 1923
Pearson, Hesketh. *Gilbert: His Life and Strife*. 1957
Sutton, Max Keith. *W.S. Gilbert*. Boston, 1975

On Gilbert's early work see
Stedman, Jane W. (ed.). *Gilbert before Sullivan: Six Comic Plays by W.S. Gilbert.* Chicago, 1967
and the Introduction to James D. Ellis's edition of *The Bab Ballads.* Cambridge, Mass., 1970

On the bibliography of Gilbert's plays:
Allen, Reginald, 'William Schwenck Gilbert: An Anniversary Survey', as above
Searle, Townley. *Sir William Schwenck Gilbert: A Topsy-turvy Adventure.* 1931

The large number of books on the collaboration of Gilbert and Sullivan includes:
Baily, Leslie. *The Gilbert and Sullivan Book.* revised edition, 1957
Cellier, François and Bridgeman, C. *Gilbert, Sullivan and D'Oyly Carte.* 1914
Goldberg, Isaac. *The Story of Gilbert and Sullivan.* 1929
Helyar, James (ed.). *Gilbert and Sullivan: Papers Presented at the Kansas Conference.* Lawrence, Kansas, 1971
Jones, John Bush (ed.). *W.S. Gilbert: A Century of Scholarship and Commentary.* New York, 1970
Mander, Raymond and Mitchenson, Joe (eds.). *A Picture History of Gilbert and Sullivan.* 1962
Pearson, Hesketh. *Gilbert and Sullivan.* 1935
Sullivan, Herbert and Flower, Newman. *Sir Arthur Sullivan: His Life, Letters and Diaries.* 1927
See also
The Gilbert and Sullivan Journal. First published 1925; continuing
The Savoyard. First published 1961; continuing

The background to Gilbert's work is covered by the following, amongst others:

Booth, Michael R. Introductions to *English Plays of the Nineteenth Century*, Oxford: vol. III *Comedies*. 1973; vol. IV *Farces*. 1973; vol. V *Pantomimes, Extravaganzas and Burlesques*. 1976

Nicoll, Allardyce. *A History of English Drama 1660–1900*: vol. V *Late Nineteenth Century Drama 1850–1900*. 2nd edition, Cambridge, 1959

The Revels History of Drama in English: vol. VI *1750–1880*. General editors: Clifford Leech and T.W. Craik. 1975; vol. VII *1800 to the Present Day*. General editor: T.W. Craik. 1978

Rowell, George. *The Victorian Theatre 1792–1914*. 2nd edition, Cambridge, 1978 *Theatre in the Age of Irving*. Oxford, 1981

Other works cited in the Introduction:

Archer, William. *English Dramatists of Today*. 1882 *The Old Drama and the New*. 1923

Binder, Robert. 'Gilbert's Other Princess', *Gilbert and Sullivan Journal* vol. X, no. 15, 1978

Gilbert, W.S. 'Actors, Authors, and Audiences', *Foggerty's Fairy and Other Tales*. 1890

Hudson, Lynton. *The English Stage 1850–1950*. 1951

Rees, Terence (ed.). *Uncle Baby: A Comedietta by W.S. Gilbert*. Privately printed, London, 1968 *The Realm of Joy*. Privately printed, London, 1969

Wells, Stanley (ed.). *Nineteenth Century Shakespeare Burlesques* vol. IV. 1978